Contested Domains

The Author

Robin Cohen is Professor of Sociology at the University of Warwick and directed its Centre for Research in Ethnic Relations over the period 1984-9. He has also held teaching posts at the University of Ibadan, Nigeria; the University of Birmingham and the University of the West Indies. Among many other professional activities, he was one of the founding editors of the *Review of African Political Economy* and *The Newsletter on International Labour Studies*, and Series Editor for the Cambridge University Press series on *African Societies Today*. His books include: *Labour and Politics in Nigeria* (London: Heinemann Educational Books and New York: Holmes and Meier, 1974, 1982); *Endgame in South Africa? The Changing Ideology and Social Structure of South Africa* (Paris: Unesco and London: James Currey, 1986); and *The New Helots: Migrants in the International Division of Labour* (Aldershot: Gower, 1987). In addition, he has edited or co-edited ten other scholarly volumes, particularly in the fields of African labour, refugee issues and the study of small islands. His research and teaching interests include the Sociology and Politics of Developing Societies, Comparative Labour Studies, the Sociology of Migration and Ethnic Relations.

Reviewers' Reactions to Previous Books

'A book of high intellectual and literary quality which can be recommended as essential reading for students of Nigerian society and politics.'
—**Dr Richard Jeffries** (SOAS, London) *African Affairs* (reviewing *Labour and Politics in Nigeria*).

'His sophisticated analysis of the role of ideology is offered with wit and insight.'
—**Professor Jack Spence** (University of Leicester) *Times Literary Supplement* (reviewing *Endgame in South Africa? The Changing Ideology and Social Structure of South Africa*).

'A dramatic and exciting work, linking together an extraordinarily wide range of themes.'
—**Nigel Harris** (University College, London) *New Society* (reviewing *The New Helots: Migrants in the International Division of Labour*).

'A wonderfully stimulating and synoptic new book ... a formidable piece of comparative sociology and history'.
—**Jeff Crisp** (UNHCR, Geneva) *Journal of Refugee Studies* (reviewing *The New Helots*).

Contested Domains

Debates in International Labour Studies

Robin Cohen

including chapters with
Jeff Henderson & David Michael

Zed Books Ltd
London and New Jersey

Contested Domains was first published by Zed Books Ltd,
57 Caledonian Road, London N1 9BU, UK, and 165 First Avenue,
Atlantic Highlands, New Jersey 07716, USA, in 1991.

Cover designed by Andrew Corbett.
Laserset by Selro Publishing Services.
Printed and bound in the United Kingdom
by Biddles Ltd, Guildford and King's Lynn.

A catalogue record for this book is
available from the British Library.

ISBN 1 85649 012 2 Hb
ISBN 1 85649 013 0 Pb

Contents

List of Tables and Figures

Acknowledgements

Two of the contributions to this book are written with friends, and I would like to thank warmly Jeff Henderson and David Michael for allowing me to publish them here.

Most of the material has been published, though sometimes only in part, or in barely accessible journals. The 'endbox' after each chapter contains details of the original publication and sometimes also indicates the relevant circumstances, or occasionally some personal details, that surround the publication of a particular version in this volume. I trust this device will both give the reader an appreciation of the original context and provide a small diversion of passing interest. The endboxes also contain the acknowledgement due to the journals of first publication.

I have felt free to rewrite sentences or paragraphs in several chapters either because I no longer agree with a particular formulation or because I have cross-referred points of interest to another place in the text.

My love and thanks go to Selina Cohen for her customary help and support. I also wish to express my thanks to the Study Leave Committee of Warwick University who gave me the time to write, and to Robert Molteno at Zed Books who was a helpful and sympathetic editor.

Robin Cohen
La Vendée and Warwick

Foreword

The chapters in this book were written over a 18-year period, from 1972-90. Some were intended as stand-alone articles, others drew on debates partly engendered by the earlier studies. Yet, despite the long period involved, the chapters are closely linked - each concerning the contested terrains in which 'labouring people' (in the widest sense of that description) are simultaneously controlled and seek to resist.

On the one hand, the studies depict the forms of domination effected by agents representing capital and the state as they strive to harness the energies and labour-power of working people to their own interests. On the other hand, they portray the forms of encounter, resistance and self-organisation that working people adopt or create in their attempts at self-organisation and political mobilisation.

'Control' and 'resistance' are closely related to the familiar social scientific dyad, 'structure' and 'agency.' These terms are in turn at least as old as Aristotle, in his musings about the limits to human beings' passions and actions in his Ethics. To address fully this issue would require exegesis not only of Aristotle, but also of Kant, Spinoza, Hobbes, Marx and Freud. This would involve too great a diversion.

It is adequate to my purposes merely to say that, in recent years, the two trajectories of social analysis, concentrating respectively on structure and agency, have polarised around the figures of Louis Althusser (1969; 1970), representing a particular version of structuralism, and Edward Thompson, defending 'the view from below' that he applied so lucidly in *The Making of an English Working Class* (1963).

As in a number of similar debates, the protagonists are wont to disinter Marx's corpse to validate their own points. According to Althusser (1970: 29), never anything but arcane, 'the affectivity of structure on its elements ... is the visible/invisible, absent/present keystone to [Marx's] whole work.' A little easier for me to understand is a powerful passage in *For Marx* (Althusser 1969: 143) where Althusser turns theatre critic and contrasts the indomitable force of war in Brecht's *Mother Courage* to the personal tragedy of her blindness. The play, he thinks, shows: 'The silent confrontation of a consciousness (living its own situation in the dialectical-tragic mode, and believing the whole world to be moved by its impulse) with reality which is indifferent and strange to this so-called dialectic - an apparently undialectical reality, [which] makes possible an immanent critique of the illusion of consciousness.'

The 'illusion of consciousness,' the elimination of the human subject from social theory, the insistence that Marx constructed a 'new science' of human practice which could be discerned from an examination of the 'totality' and finally the dismissal of 'history' as an object of study in itself - all this proved too much for Thompson. In a sustained and bitter polemic (1978), which somehow combined the barbs of a Swift, the logic of a turn-of-the-century German revisionist and the moral indignation of a Leveller, Thompson contested the substance and the implications ('Stalinist' was used more than a few times) of Althusser's arguments, at times line by line and phrase by phrase. The savagery of Thompson's attack won the day for many historians and social scientists, repelled as they were by the undoubtedly unnecessary obscurantism and dogmatism of Althusser's brand of structuralist theory.

In retrospect, however, a more balanced judgment seems appropriate. While the Althusser/Thompson debate held centre stage for Marxists and social historians, Giddens (1979), working in a mainstream sociological tradition, provided the first exposition of what was to become a more sophisticated and elaborated theory of 'structuration.' Three key elements of his theory involved connecting 'human agency' with the notion of an 'acting subject'; situating action in time and space 'as a continuous flow of conduct' and seeing structure 'as both medium and outcome of the reproduction of practices' (1979: 2, 5). While Giddens is prepared to accept a complex interactive model, he firmly rejects functionalist theories of structure. (He does not add, but I will, 'like Althusser's'). Describing his arguments as a 'non-functionalist manifesto,' he writes (1979: 7): 'According to the theory of structuration, social systems have no purposes, reasons or needs whatsoever; only human individuals do. Any explanation of social reproduction which imputes teleology to social systems must be declared invalid.'

Much as I am tempted to pursue this debate as pure theory, my purposes in this book are more limited. My broad sympathies lie very much with Giddens. Collapsing all human action, motivation, intention, even consciousness, into an Althusserian totality seems to me to be both futile and wrong-headed. By contrast, Thompson probably exaggerates the transformative possibilities of human beings in general and labouring people in particular. One does not have to be a structuralist to accept that those in charge of the modern Leviathan *do* have a sophisticated military, police, bureaucratic and ideological apparatus at their disposal. (How quickly it tumbled in

Romania or Czechoslovakia in the last months of 1989, those defending human agency might declare. How long did it sustain, and will not the structures reassert themselves, the structuralist might reply.)

Within the domain of the workplace, employers have evolved powerful means of habituating workers to their tasks and, almost without exception, have stabilised the industrial order. In short, there are awesome constraints on the freedom of human beings, however class conscious, angry or organised, to alter the basic economic, spatial and systemic 'facts of life.' Views from below are simply inadequate to take account of such processes as the spread of information technology, the arms race, the international division of labour or the globalisation of production - which have so profound an impact on the possibilities of galvanising a sufficiently coherent base for common social action.

What I have tried to do in this book is to provide a meaningful gauge and fair assessment of the limits of class action designed to oppose these controlling forces. Thus, for example, I am very sceptical of the possibilities of political action on behalf of US agricultural workers (Chapter 4), or the urban poor in Third World cities (Chapter 7). By contrast, African workers are shown to be capable of localised informal protest, even in the most adverse circumstances (Chapter 6), though their resistance does not ineluctably or self-evidently lead to a revolutionary outcome.

I would describe my stance here as a form of 'socialist realism,' not of course in the sense of the brutal figures on post-revolutionary Soviet posters, but in the sense of being concerned to examine the aspirations and organisations generated by working people, without falling into the trap of romanticising the proletariat or exaggerating the possibilities of it fulfilling its ascribed role as an unfailing and exclusive vanguard for a global revolutionary project.

On the side of the constraining or controlling forces, I have sought to avoid the over-determinancy of systems of thought such as Althusserian structuralism, Wallersteinian world systems models or Latin American *dependencia* theories. I find more flexible and useful concepts in the 'changing international division of labour' (Chapter 8) and in more modest units of analysis, like 'regional political economies' (Cohen 1987: 25-6). Equally, I use the expressions 'state' and 'capital' not in any theoretically-inflated sense, but simply as a shorthand way of referring to a particular administration or government, or a constellation of interests of a particular group of employers. Where it is possible to avoid these overburdened terms, I try to specify 'the Governor-in-Council in Hong Kong,' 'the Ford Motor Company,' or some other exact description. (Frequently, however, I have had to deploy the short-hand version 'state' and 'capital' simply to avoid penning a grossly unwieldy sentence.) I also eschew most usages of the expression 'modes of production' when it is clear that the writer is simply referring in a pretentious way to a particular country or region. In short, in delineating structures, I have a preference for real agencies and real interests rather than vaguely-defined Procrustean beds that trigger meaningless 'discourses' about invisible objects.

In sum, I would hope these essays could serve as both an analytical and empirical contribution to the reassessment of the historic role and transformative and liberatory possibilities of labouring people in a number of international and national settings. In making this contribution I hope that I have neither stumbled into the Scylla of proletarian messianism nor fallen into the Charybdis of a passivity and fatalism generated by the apparently indomitable force of capital and state.

1

Theorising International Labour

Introduction

In introducing the theme of 'international labour' it would be appropriate to make some assessment of the present fortunes and ultimate fate of the working class, a group marked out by Marx as the bearer of freedom for humankind. But the century of experience since Marx's death provides neither unambiguous evidence to support his vision, nor sufficient testimony to refute it. The story of international labour has been one of disappointed hopes and frustrated dreams, as well as one of stirring acts of solidarity and fraternity.

As socialist experiments have proliferated, so the message has become fragmented and diluted. The seizure of state power, the anti-imperialist struggles and the expropriation of the means of production by revolutionary parties have liberated many working people from the worst excesses of colonialism and private profit. But these advances have often been accompanied by ideological rigidities, the unrestrained hegemony of the state's bureaucratic apparatus, and restrictions on workers' rights to self-expression and autonomous organisation. All over the socialist world the people in whose name the party has acted have rebelled against the constraints of state socialism. Sometimes, as with *Solidarity* in Poland, the labour movement has been able to place itself at the forefront of such a democratic movement. But more frequently the labour movement itself appears to have been left behind in the rush towards direct representation and popular control.

Within the domain of world capital, more and more workers from the far-flung reaches of the multinationals' new 'empires' are brought into commercial agriculture or sucked into the vortex of manufacturing production. But this process is also far from homogeneous. Instead, the uneven spread of capitalist relations of production seems to separate the interests of rural from urban workers, men from women, old from young, black from white, and

1

the metropolitan from the peripheral working class. The reality of
international labour is therefore a mixed and complex one, and the
movements that seek to organise workers seem to divide and
fracture class solidarity, even as they attempt to cement it.

The theoretical ordering of this mixed reality reflects a similar
complexity. Outside the ranks of the labour movement itself,
scholarly and political engagement with the issue of international
labour has generated three broad lines of argument and analysis,
each with its corresponding political implications and practice.

The first, stemming from orthodox studies of industrial relations,
explicitly recognises the need for comparative analysis, but is quick
to reject the notion that workers are, or ever could be, revolutionary
agents, let alone capable of action on a global stage.

The second line of analysis, stemming from orthodox left-wing
theory about the working class, is magnetised by Marx's original
vision of a revolutionary working class, but is pulled so decisively to
the positive pole that it fails adequately to take account either of the
limits of grassroots worker struggles or the real distinctions of
nationality, race, gender, skill and status that separate worker from
worker and inhibit the construction of international labour
solidarity.

The third position reflects a cautious reappraisal of the
international role of the working class and an attempt by academics,
intellectuals and labour activists to define a new *modus vivendi*. This
alternative approach we called (at a 'state of the art' meeting in
Montreal in 1980) 'the new international labour studies,' a paper by
myself (Cohen 1980) having set out a preliminary definition of the
concept.

After reviewing these three broad lines of argument and analysis,
together with their implicit or consequent political practice, I draw
attention to some of the chapters in this book that sustain or extend
'the new international labour studies.' A brief conclusion follows.

The industrial relations tradition

The domain imagined by Industrial Relations (IR) specialists is a
formal, carefully constructed, but often ahistorical world. Therein is
found a tight bargaining environment where collective agreements,
grievance handling, arbitration and conciliation procedures,
contracts and negotiations take place. It is a world where 'labour'
normally means a middle-aged, male, trade union bureaucrat in the
capitalist West negotiating with his management counterpart. It is
also a world where the principal organs of the working class, the
trade unions, are accepted parts of the industrial landscape,
institutionally protected but legally regulated and constrained.

Those from this tradition of scholarship who deal with international and comparative issues are perhaps more adventurous than their nationally-oriented colleagues, but they remain uneasily imprisoned, I shall argue, in the largely phoney world of workplace collective bargaining.

I want briefly to address the conventional IR approach through the most synoptic work of a representative figure, Adolf Sturmthal (in Sturmthal & Scoville 1973), a leading mainstream theorist of comparative labour and industrial relations. Though the possibilities of including other figures involved in the same kind of discourse are legion, Sturmthal has the great virtue of both commanding his version of the field, and showing some sensitivity to the political and ideological contexts from which his arguments are assembled.

At the core of his model is a fierce defence of the efficacy of collective bargaining celebrated by writers such as Perlman (1949) who, in Sturmthal's words, proclaims that a 'mature' labour movement, 'freed from the ideological freight which intellectuals have imposed on it, would abandon its political aims and methods and rely upon its economic power. Collective bargaining would become its main activity' (Sturmthal & Scoville 1973: 4). For its advocates, collective bargaining became largely a means of defusing political, ideological and industrial conflict by institutionalising and, by so doing, containing the relative power of bosses and workers. But containerisation had another desirable effect: the world of work could be insulated from the 'passionate debates of the syndicalists' (as Sturmthal describes them) who announced the virtues of 'revolutionary action by unions culminating in a series of general strikes,' or the Marxists who advocated 'political action [as] the main instrument of working-class liberation' (Sturmthal & Scoville 1973: 3). The world of work was not only separated from politics, it was separated from society. Discussions of the relation between reproduction and production, or of the way in which the world of industry is parasitical upon, or interdependent with, the world of domestic and peasant labour, do not appear in traditional IR research. In marked contrast to some of the newer work on international labour studies reflected in this book, in IR circles the bargaining environments of the workplace or industrial sector provide the agreed parameters of their concerns.

Unfortunately for such restricted models, what muddied the waters was that, as *laissez-faire* capitalism and its accompanying ideological support collapsed in the face of increasing government intervention, so too did the notion of exclusive employer-employee bargaining - even in the limited Euro-American contexts where the system had taken root. The 'government' or the 'state' had, in reality, effectively intervened as a third agent from at least the 1930s in all major industrial powers. Thus Sturmthal's attempt to try to rescue some pure form of collective bargaining from the numerous exceptions and special conditions under which it applies, is doomed to failure (Sturmthal & Scoville 1973: 5-11). 'Collective bargaining' is better conceived as a limited case, rather than a universal form of employee/employer relations. In practice, even in the Euro-American model, the third party, the state, always sets the limits to the bargain - whether by minimum wages, industrial relations legislation, regional policies, immigration rules, incomes policies or, more recently, monetarist cash limits.

Given that the role of the state is often recognised by IR scholars, a curious double-talk ensues. The virtues of free collective bargaining are preached from the mountain tops, yet everybody with even a superficial knowledge of the conditions under which wages and conditions of work are determined knows the legal, political and empirical limits to such an exercise. Despite this, Sturmthal implausibly argues that incomes policies and legal minima are exceptional measures to meet extraordinary situations and are designed to provide help to 'weak social groups' until 'they too could develop the strength necessary for a full enjoyment of the blessing of collective bargaining' (Sturmthal & Scoville 1973: 8). It is doubtful that Sturmthal actually believes that such forms of state intervention are temporary benevolent measures, for he reverses his position immediately by saying that, if we compare the Anglo-American ideal with the reality of large parts of the contemporary world, 'we find a variety of departures and contrasts' (ibid.).

Though a large enough concession, this still somewhat understates the nakedness of the argument. For example, the most prestigious international organisation concerned with labour questions, the International Labour Office, explicitly rejects the bipartite model of collective bargaining in favour of a tripartite (including the state) structure. Let us add to this renunciation the fact that Sturmthal accepts that collective bargaining does not apply to situations where there are unlimited supplies of labour, where there is uncontrolled immigration, where (as in developing countries) 'political unionism' obtains, or where there are 'lags' or 'adaptations' (Sturmthal & Scoville 1973: 11-18, 20-7). In short, *all* we have is variety and contrast: the degree of conformity of the conservative model to reality is so minimal that we may as well ignore it for comparative analytical purposes. Sturmthal and his co-editor Scoville (1973: 286) indeed ultimately reach this conclusion in a postscript to their joint collection, where they write: 'the migration of ideas, the fact that people - even governments - learn, will lead to new and different institutions or processes in response to national conditions. But whatever these new institutions and processes are, *they are not likely* to resemble the classical paradigm of "free collective bargaining"' [emphasis added].

Faced with such an extraordinary display of self-immolation from scholars within the mainstream IR tradition, we can only ask why the naked Emperor is still wheeled out for public display. A part of the answer has already been suggested - and it turns on the ideological and political implications of the model. At a national level, within some Western industrial countries, the model of collective bargaining acts to insulate the industrial environment from its social and political contexts. At an international level, the ideological instrumentality of 'collective bargaining' has to be seen as allied to the cognate conservative version of 'independent trade unionism.' Together these notions have provided an important underpinning defining the distinctiveness of the Western position during the periodic upsurges of the Cold War.

Since 1949 the international trade union movement has been totally riven by the force of super-power rivalries (see, for one account, Levinson 1972). The International Confederation of Free Trade Unions (ICFTU) and the Christian internationals overwhelmingly organise workers in Western industrial countries and declare their distinctive ideological commitments to be the freedom from party or governmental control and the primacy of the industrial bargain. For its part, the World Federation of Trade Unions (WFTU) has been reduced to an international body largely federating unions in state socialist societies, where the assumed harmony of interest between state, party and working class is said to obviate the need for independent trade unions. With the collapse of party hegemony in Eastern Europe, the WFTU is likely to have difficulty surviving in its present form.

The immense gulf between the major international trade union federations is reinforced by a veritable panoply of supra-national agencies. Some, like the American Institute for Free Labor Development, the African-American Labor Center, the Asian-American Free Labor Institute and the Inter-American Regional Labor Organization, are largely vehicles for overt foreign policy objectives funded by the State Department or the US Agency for International Development. These organisations, and other US bodies, also provide fronts for covert actions carried out by the CIA.

By contrast, the 20 or so International Trade Secretariats have deeper and more autonomous roots, some dating back to the 19th century. In recent years, however, they too have been heavily influenced by their wealthiest affiliates, often conservative US or German unions. Regional organisations, or bilateral foreign associations by strong metropolitan unions, also interlace with other forms of organisation (see Busch 1980). So multifarious have these organisations become, so entrenched the international trade union bureaucracy, that it is sometimes difficult to see through the mist to newer, more relevant forms of international organisation. Olle &

Schoeller (1987), for example, draw our attention to the World Corporation Councils set up under the aegis of the ICFTU since 1966. Though they almost certainly exaggerate the importance of the World Corporation Councils (Baker 1978) their work is important in sensitizing us to the varieties of existing and possible forms of multinational bargaining outside the established structures.

While new global labour institutions are emerging as a (as yet partial, weak and delayed) response to the growth and flexibility of multinational capital there has been no corresponding theoretical advance by the more conventional school of IR theorists. As yet there has been little appreciation of the way in which transnational sector or firm agreements will further damage the notion of plant-level collective bargaining. Just to illustrate some complexities: multi-national agreements might well fundamentally alter national wage relativities and comparisons between worker and peasant incomes in the interests of secure and internationally agreed 'rates for the job.' The parties to the bargain might well involve, in addition to the firm and a variety of unions, international agencies and governments from 'First,' 'Third' *and* Second Worlds. Again the items under negotiation might include such facets as foreign investment policies and job exports.

In short, the structural variables, which provide the surrounding context for an industrial bargain, have simply become too complex and too determinant for the IR models to encompass. What remained, at least in the 1980s, were the still potent ideological functions of the notions of 'collective bargaining' and 'independent trade unionism.' We witnessed, for example, their continuing political resonance in statements by President Reagan and Mrs Thatcher in the early 1980s, who announced their profound sympathy with the aims of *Solidarity* in Poland while simultaneously breaking a strike of air-traffic controllers in the US and unveiling a package of the most openly anti-trade union legislation seen in Britain in living memory.

Is it legitimate, however, to link such gross political hypocrisies with the tradition of scholarship I have discussed? My argument here is essentially threefold. In so far as those committed to IR research have acknowledged that their major explanatory framework - the evolution of collective bargaining - no longer corresponds with observed reality or comparative examples, they have left a theoretical structure in place that is open for manipulation as a political totem. In so far as their work defies a consensual framework in which all interests (workers, employers and, later, governments) are ultimately reconcilable, they leave no space for examining the liberatory possibilities of worker internationalism. In so far, finally, as their ideas have provided ready ammunition for Cold War warriors and the agencies of foreign policy in a handful (but a powerful handful) of Western nations, the extent to which comparative IR research can be seen as anything more than an ideologically limited and culturally and historically specific form of discourse, must be raised.

The orthodox left tradition

Where IR research pretends to scientific neutrality, orthodox left-wing writing on the subject of international labour is overtly engaged and committed. Where the IR tradition is open to political manipulation by the right, much of the traditional communist and socialist literature is open to the self-delusions wrought by confusing the 'ought to be' with the 'is.' The tradition normally invoked is a hortatory and heroic one, which stresses the achievements of the working class in the quest for self-organisation and international solidarity. As these themes are so much part of the warp and woof of the pronouncements of revolutionary parties, radical trade unions and communist intellectuals, there is no one representative figure (but see, for examples or relevant discussion, Lenin 1918; Borkenau 1962; Carr 1951-64, 1982; Degras 1956-65; *Communist International* 1919-40; Padmore 1971).

It is not my purpose here to examine this literature in detail. No doubt some of it authentically distils worker experiences and ideas. Some again is a necessary dose of rhetoric to stiffen resolve and stir the heart, not to mention its function as a necessary counterblast to crude pro-capitalist propaganda. But there remains a sense in which communist intellectuals and revolutionary parties need now to supplement the heroic tradition with a careful examination of the historical limits to previous international organisation, so that these limits can be transcended in the light of prevailing circumstances.

One of the first, and all too easy exaggerations perpetrated, is the substitution of the words of the Communist Manifesto for an actual analysis of the conditions under which, 16 years later in 1864, the International Working Men's Association, was formed. Though it was an achievement of some note, an examination of the record of the First International shows that it was hopelessly split between Marxists and the followers of Proudhon or Blanqui or Bakunin. Powerful English and French trade union leaders dominated the Council and the work of the International never spread much beyond Europe in the eight to ten years of its existence. Moreover, as Olle & Schoeller (1987) point out, the appeal of internationalism to English workers was largely predicated on the experiences of London building workers during 1859-61, when employers threatened to import cheap European labour to break the strikes of those years. This threat to one section of the international working class by the spread of capitalism to Europe and the use of a common labour pool, provided the material basis for some kind of unity across national lines.

A second common error of the orthodox left is to exaggerate the power and effectiveness of the internationals. In fact they were (at least until the twentieth century) patchy affairs with limited memberships nearly entirely confined to Europe. The First International had a hard-core membership of a little more than 20,000. Its annual income rarely exceeded £100. The Second International, which had an effective life from 1889 to 1915, expended much of its energies renouncing the Anarchists who had taken over and ultimately destroyed the First International after The Hague Conference in 1872. Despite this diversion, some of the leading members of the Second International held that if the forces of worker internationalism could triumph over the inter-imperialist and nationalist rivalries of the European powers, the decisive battle with capitalism could be joined. That at least was the conviction of Lenin, Luxemburg and Martov who sponsored a resolution at the International (in 1907) that the coming European war, which was already visible on the horizon, should be the occasion for fomenting a global (by which they largely meant a European) revolution. In the event, most of the International's affiliates fell meekly in line behind their national governments, some embraced pacifism and only a handful of parties and unions (in Russia and Serbia notably) sought to follow the spirit of the 1907 resolution. At the grassroots, the decisive majority of the European working class lined up behind the banners of the Kings and Kaisers, rather than behind the divided slogans of the International.

It was a crushing defeat from which the spirit of worker internationalism has never fully recovered. The Comintern (the Third International) was always too much of a Moscow-centred organisation (for one account see Carr 1982). Over its 20 years of effective existence (1919-39), trade unions became subordinate to communist parties, communist parties became subordinate to the Soviet communist party, and that party in turn was dominated by the force of one man, Stalin. There were momentary flurries of zeal in the trade union section of the Comintern, the Red International of Labour Unions, but all conflicts of interest were subordinated to the need for 'socialism' (as it was deemed) to survive in the Soviet Union. It is perhaps worth mentioning that despite the Comintern's shortcomings, Trotsky none the less at first opposed starting a rival body on the grounds that a significant section of revolutionary parties was still aligned to the Comintern. It was only because of the need to oppose fascism more decisively after Hitler's rise to power that he lent his authority to the creation of a Fourth International. Though its ideological pronouncements and general level of analysis undoubtedly carried considerably more conviction than the

Comintern's opportunistic pronouncements, the Fourth International was destined to remain largely a haven for dissident intellectuals, minor tendencies and parties, and Trotsky's epigones.

Other than the small Trotskyist left, the major grouping opposing the communists in the Internationals were the socialists. Some sort of unity between communists and socialists was patched together in the International Socialist Bureau, but the 1914-18 war rapidly saw the separation of figures like Stauning, Branting and MacDonald (later the Prime Ministers of Denmark, Sweden and Britain respectively) committed to the 'parliamentary road to socialism,' from communists such as Lenin, Luxemburg and Rakovsky (Vandervelde 1929: 511, 512). Though the social democratic and labour parties were to found a still vibrant Socialist International in the period after 1919, in practice the Socialist International became a forum for parties, rather than labour movements. Likewise, ameliorist politics at home became a far more important issue than worker solidarity abroad. This was a logical consequence of the abandonment of the revolutionary road. The plain fact was that the working class at home had a vote, while its counterparts abroad had none. In effect, electoral politics was bound to subordinate the international to the national level.

So despite the success of social democracy in electoral terms (particularly in Europe), it is to the communist left that we must return to assess the experience of labour internationalism. Some may argue that it is too premature to give any final judgment on this question, but after nearly a century and a quarter of attempts at organising the workers globally it is difficult to escape a negative assessment. From within the ranks of the communist movement displays of internationalism remain fragmented and episodical (the Spanish Civil War, Cuba, Vietnam, Angola) and more often than not it was the foreign policy interests of state socialist countries that motivated acts of fraternity rather than the need to respond to worker demands for solidarity. The experience of the Soviet state in the Third International may present an especially cautionary tale in this respect, but the point is a more general one. Those who are preoccupied with international diplomacy, military power, trade, aid and investment are not likely to act effectively to promote worker internationalism.

Whatever the limitations of the pre-1914 Internationals, they were labour-movement led and did reflect some rank-and-file opinion. In retrospect, it is clear that the interests of the various movements were distinct and separable from the interests of revolutionary parties, which were concerned, above all, with the achievement and consolidation of state power. The period after the consolidation of Soviet power illustrates the point most forcibly. Any state, 'socialist' or not, acts in the interests of state power and cannot put itself at the head of a movement for worker global unity with any credibility. Though there are some reactionary or negative features of the Polish *Solidarity* movement, its central virtue is that it showed that it is possible, even under state socialism, to destroy the myth that the party is the vanguard of the working class. But just as one swallow does not make a spring, one independent worker movement from within the centralised state economies is insufficient to demonstrate that the cause of worker internationalism will be better served in the future by what remains of the orthodox left than it has been in the past.

The new international labour studies

It is partly because of the limits, in theory and practice, of comparative industrial relations and the orthodox left traditions, that an alternative theoretical approach to questions of international labour began to emerge in the 1970s. I cannot now repeat the arguments I advanced earlier (Cohen 1980) in detail. Suffice it to say that my definition involved negative elements - the new international labour studies was different from and could not be reduced to industrial relations, trade union studies, labour history or the sort of technicist studies carried out by bodies like the ILO.

More positively, a rough agenda of common concerns was beginning to emerge. In metropolitan societies, scholars in the new mould were concerned with the changing ethnic and sexual composition of the labour force, structural unemployment, the relocation of industry and the emergent forms of worker consciousness. In state socialist societies, the role of the working class in national liberation was important, as was the possibility of non state-sponsored organisation. Within peripheral capitalist countries scholars were concerned with the processes of proletarianisation, the nature of worker struggles and their relationship to the peasantry and urban poor. And this does not quite exhaust the list I prepared. Some of these themes are picked up by the essays collected in Boyd, Cohen & Gutkind (1987), which form part of the new international labour studies approach and will hopefully help to adumbrate and extend it.

The dissatisfaction with existing approaches was conditioned by a sense (experienced both by scholars and labour activists) that there had been important changes in the objective circumstances confronting international labour but that these were inadequately addressed in conventional ideas and practices. In the post-war period large-scale labour migration, particularly to Europe and North America, had brought metropolitan and peripheral sections of the global labour force together - with all the consequential possibilities for inter-racial subordination, tension and sometimes cooperation (see Cohen 1987). Later, in the mid-1970s, as labour imports slowed up, capital exports generalised commodity relations beyond Europe and the US to nearly all parts of the globe. The rise of the transnational enterprise, the creation of what has rather exaggeratedly been termed 'the global assembly line' and the consequent changes in the international division of labour (see Chapter 9) all provided a different material basis for cross-national worker solidarity. It is arguable that this underlying basis provides not only a different, but also a far stronger, foundation for collective organisation than the early Internationals.

On the other hand, many observers noted that the existing international trade union organisations were too infected by the viruses of the Cold War to command general support across bloc lines. This did (and does) not exclude the possibility of trade secretariats or other sectional bodies becoming more relevant than their parent or umbrella organisations. However, after the Second World War the structures of leadership of the large federations (WFTU, ICFTU, WCL) were too dug into entrenched ideological positions to transcend their origins in Cold War rivalries or to take advantage of the new possibilities of worker internationalism.

Amongst progressive scholars and revolutionary intellectuals an implicit consensus therefore developed in the 1970s. Greater worker internationalism was possible, but there were no likely contenders for assuming the organisational function. But it is important to point out that the argument was not confined to the intelligentsia. There were many initiatives from within the ranks of the movement, for example, the promotion of visits by shop stewards from different countries to branches of the same firm; the convening of industry-specific conferences (a notable example is the sugar industry where refinery workers meet cane cutters); the growth of multinational bargaining; dockers preventing the import of products from repressive regimes like Chile and South Africa; and so on. The flowering of an independent trade union movement in Poland also led to numerous acts of solidarity and support.

The growth of these and related manifestations of worker internationalism will in the long run be the decisive indicators of whether a greater level of organisational and political coherence is possible. For the moment all one can advance is a more cautious and qualified reappraisal of the idea of a liberatory working class. In trying to identify and characterise a similar group of scholars sharing a similar interest in re-theorising the role of international labour in my earlier paper (Cohen 1980), I point to a sudden surge of academic interest in the international labour studies in Venezuela, Mexico, South Africa, Britain, the US, Scandinavia, Germany, Holland and Canada.

Amongst what are no doubt numerous other examples, I am familiar with the following scholarly initiatives commencing in the 1970s.

In Venezuela, a labour history group comprising scores of researchers was formed in 1977 at the Central University in Caracas. In Mexico City, a number of studies were initiated bearing on the response of the Mexican, Central and Latin American working class to successive phases of imperialism (Chilcote 1979). Again in Mexico, the *Instituto Nacional de Estudios del Trabajo* together with the *Centro de Estudios Sociológicos* launched a pamphlet series on labour conditions in each of the Latin American countries, a project later extended to cover the Caribbean.

Even in the repressive climate of South Africa, a radical and active journal, the *South African Labour Bulletin*, linking academics to the emerging trade union movement, was launched. Radical academics also organised large conferences on *Labour History* and on *Labour, Townships and Patterns of Protest*, at Witwatersrand University which generated books under these titles (Bozzoli 1979; Webster 1978). In December 1983 a research group on international labour issues was established in Cape Town as a service to the unions.

In Britain, the History Workshop based at Oxford, by its meetings and a widely-read *History Workshop Journal*, has succeeded in legitimating the oral history of working people and freeing labour history from the more formal debates of economic historians and the officialese of trade union-sponsored histories. Also at Ruskin College, Oxford, the Trade Union Media Group changed its name in 1977 to the Trade Union International Research and Education Group to reflect more accurately its changed perception of its role. In January 1984, a new journal, *International Labour Report*, was launched by trade unions and others in North West England to 'encourage awareness, discussion and activity on international labour issues at all levels within the trade union movement.'

In the US, the Study Group on International Labor and Working-class History (affiliated to the American Historical Association) has produced a biennial journal, *International Labor and Working-class History* (*ILWCH*), dedicated to the advancement of labour studies since 1972, which has now specifically extended its coverage to areas other than the US and Europe. In one issue Winn (1979) reports on the convening of an international workshop on 'The Urban Working Class and Social Protest in Latin America' held at the Woodrow Wilson Center in Washington DC. His description of the meeting is interesting in that it independently echoes the idea of a newly founded and distinctive academic interest in international labour issues. Winn, however, confines what he explicitly calls 'the new labour studies' to Europe and the US to which he contrasts 'the

traditional [i.e. Latin American] focus on unions, parties and leaders.'
He continues:

> The workshop prospectus, prepared by Sofer, had encouraged
> participants to abandon this older perspective in favour of the concern
> with culture and consciousness viewed from below, that typifies the new
> labor studies in Europe and the US. It was striking how difficult this re-
> orientation proved to be in practice.

Other more radical groups, such as the North American Congress on
Latin America and the Institute for the Study of Labor and Economic
Crisis (San Francisco), and radical journals, such as *Latin American
Perspectives*, *The Socialist Review* and the *Review of Radical Political
Economics*, have all increasingly published material or initiated
projects on international labour issues.

In Sweden, a group identified by its Swedish acronym AKUT,
which forms part of the Political Science department at Uppsala,
changed its focus from 'development studies' to 'labour studies' to
reflect the switch in emphasis and orientation of its work (AKUT
1983). In Copenhagen and Oslo, a similar reorganisation of scholarly
work was reported in 1982 (Waterman 1982).

In Germany, there are numerous related initiatives, perhaps the
most notable being the work of the researchers at the Max Planck
Institute at Starnberg, on 'the new international division of labour'
(Fröbel et al. 1980), discussed in Chapter 9 of this book.

In Holland, under the energetic leadership of Peter Waterman, a
conference on strikes in the Third World was convened in 1977 (a
selection of the papers was published in *Development and Change*
(April 1979)), while Waterman was again instrumental in founding a
Dutch Labour Studies Group, which includes trade union
participation, concentrating on international issues. His home
institution, the Institute of Social Studies, offers a Masters' degree in
Labour Studies with a thesis to be written in the area of International
and Comparative Labour Relations, Workers' Participation, Self-
Management and Producer Cooperatives and the Trade Unions and
the Labouring Poor.

One can go on. Many of these developments were reflected in the
pages of the Dutch-based *Newsletter of International Labour Studies*
and the Canadian journal *LABOUR Capital and Society/TRAVAIL
Capital et Société*, launched in 1979. The journal is a
transmogrification from the title *Manpower and Unemployment
Research*, itself a widening of the regionalist title, *Manpower and
Unemployment Research in Africa*. That a new direction was
anticipated can be seen in the editor's introduction to the first
number under the title, 'The new title is indeed a bold step.' She
writes, 'the old title was useful but needlessly restrictive since it
addressed itself to only one aspect of labour problems, namely

unemployment... we shall widen our purview to include all aspects of worker problems in the Third World, particularly within the context of the International Community' (Boyd 1979: 1). *LABOUR Capital and Society* also began publishing an annual *Register of Ongoing Labour Research* in 1979.

In his concluding bibliography to Boyd et al. (1987), Waterman lists no less than 37 periodicals, many of them mushrooming since the mid-1970s, concerned with regional or international labour issues. Student access to this literature is best gained through the excellent synthesis of the field provided by Ronaldo Munck (1988).

The themes of this book

Clearly, the efforts to establish a 'new international labour studies' are not all of equivalent significance, nor do they stem from identical pressures, nor again are they yet that well-organised in terms of a programmatically-agreed scholarly endeavour, or in that of a professional association or organisation. None the less, my own work falls very much within the broad pattern of international labour studies described above. In this selection (and in the subsequent revisions) of my work, I have sought to focus on one overall theme and three subsidiary themes, as detailed below.

Contested domains

The overall theme of contestation by labouring people on the one hand and representatives of the state and capital on the other is reflected in the title of the book and the comments already made in the foreword. The central problem alluded to here is the respective weight of determination from outside ('control') and the level of intervention to open out a greater range of choice ('resistance'). The same problem can be expressed, to paraphrase Marx, in this way: 'workers can make their history but they cannot make it in the time and circumstance of their choosing.'

The various institutional domains where the contest takes place ('structure') both channel and provide limits to the expression of class consciousness and action ('agency'). In particular, two major features of 'structure' assert themselves - the composition of the state and the organisation of capital. But instead of leaving the argument at that general level - which falsely ascribes a uniform capacity to each of these structures, in my text I have specified *which* states at *what* time and *which* employers with *what* purpose act in support of the structure.

Thus, in Chapter 3, we see the US state inducing a sense of national consciousness and citizenship among the industrial workers drawn from Eastern Europe at the turn of the century. These workers came from backgrounds so ethnically diverse that they threatened to undermine the dominant Anglo hegemony of political office, capital and culture, to which they now had to be made subject. By contrast, the colonial state in Africa (Chapter 5) sought to establish a delicate balance between peasanthood and proletarianisation, precisely because the possibility of the modern worker movement linking with nationalist elements threatened the authority of colonial rule. Again, in the case of modern Europe (Chapter 9) the state is seen as multiplying, rather than unifying, definitions of citizenship and belonging.

Pari passu, employers do not habituate and control workers in an identical way. In the case of US agricultural labour (Chapter 4) we notice the employer associations seeking to perpetuate deference to their power by prolonging the migrant status of their labourers. In the Newly Industrialising Countries (NICs) of South East Asia, however, employers seek to substitute their paternal authority over young women workers for the authority of the women's fathers in the villages (Chapter 8).

The point of these examples and others provided in the book is not simply to provide a sort of democratic hotchpotch of every case under the sun, but to lend much greater specificity as to how control is effected and maintained and how, *per contra*, resistance is organised and advanced. This sense of cut and thrust, response and counter-response is sadly lacking in many left writers. In my view it is insufficient to cry 'conspiracy' when talking of employers, 'hegemony' when talking of the state and 'revolution' when referring to workers. Instead, as I try to demonstrate in this book, the responses of state, capital and labour have to be more subtly theorised as the interplay between control and resistance unfolds in the real world.

Objects and subjects

Within the wide-ranging theme of contested domains it is necessary to express more precisely who it is we are speaking of. A number of the chapters here thus seek to explore the definition of the 'object' of study. For example, Chapter 2 identifies a number of categories of workers in the Third World (rural/urban/migrant) and compares and contrasts their sociological characteristics with the more familiar cases of the UK and the US. The classical urban/industrial proletariat of these countries is described in Chapter 3, to which is added the lesser-known case of US agricultural labour (Chapter 4).

Subsequent chapters deal with the contrast and similarity between a state of peasanthood and that of a proletariat - and with the emergence of an intermediate category between these forms. The distinction between the lumpenproletariat or subproletariat and the proletariat 'proper' is pursued in Chapter 7, while yet another contrast between a 'helot' and a 'citizen-worker' is established in Chapter 9.

Discussion of all these categories and sub-categories is the necessary sociological precursor of a more political discussion of the capacities and potentialities of the various groups to act in defence, or in advancement, of their group interests. The 'objects' of study become the 'subjects' of history.

Treating categories as both objects and subjects is vital to my wider purpose. On the one hand, I try to convey the contexts in which volition and group-will are insufficient (because of overwhelming structural constraints) to the exercise of a radical political purpose. On the other hand, I portray the contexts in which a favourable setting is left unexploited through a lack of organisation, direction and political contestation. For example, in Chapter 8, David Michael and I challenge the 'Fanonists' for believing that the lumpenproletariat can be galvanised to fulfil a revolutionary purpose - for this category, we argue, mere will will not suffice to find a way. A contrasting example is found above, where I argue that the objective conditions for greater worker internationalism have been created by increased capital mobility and labour migration, but that international worker organisations are ineffective and out of date. (They continue to divide, for instance, on Cold War lines even after the Soviet Union and the US have declared the war over.)

Overt and covert protests

The notion that the objects of analysis can transmute into acting subjects advancing a cause, implies awareness, motivation, consciousness. These are words that all too easily drag a writer into a quagmire. Can there be such a thing as 'false' consciousness, as Marxists want to assert, or is this not a contradiction in terms? And what of the unconscious probed by the Freudians and current-day psychoanalysts? Can the unconscious (or more pristinely, instinct) impel actions more powerful than the expressed consciousness of a political movement or a trade union?

I do not address these issues through some prior understanding of 'human nature' or through the lens of a psychologist, but through inference - using conduct and behaviour as a guide to motivation, intention and 'consciousness.' Thus in Chapter 4, I discuss the 'habituation' of agricultural labourers, using this term to capture the slow, dripping, disabling features that surround the life of farm workers in the US. Poor housing, adverse health conditions, low pay, bad food, dangerous conditions of work and a number of other aspects are discussed, each enfeebling the human spirit and its will to resist. I also deploy the cognate notion of 'interior determination' to illustrate how some aspects of the external oppressive world are internalised and reproduced by the workers' own culture and sub-culture. This then is the most insidious form of control - with the victims inhibiting their own possibility for escape or rebellion.

But if my empirical material can yield such a depressing outcome, it can also demonstrate a rich and wide variety of protest. Resistance can be a subtle matter - apparent compliance can conceal passive rejection, individual acts of rebellion and more complex patterns of group mobilisation. In Chapters 3 and 6, I attempt a systematic review of the various forms of resistance and encounter - covering such issues as theft, desertion, absenteeism, drunkenness, lateness, drug abuse, sabotage, go-slows and other manifestations of worker dissent that have nearly always failed to reach the textbooks of industrial relations.

Of course pay disputes, grievance handling, strikes and other open manifestations of worker resistance are also important and need to be analysed and discussed in their own right. The difficulty of concentrating *solely* on overt forms of protest is that the hidden forms may escape notice, even where (as in contexts where open organisation is legally repressed) they are the more potent form of struggle. Normally both forms of struggle coexist - and the difficult theoretical problem, addressed several times in the text, is to explain and analyse the rhythm of their mutual interaction.

Paradigms and pre-paradigms

The word 'paradigms' has become in recent years a rather pretentious way of saying 'ideas,' 'models' or 'theories.' But, without assuming a full Kuhnian meaning, it is useful here to characterise 'the new international labour studies' as in a 'pre-paradigmatic' stage. Those pursuing the study of labour in the new mode are still dependent on, but likely to soon break free of, the more developed cognate fields of labour history, trade union studies, industrial relations and what I call in this chapter 'technicist labour studies.'

The new international labour studies is pre-paradigmatic in another sense too, in that the 'internationalism' of 'international studies' remains under-theorised. Elsewhere in this book I show how the globalist and international (they are not necessarily one and the same) perspectives of recent years have proved difficult models for the emerging conceptions to model themselves on. In Chapter 8, I put the usual cast of more developed paradigms through their paces - covering in rapid order modernisation theory, dependency theory and world systems analysis. Again in Chapter 8, I suggest that while none of these perspectives is adequate to our purposes, a modified version of the 'new international division of labour theory' may well prove to be a compatible paradigm, complementing at the level of world capital what we are trying to achieve with respect to world labour.

Conclusion

The 1980s have proved to be an infertile decade for the development of critical, let alone Marxist, social theory. Everywhere, and not least in the nominally socialist states of Eastern Europe, 'the market' is triumphant. The fetishism of the market has been turned not merely into the *deus ex machina* of a resurgent capitalism, but into a universal law supposedly governing the dynamics of all societies.

In such an impoverished notion there is little room for theorising 'international labour' - except in two respects. First, international migrants (discussed in Chapter 9) can be seen as responding to market forces in leaving countries without jobs in favour of those with job vacancies. Second, improvements in pay and conditions (or the reverse) can be assessed as adjustments to labour and skill shortages or surpluses.

I would regard such a view as inadequate. While it may be correctly asserted that Marx and Engels wholly exaggerated the potential for organised labour to lead a liberatory struggle for humankind, the counter-exaggeration (that working people have no special role above the sale of their labour-power as a commodity in the market place) is clearly untrue too.

All over the world (I have discussed in some detail in this book the situation in over 15 countries) labouring people *have* galvanised some level of opposition to the control of the employers and the state. Nor can this opposition be reduced to mere bargains struck in the marketplace. In the development of their consciousness, organisation and practices working people have found a voice (often a hesitant and uncertain one) that speaks to humankind in a different pitch and tone to that of their employers. Occasionally this resonates outside the ranks of working people - to allied classes, sympathetic intellectuals and progressive sections of the capitalist world order. It is to capturing this voice, this intimation of an alternative future, that this book is dedicated.

Bits of this paper have been bent to serve a number of purposes. I drafted it first as an internal paper at Warwick University which sought to differentiate 'international labour studies' from 'comparative industrial relations.' Industrial Relations is particularly strongly and diversely represented at Warwick - at the Industrial Relations Research Unit and elsewhere in Industrial and Business Studies. I mention this, as I wish to make clear that I do not direct the charges I make against the IR tradition to my immediate colleagues, but rather to the more orthodox traditions in the US and elsewhere in the UK. At the same time, there is no doubt that all IR theorists find it difficult to move in a comparative direction beyond Europe, the US and the colonies of Anglo-Saxon settlement and beyond such obviously comparable elements as strike statistics, labour law and the rates of union membership. As explained in the body of the chapter, the paper was extended in 1979/80 to become the introductory 'keynote' paper underlying a series of seminars at McGill University. It was published in this early form as a Working Paper under the title of 'The "New" International Labour Studies,' No. 27, Centre for Developing Area Studies, McGill, *1980. Subsequently the paper was adapted for publication in R.E. Boyd et al.* International Labour and the Third World: the Making of a New Working Class, *Aldershot, Avebury, 1987, 3-17.*

2

Workers in Developing Societies

Definitions

To talk about a 'working class' in the developing societies of Africa, Asia, Latin America, the Caribbean and the Middle East might initially appear premature, both in a numerical and sociological sense. It has become embedded in the popular consciousness of metropolitan societies that developing nations are 'peasant' societies, locked in a rural universe and producing goods won from the soil in the 'traditional' manner of generations of tillers.

Few contemporary scholars of peripheral societies would now be insensitive to the massive changes in rural lifestyles wrought by the expansion of the capitalist world system since the sixteenth century. Communal systems of land tenure have been all but totally undermined. In many countries landholdings have become consolidated, crops are produced for reasons of commerce rather than subsistence, while the processes of urbanisation, migration and industrialisation are everywhere visible and accelerating rapidly. Despite these observed processes, however, there remains a curious reluctance to accept that a new working class of considerable dimensions and with a potentially great political significance has already been created in the fields, factories and backyard slums characteristic of peripheral cities.

The scholars' reserve is, in a sense, understandable - for the initial problems of definition of what constitutes a 'working class' in such an environment are indeed formidable. If we accept only a minimalist view, for example 'those working in full-time wage employment in establishments employing over ten persons' (a definition often favoured in labour legislation and by planners and international agencies), the number of 'workers' in peripheral societies is indeed low. However, such a restrictive definition ignores the fact that the land is often deserted in favour of contract, seasonal, or temporary wage labour. There is, in short, a large group in the population that is simultaneously and ambiguously 'semi-proletariat' and 'semi-peasant,' whose situation is described below. Equally, in the *favelas* and shanty towns large numbers of individuals are sometimes designated as 'unemployed' or as a 'subproletariat' or 'lumpenproletariat', but are in fact intermittently employed performing services or in small workshops employing a handful of workers and apprentices. In the case of this group the ambiguity arises from the fact that it comprises people who can at the same time be considered self-employed and employees.

Misconceptions

So long as the definitional parameters of the working class in the periphery remain restricted by the model derived from contemporary industrial societies, the importance of workers will be minimised. But the relative invisibility of the working class in developing societies also arises from persistent misconceptions at the political and ideological levels. The first misconception is that the working class is not only small in numbers but is also 'privileged,' especially in relation to the unemployed, petty traders and rural dwellers. This view is often simply held as self-evident; at the level of the peripheral state it is frequently invoked to hold down wage demands in the interests of 'development.' But it is also given theoretical status by a number of authors, Fanon (1967) being a notable example of a polemicist who holds that the working class can be seen as 'bourgeois.' A similar notion of privilege in relation to other segments of the population is seen in the use of the concept of a 'labour aristocracy,' initially used to distinguish craft from manual workers, then by Lenin to typify metropolitan workers fattened by imperialism and now to characterise a section of - or indeed the total - wage labour force in the periphery. From the notion of privilege stems a second ideological misconception, this time found in the writings (or more often the commentaries on the writings) of practising revolutionaries on three continents - including Mao Zedong, Che Guevara and (again) Fanon. The common conception is that revolutions in the peripheral countries are 'peasant revolutions'; the role of workers is therefore seen as marginal or irrelevant. The study of peasants as revolutionaries has acquired formidable academic support (for example Moore 1966; Wolf 1966; Shanin 1971a; Alavi 1965). But by over-reacting to the Marxist view of the exclusive authenticity of proletarian struggle in favour of a peasant-led explanation of major social changes, there is a danger of underestimating the real level of worker participation.

Rural workers

Other serious reservations about the prevailing orthodoxies can be indicated. Take, for example, the initial conventional wisdom that capitalist social relations have not seriously penetrated the countryside. In terms of our present concern, the major index to refute this claim would be evidence of the extent of wage employment in the countryside. One interesting, if still controversial, viewpoint is that there existed a proletariat of a kind (in respect of the typical labour process, with 'hidden' wage and work practices) in the plantations of the New World - in Brazil, Central America, the US South and the Caribbean - either earlier or at roughly the same time as the European proletariat emerged (Mintz 1974).

While the delineation of a 'plantation proletariat' in the New World can perhaps be considered rather esoteric, there seems little doubt that the intensification of commercial agriculture, combined with population pressure, has led in recent decades to the emergence of millions of new agricultural labourers compelled to work for wages. The process is dramatically evident in India - surely the 'peasant' country *par excellence*. There, even allowing for problems in the definition and collection of the statistical evidence, Sau's (1979) conclusions from his comparisons of the 1961 and 1971 decennial censuses seem inescapable. Of the three categories ('cultivators,' 'agricultural labourers' and 'other workers') comprising the rural work-force, the number of cultivators and other workers has stabilised, while 28 million more agricultural labourers have appeared over the ten-year period - exactly the same increase as that in the rural work-force as a whole. Thus, in the case of India alone, assuming the trend continued through the 1970s, roughly as many rural labourers (who have virtually escaped any Western sociological attention) have been created as comprise the total population of France.

Finally, with respect to the development of a rural working class, it is necessary to note how the enormous expansion of agribusiness in the post-1945 period has created a modern plantation system and numerous agriculturally related jobs. The case of Del Monte, the California-based transnational, is instructive. By 1967 the company owned canneries and plantations in 20 countries - including Kenya, the Philippines, Guatemala and Mexico. In the Bajo Valley of Mexico alone, 5,250 workers are employed in Del Monte's field-factory (NACLA 1976).

If the existence of a working class in the countryside can now be roughly documented, it is clear that it has not been adequately theorised, either politically or sociologically. Lenin, for example, tended to assimilate the 'rural proletariat' into the urban one and drew no firm distinction between the forms of struggle characteristically found in urban and rural areas. The initial form of resistance by a rural community is indeed to try to cling to its own means of production (land, tools and labour-power) and thereby prevent the full process of proletarianisation from unfolding.

It is for this reason that most colonial governments resorted extensively to forced labour, rather than the 'lure' of wages. In another sense, it was not in the interests of colonial capital (in particular) to detach workers too violently or completely from the land: their low-wage policies could then be justified by reference to the idea that workers had a supplementary income from their agricultural produce. The contradiction between a necessary supply of labour-power to the towns and plantations and the benefits that a viable peasant economy conferred by subsidising the cost of the reproduction of labour was partially resolved by the development of migrant labour systems. The individuals enmeshed in these systems became, as it were, 'peasant-workers,' or, if one prefers an even more adventurous term, the 'peasantariat'. In the countryside peasant-workers resisted recruitment by communal flight, evasion of the taxes designed to draw them into the wage economy, and desertion from the labour gangs. At the point of production they evolved an ingenious set of strategies, graphically described in the case of Southern Rhodesia by van Onselen (1976), involving symbolic and cultural protests, theft, sabotage and the reduction of tasks, labour time and productivity.

Protests against the migrant system were normally constrained by the inconsistent relationship the peasantariat had to the means of production - a relationship that led to sporadic, localised and individualistic forms of class consciousness. The importance of an attachment to the land, albeit increasingly only an emotional one, has led Shanin (1971) to argue that even in the case of post-war migrants to Europe, 'in their social and political characteristics, labour migrants carry aspects of peasanthood not only in the traces of the past in the present, but also in terms of actual relations and contacts, both real and imaginary.' While the 'traces of the past' typically act to mediate the development of a full proletarian consciousness, an important limiting case is one where the retention of an independent means of production causes workers to take *more*, not fewer, risks and to adopt more militant postures than those of their co-workers with fully urban backgrounds (Sandbrook & Cohen 1975: 312). This case was repeated in Iran in 1980, where construction workers, with a base in the villages to which they could retreat, openly challenged the post-revolutionary regime with respect to its economic and employment policies.

Urban workers

As well as creating a dependence on wages in the countryside and a class of peasant-workers, the spread of capitalist social relations into peripheral societies has propelled the growth of more conventionally described urban and industrial workers. The pattern of industrialisation exhibits large regional variations, but Ranis (1979) provides a useful generalisation in the case of Latin America. He identifies three phases:

—First, the 1880-1930 period, when a small light industrial sector, concentrating on clothing, textiles, handicrafts and furniture, developed.
—Second, from the Depression of 1930 to the early 1940s, when the strategy of import substitution was predominant and household and consumer goods were produced locally.
—Third, from the late 1950s to the 1960s, when infrastructural and heavy industrial plant was laid down while employment in the service sector showed explosive growth.

The Latin American pattern can be contrasted with the subsequent expansion of export-oriented manufacturing in peripheral capitalist countries (a trend perfected in the four Asian 'tigers' - Hong Kong, Singapore, Taiwan and South Korea). Other notable export-geared manufacturing bases have been established in northern Mexico, Malaysia, the Philippines and elsewhere. As the editors of a collection on workers and peasants note (Cohen et al. 1979), 'there is no doubt we are in the midst of a substantial relocation of industries on a world-wide scale, a trend being orchestrated and led by transnational companies.' The Brandt Commission (1980) popularised the term 'newly industrialising countries' to cover such structural shifts in global manufacturing.

The working class in peripheral countries is thus set for an enormous quantitative expansion, especially if the number of workers in the small open-air sweat shops (the so-called 'informal sector') is considered. The informal sector is, in addition, likely to experience greater growth as rural populations are further displaced and as planners expect to assist the informal sector through easier access to credit, training to upgrade skills, technical advice on product improvement and the provision of better tools and infrastructural facilities (Brandt Commission 1980: 130).

An expanded notion of the working class must also include those from peripheral zones who have been sucked into the central economies - the advanced capitalist societies - as temporary migrants or immigrant settlers. The migrants are normally escaping a reproduction sector that does not even permit the replacement of labour-power at existing levels of nutrition and they are destined for jobs that are dirty, unskilled and dangerous, with low status and poor pay, at least by metropolitan standards. The numbers involved are considerable. By 1975 workers from peripheral zones constituted 10 per cent of the labour force in western Europe as a whole. In France they represented 11 per cent of the total labour force, while in Switzerland the proportion surpassed 25 per cent. Since the mid-1960s, the US has also experienced a huge influx of workers from the Caribbean (including Puerto Rico) and Mexico. Illegal migrants alone are estimated at anything from two to seven million (Piore 1979: 1). These migrants are paralleled by migration to industrially active zones within the periphery. The Iraqi invasion of Kuwait in 1990 brought to public attention the enormous inflows of labour from Asia and Egypt to the Gulf states. Similar flows exist from Colombia to Caracas in Venezuela and from neighbouring countries to South Africa, particularly to the Rand area.

Politics

Given the limited political and civic rights and low levels of organisation characteristic of a work-force that can easily be expelled from production, there is frequently a low level of political organisation and consciousness among migrant workers. Castells (1979) goes so far as to argue that the use of migrants has become a structural requirement for monopoly capitalism, both in the sense that they help to iron out the stops and starts of the economy, and in that they help to fracture the class composition of indigenous workers. Migrants, however, have begun to organise defensively within their communities and at their places of work around such issues as residential and legal rights and the need to join or organise trade unions. These modes of organisation are slowly cutting into the capacity of the advanced capitalist states to use migrants as a flexible 'reserve army.'

But what levels of consciousness and forms of organisation and action can be anticipated from workers within developing countries themselves? It is first necessary to discount the argument that they constitute a privileged group *en masse*. Such a characterisation may be applied, with reservations, to a narrow band of salaried workers and to exceptional cases like that of the white working class in South Africa. But the bulk of unskilled and semi-skilled workers have been wrongly compared to the peasantry in terms of the income of the employed head of an urban household, ignoring the fact that this relative advantage is offset by the higher cost of living in the towns, the practice of transferring income from urban to rural households and the larger size of the dependent urban household (Sandbrook & Cohen 1975: 3). This last point is particularly important in understanding the political and social role of workers in peripheral capitalist societies. There is little evidence to suggest that the urban poor, the small-scale traders, or the peasantry have accepted the image of selfish unionised urban workers held by planners, officials and politicians. On the contrary, there appears to be a wide acceptance of workers and their principal class organs, the trade unions, as articulators of a wider set of grievances and ideologies than those that can simply be reduced to a wage demand.

In Latin America, workers have been deeply influenced by anarchist, syndicalist and socialist views, and strikes and other manifestations of dissent often spread far beyond the confines of the dues-paying membership. In the Buenos Aires General Strike of 1970, for example, a socialist newspaper estimated a participation of 93,000 workers in 16 trades (Spalding 1977: 24). Of these, some 31,000 had participated actively in union activities, while only 10,000 regularly paid dues. In Africa and Asia worker organisations were usually in the forefront of anti-colonial and nationalist struggles, even though a good deal of disillusionment with the leadership of the post-colonial states soon set in. On the other hand, workers in peripheral capitalist societies have rarely succeeded in establishing viable worker parties or in influencing the character or policies of socialist parties (though some exceptions to this statement can be recorded in Argentina, Mexico and Chile).

Workers have tended instead to participate in politics on the basis of immediate grievances, with actions including rent strikes, marches, demonstrations and strikes. Workers in larger establishments in particular have shown a capacity to participate in class action and to achieve a political impact quite disproportionate to their relatively small numbers. Their strategic concentration in big towns and cities close to the centres of power has allowed workers to damage severely the credibility of post-colonial governments, especially those of recent provenance. Worker-led protests have culminated in a change of government in a significant number of countries. In the late 1970s alone a strike movement in Egypt, starting in January 1977, escalated into an uprising of the urban and rural poor. One year later the national trade-union centre of Tunisia, previously known for its moderate character, enraged the government sufficiently for its protests to be treated as tantamount to an insurrection (Waterman 1974: 177). The revolutionary movement in Iran, it is now (in 1990) easy to forget in the turmoil of events, was also triggered by strikes by petroleum workers. In the late summer of 1978 guerrilla action in Nicaragua was followed by a general strike which led ultimately to a civil war and a rupture with the US. The contagion spread, mainly through the agency of workers and students, to other Central American countries. Strikes in what Western newspapers called 'Africa's most stable country,' Liberia, led to the collapse of the legitimacy of the True Whig Party and the assassination of its president in a *coup d'état* in April 1980. The subsequent collapse of the country into civil war demonstrated how narrow a political base was commanded by the Americo-Liberian kleptocracy.

Finally, in this brief review there remains only the task of making a few remarks about the role of workers in peripheral socialist societies. It has already been argued that the participation of workers has been downgraded by those who have interpreted revolutionary political action as stemming largely from the peasantry. Detailed studies of the Algerian, Cuban and Chinese cases confirm the errors of this view (Clegg 1971; Zeitlin 1967; Chesneaux 1968). But it is important to emphasise (as does Petras 1975), that there is an interaction between potentially revolutionary classes and fractions of classes. While the impetus, organisation, ideology and leadership of a revolutionary struggle might begin in the urban areas, the success of revolution in the periphery seems to depend on its linking with the bulk of social forces located in the countryside.

My good friends and colleagues, Teodor Shanin and Hamza Alavi, both then at Manchester University, persuaded me to write this short piece for their edited collection Introduction to the Sociology of Developing Societies *(Basingstoke, Macmillan, 1982, pp. 279-86). As they put it, they wanted an encyclopaedia entry, short, to the point, but alluding to all the essential arguments. That is always difficult to do and I reproduce the chapter here, as, to my own mind, I have squeezed in most of the key points in recent debates about workers in developing countries, if only very briefly. It testifies greatly to Hamza and Teodor's ability to see other arguments that they accepted my contribution without demur even though, in Teodor's case, he is much more inclined to argue that some of the people I define as workers are in fact temporarily displaced peasants. His article (1978), with its characteristically ironic title, 'The Peasants are Coming: Migrants who Labour, Peasants who Travel and Marxists who Write,' contains one of the clearest statements of his extended definition of the peasantry. Both Teodor Shanin and Hamza Alavi provided crucial contributions to peasant studies in the UK, the former with his oft-cited reader* Peasants and Peasant Societies *(1971 and subsequent editions), his major work on Russia and his contributions to* The Journal of Peasant Studies; *the latter with his influential work on rural social differentiation in South Asia and the role of peasants in revolutionary movements. Despite my admiration for their work, the drift of my arguments goes off in an opposite direction. Instead of describing modern neophyte workers as 'peasants who travel,' I am more inclined to see the process of proletarianisation as penetrating the countryside. This line of analysis is visible in the above chapter, but asserted much more forcibly in Chapter 5, where an intermediate category of peasant-workers is also discussed.*

3

Work, Culture and the Dialectics of Proletarian Habituation

with Jeff Henderson

Introduction

As Braverman (1974: Ch. 6) argues, with each generation capital has to renew its attempt to habituate workers to a capitalist mode of production. Young workers are 'plunged into work from the outside, so to speak, after a prolonged period of adolescence during which they are held in reserve.' This stress on the continual need for capital to coerce or manipulate the proletariat to accept the industrial work ethic is an element in the process of reproduction that was not, at first, emphasised by Marx. His central project in *Capital* was to analyse the ways in which competitive capitalism is able to reproduce the *means* of production fundamental to its epoch. Marx's discussion of the reproduction and extraction of labour-power is therefore concerned, firstly, with the physical reproduction of the labour force and, secondly, with developments in the labour process designed ever to increase the rate of exploitation.

By 1863, however, Marx saw that the realisation of the capitalist mode of production depended not only on its capacity to reproduce the means of production, but also required reproduction on a more total plane. In the context of an analysis of Quesnay's Economic Table, Marx introduced the concept of the 'whole process of reproduction' (Marx & Engels 1965: 142-4). Here he seems to be pointing not only to domination in the sphere of production, but also to the whole matrix of work orientations, and the social processes through which inequality and exploitation come to be legitimated. These comments, however, amount to no more than an indication that he was aware of the problem of the reproduction of the *relations* of production, the issue with which we are centrally concerned.

31

We begin by following Lefebvre's (1976) distinction between 'exterior conditioning,' which consists, as we understand it, of the overt moves by capital directed against labour, and normally at the point of production; and 'interior determination' - those elements of culture and ideology which become accepted and transmitted, or even generated, by the institutions of proletarian culture itself. In seeking to demonstrate the ways in which the habituation of workers to industrial labour have varied as the capitalist mode of production has been realised, we have drawn briefly on the habituation experiences of African workers and more extensively on the historical experience of British and US workers. Our initial interest in habituation at the point of production is followed by an analysis of reproduction through interior determination in which we pay particular regard to the early British case, to the particular situation of immigrants in US industry and to the role of the state in reproducing the relations of production outside the work place. Reproduction also takes place *within* the social institutions of the proletariat itself - as our discussion of family and community indicates.

In our concluding section we suggest some reasons why the processes of habituation have remained a problem for capital in its contemporary period and identify three principal fractions of labour - migrants, young workers and Third World workers, where the issues of habituation remain unsolved for capital.

Exterior conditioning

Before capital can subjugate a work-force to the demands of industrial production, it has first to create and control a stock of labour-power, separating peasants and artisans from their own means of production and forcing them to sell their remaining asset - their labour-power - as a commodity.

Early examples of worker resistance to the process abound. Research on African labour history, for example, shows that many African communities feared the encroachment of metropolitan capital as they once did the slavery of the mercantilist period (Sandbrook & Cohen 1975; Gutkind et al. 1979). Desertion from work and self-mutilation to escape service in the colonial armies were common. Whole communities fled into remote regions to escape 'blackbirder' recruiters and the colonial soldiery, who were acting for labour-hungry farmers and colonial states initiating public works - railways, roads, ports. Sustained wars of 'pacification,' which were spuriously represented as 'stopping tribal wars,' were designed to subjugate recalcitrant communities. Often the peace terms included a provision that the defeated communities had to provide labour for neighbouring public works. In conjunction with wars of pacification, forced labour was used, while 'hut and poll' taxes were imposed, taxes which, needless to say, could only be paid through money earned in wage labour.

Where the work was particularly dangerous or enervating, as in mining, colonial companies evolved a vicious 'compound' system to habituate workers. In a powerful study of the system of migrant labour to the Rhodesian gold mines, van Onselen (1976) points to the centrality of the compound as a habituating mechanism. Mine-owners exerted an almost 'military discipline' in the compounds, regularly fined workers for 'misdemeanours' and permitted assaults on them. More subtle, but no less obnoxious means of subordination were also used. The credit system (a twisted variation of a company store operation), the provision and production of alcohol, drugs and sex, religious education, dancing and sports - all these were manipulated by mine managements to induce patterns of obedience, servility and, finally, acceptance of the debilitating conditions of work. Workers responded with desertion, theft, individualised pleas for justice and time bargaining (called 'loitering'). As van Onselen (1976: 239) argues, 'compound police, spies, censorship and the *sjambok* (whip) do not produce an environment conducive to the development of public ideologies, organisations, meetings, petitions or strikes ... the pattern of resistance should be looked for in the nooks and crannies of the day-to-day situation.'

Similar early forms of resistance were evidenced by workers in Britain, the US and other industrial countries. Attempts by early industrialists to forge a first-generation working class for their new factories were met by massive absentee and worker mobility (labour turnover) rates, the latter often in excess of 100 per cent per annum. Workers often stubbornly resisted the cultural shifts necessary for them to become effective proletarians, often preferring to adhere to folk customs at odds with the rigorous schedules of factory production (see Pollard 1965; Thompson 1967; Dubofsky 1975; Gutman 1976).

On occasion, individualistic responses to the experience of industrial labour and the erosion of craft skill, which were being produced by the increasingly minute division of labour, coalesced into collective struggle. Perhaps the most famous expressions of this sort in Britain were the Luddite movement of 1811-12 and the Plug Plot riots of 1842 and, in the US, the Lynn shoemakers' strike of 1860, the activities of the Molly Maguires in the Pennsylvania coalfields of the 1870s, and the railroad strikes of 1877 (Thompson 1963; Mather 1959; Dawley 1976; Lens 1974).

It is significant that many of these struggles involved the use of industrial sabotage against capital. The struggles of newly proletarianised workers have a dual logic. On the one hand they express the logic of escape - escape from the work situation - and, on the other, the logic of control - the struggle to stem their diminishing control over the labour process. The logic of escape is clearly expressed in actions such as absenteeism and worker mobility. The early proletarians either moved from one mine, mill or foundry to another, partly out of the belief that the work experience must be better elsewhere, or they simply adhered to their traditional rural customs and periodically (for example, during harvest) returned to a work experience they considered more enjoyable and over which they had more control (Pollard 1965: Ch. 5). The logic of control in these early industrial struggles was of significance where substantial deskilling was involved, as in cotton and woollen manufacture in England, and shoe manufacture in Massachusetts. Where strikes took place the driving force was often skilled craftsmen anxious to re-establish their control over the labour process and hence improve their bargaining position in the labour market. Sabotage was (and is) a form of industrial action that bridges both these logics. On the one hand, sabotage is a symbolic indication that the worker is still the ultimate master over the machinery he services (and which one day may displace him) and, on the other, it gains the worker respite from the monotonous rigours of factory labour.

Manipulation of the labour process was historically the first means adopted by capital to habituate people to industrial labour. Marglin (1976) shows that the first factories in Britain were created, not so that new technologies could be efficiently exploited (for factory production developed prior to the advent of the technology necessary for machinofacture), but rather so that the first industrial capitalists could exert more control over the labour process and increase the rate of exploitation by means of close supervision in the context of an extended division of labour. Mill and foundry workers were often brutally 'driven,' and were subject to dismissal for bad work, and fines for lateness, opening a window or talking.

Another quite early innovation in the mechanics of 'exterior conditioning' was the manipulation of wage-payment systems, primarily through the application of piece-rates. The piece-rate system had a number of advantages from the point of view of habituation. Firstly, it tied worker remuneration to the amount of effort expended and, hence, served to reduce the amount of direct supervision required. Secondly, it was frequently used to ensure that a worker's wage packet partly depended on labour-power extracted from another worker, as where a child was tied to an adult labourer and the adult's wage in part depended on his exploitation of the child. Thirdly, the piece-rate system was a useful way of instilling the centrality of the cash-nexus into the consciousness of workers and, as such, can be seen as having some limited impact on the interior determination of reproduction.

Disciplining workers for trivial (though for capital inconvenient) behaviour has persisted to the present day. As late as the 1930s, for instance, Ford workers were fined for talking in the shop (Beynon 1973: Ch. 1) and the practice of docking 15 minutes' wages from workers who arrive more than two minutes late is standard in British industry.

Similarly, the use of wage manipulation as an habituating technique remains significant. Productivity and bonus schemes abound, though the piece-rate system has fallen out of favour with Western employers over the last ten years or so. A system designed partly to decompose the basis of worker solidarity and to communicate the benefits of individual competition was recovered by the workers and used to their own ends. Workers on piece rates tend to produce only enough to provide what their work group considers an adequate wage (see Roy 1952). The recovery of the piece-rate system, which began in Britain in the 1950s, resulted in a substantial wage drift, coupled with only limited increases in productivity. The response of capital, starting with Chrysler (UK) in 1967, has been the introduction of measured-day work systems.

Perhaps the most significant agent available to capital for habituation at the point of production has been technology. The application of technology to production has, of course, enabled a vast increase in the rate of exploitation, reduced the numbers of labourers required and, via its deskilling capacities, reduced the unit cost of labour (the 'Babbage principle'). As important as these 'advantages' of technology, however, has been the fact that machinery works with a stable and predictable rhythm and can be operated for long periods of time. Through the use of machinery the capitalist is able to set the pace at which the labourer works. The resultant speed-up comes to be perceived by the labourer as the inexorable consequence of the essential application of science to production, thus diverting hostility away from the relations of production.

The habituating capacities of technology were not lost on that early management consultant, Charles Babbage. 'One great advantage which we may derive from machinery,' Babbage (1832: 52) suggests, 'is from the check which it affords against the inattention, the idleness or the dishonesty of human agents.' Nor were they lost on that more blunt ideologue of early capitalism, Andrew Ure (cited in Marx 1967: 437), who saw machinery as 'a creation designed to restore order among the industrious.... This invention confirms the great doctrine... that when capital enlists science into her service, the refractory hand of labour will always be taught docility.'

Not only has technology, in the context of the capitalist division of labour, been a useful means of decreasing worker control over the labour process, but it has also been useful in decomposing the basis on which class struggle is possible in a given period. As Marx (1967: 435-6) points out, machinery 'is the most powerful weapon for repressing strikes.... It would be possible to write quite a history of the inventions made since 1830 for the sole purpose of supplying capital with weapons against the revolts of the working class.' A classic example of the naked use of technology to decompose a work-force occurred in 1885 at the Chicago plant of the McCormick Harvesting Machine Company, a forerunner of International Harvester. Unproven pneumatic moulding machines were introduced into the plant's foundry to eliminate the need for skilled iron moulders who, until that time, had been the most militant section of the factory and had frequently operated as a 'wage vanguard' for the rest of the workers in the plant. By re-equipping the foundry with the new technology (which, due to the inefficiency of the machines, *increased* the cost of castings), McCormick was able to fire all 91 moulders and to replace them with unorganised unskilled labourers (Ozanne 1967: Ch. 1).

It is a direct line from the decomposing effects of the pneumatic moulders on McCormick's work-force to the application of the automatic welding machines (the 'unimates') on the Vega assembly line at General Motors, Lordstown, for essentially the same reason (Rothschild 1973). The intervening 80-odd years had seen the consistent use of new technologies, partly indeed to increase the rate of exploitation, but also partly to discipline and decompose labour. It seems plausible to argue that the rapid technical development of US industry, relative to Europe, resulted in part from the need to habituate successive waves of first-generation working people throughout most of the twentieth century.

The creation and control of a stock of labour-power, the organisation of the labour process within the workplace, wage manipulation and, finally, the use of technology, constitute the weapons capital deploys to habituate a proletariat trying to escape control by capital over its skills and means of subsistence. At an ideological level, Taylorism and Fordism provide the most sustained elaborations of capital's industrial strategy. Yet, as Braverman (1974: Ch. 6) argues, however crude or sophisticated the industrial psychologists' attempts to induce a greater acceptance of managerial authority, academic studies yielded little to management in the way of solid and tangible results. Habituation, he goes on to argue, is not effected by manipulation or cajolery, but by socio-economic conditions and forces. In our view, this formulation of the problem both undervalues the importance of direct initiatives by capital and is overdeterministic in assigning the problem solely to the realm of the substructure. If the dialectics of proletarian habituation are addressed more comprehensively as a problem of the reproduction of the relations of production, we need consider not only conditions and forces of production, but also the manner in which proletarian consciousness and culture articulate with these forces.

Interior determination: early phase

In pre-capitalist epochs, the substantial control peasants and artisans exercised over the labour process, together with the relative absence of a commodity market, meant that the habituation problematic lay not so much at the level of exterior conditioning, but rather at the level of interior determination - and in particular in terms of the work-culture of those destined to take their place as farmers or craftsmen.

Discussions of peasant economies and artisan production suggest that the experience of work was of an activity not substantially detached from the other activities of everyday life. The household was the locus of production and as a result there was an easy, free-flowing relationship between 'work' and 'play.' There was little compartmentalisation of life into separate spheres to be pursued at different times of the day or week (Hilton 1975: Chs. 2 and 3; Thomas 1964; Baudrillard 1975: 96-9; Mallet 1975; and Dawley 1976: Ch. 2). In peasant and artisan economies, production and consumption took place primarily within the collectivity, be it household or village. This autarkic picture was severely disrupted by the growth of capitalist agriculture and the 'putting out' system of manufacture.

In countries peripheral to the centres of capital, merchant capital, though at first only operating in the sphere of exchange, soon transformed both the commodities produced and the relations of production. None the less, one can postulate a period and a mode of production in which there was relatively little division between work and everyday life, between producer and consumer, and between the household hierarchy and the production hierarchy. In such circumstances the interior determination of labour was almost automatic.

The fragmentation of work, the gradual splitting of the internal dialectic between mental and manual labour (which was a consequence of the division of labour initiated with embryonic industrial capitalism), and the location of labourers in factories detached from the community (and hence destroying the cultural unity between work and everyday life), all raised serious problems of proletarian habituation at the point of production. Ever since the last decades of the eighteenth century, strenuous efforts have been made, sometimes by capital alone, sometimes by capital in conjunction with the state, to synchronise the culture and consciousness of proletarians to the demands of factory production. As our analysis of developments in the reproduction of the relations of production progresses, it becomes clear that capital was assisted in its tasks by contradictions inherent in the institutions of proletarian culture. To put it another way, the world's working class did in part make itself, but aspects of its 'making' involved an unconscious complicity in its oppression.

From the beginning ideology played an important role in the interior determination of habituation. To demonstrate this our empirical reference is primarily nineteenth-century Britain and we address ourselves to three ideological forms - the work-orientations of skilled artisans, religion and moralism.

Work-orientations were one way in which the first proletariat had complicity in its own oppression. One component of the attitude a skilled artisan had to his work, which was a remnant from the pre-industrial craft experience, was pride in the job. It was the tradition of the skilled artisan to do a 'fair day's work,' for which he expected a 'fair day's pay,' namely the customary differential of about twice the wage of an unskilled labourer. When at work (i.e. when not observing 'St Monday' or the traditional feast days) artisans expected to work hard. Their interest in hard work and the possibility of having pride in their work of course stemmed directly from the relatively high degree of control they were able to exert over the labour process. This ideological remnant from a pre-industrial period - a remnant which still persists among many skilled and semi-skilled workers - was on occasion of considerable assistance to capital in its attempt to create a stable, efficient work-force. Hobsbawm (1964), for instance, reports that the boiler-makers' union had strict penalties for members who produced bad work, and that conscious and systematic slacking generally produced considerable moral indignation from skilled workers.

Another way in which self-image, particularly of the working-class male, assisted his habituation to factory labour was the 'machismo' association between hard work and virility. To be able to work hard was a necessary component of masculinity, just as the ability to consume vast amounts of beer had a direct association with masculine virility in many working-class cultures (Harrison 1971: 39).

A significant ideological input into the habituation process originating from outside proletarian culture came from the various varieties of Puritanism. The configuration of values known as the Protestant Ethic not only provided, as Weber (1958) shows, the motivational basis for entrepreneurship and the accumulation of capital. For working-class people it had the effect of delegitimating their attachment to pleasurable, hedonistic activities of both a social and sexual kind, and also helped instil the need for time-discipline - an essential attribute of an efficient factory worker. In England, as Thompson (1967; 1963: Ch. 11) argues, Methodism, both from the pulpit and in the Sunday Schools, transmitted the time-as-currency imagery. It emphasised the productive use of time and the sin of time 'wasting' - in effect the sin of pleasure. This was clear in Wesley's own teaching (quoted in Thompson 1967: 88): 'See that ye walk circumspectly, says the Apostle... redeeming the time; saving all the time you can for the best purposes; buying up every fleeting moment out of the hands of sin and Satan, out of the hands of sloth, ease, pleasure, worldly-business.'

Puritan moralism was also used to rationalise attacks on traditional social habits and customs. These attacks were directed against traditional feast days, holidays and indeed almost every aspect of rural culture that inhibited the effective operation of people as mere labour-power. The attacks of the various Puritan-moralist associations were directed particularly against alcohol consumption.

As Harrison (1971) points out in his instructive book on nineteenth-century attitudes to alcohol consumption, it is difficult to make any simple link between the Puritan-moralist attack on drink and industrial interests. He does suggest, however, some connection between textile manufacturing and the emergence of the anti-spirits movement in the 1820s and 1830s, particularly in Glasgow, Preston and the West Riding of Yorkshire. Whether or not the temperance movement was directly manipulated in the interests of capital, its effects were undoubtedly beneficial to capital accumulation. The traditional consumption of alcohol by the labouring classes contributed substantially to the high rates of absenteeism or late time. A movement with the potential of rooting itself in working-class culture that proclaimed the evil of drink could not but assist in the creation of a stable, disciplined labour force.

Though the connection between industrial capital and the temperance movement is somewhat ambiguous, the fact that the capitalists themselves took steps to adjust the culture of their labour force is beyond question. People like Owen, Salt and the Cadburys developed institutional arrangements, as adjuncts to their factories, which looked after the welfare of their workers from birth to the grave. The communities of New Lanark, Saltaire and Bournville were, of course, in part products of capitalist philanthropy, but by providing churches, educational institutes, meeting places and company houses for their workers, and by banning the sale of alcohol, these communities also generated the structural context within which the sober, hard-working, respectful (of authority) proletarian could be created. It is in this sense that the philanthropic worker communities of the mid-nineteenth century must be regarded as a significant (and effective) form of managerial control. They can be seen as one of the first attempts by capital to structure family life, leisure and the personal experiences of working people according to the demands of factory production. The state during the first phase of British industrialisation was not without a role in the reproduction of the relations of production. The first half of the nineteenth century, for instance, saw the codification of the Master and Servant Law, which penalised breaches of contract more severely for workers than for masters. Throughout this period systematic attempts were made to outlaw unions and strike action, a strategy which not infrequently produced folk heroes, such as the 'Tolpuddle Martyrs,' and the state often sanctioned long-term inflexible work contracts, such as the miners' yearly bond (Hobsbawm 1964).

Finally we might mention that insidious piece of legislation, the New Poor Law, which was designed to render poor relief financially viable. By interring people in workhouses the state sought to transmit the reality that the only way they could escape and survive in the outside world was by accepting the rigours and discipline of oppressive, monotonous work.

Interior determination: later phases

So far we have discussed some of the problems confronted by capital in its attempts to habituate proletarians at the levels of both 'exterior conditioning' and 'interior determination' to a developing labour process which was increasingly rooted in the overthrow of the dialectical unity of work and culture (a dialectic paralleling that between mental and manual labour) and in the fragmentation of labour. To observe more fundamental changes in the labour process and to examine the special problem of the immigrant worker, our historical emphasis must now shift to chronologically later phases of industrialisation, in both Britain and the US. As such, it will involve us in making sense of the actions not only of a first-generation working class (as with the US immigrants), but also of a 'mature' working class in both countries.

Unlike their counterparts in Britain and Western Europe generally, US industrialists were confronted with the unique situation of having to habituate a first-generation working class at almost every stage of industrial development. In no other country was the motor of industrial expansion so dependent on successive waves of immigrant rural labourers and artisans. In the first decades of the nineteenth century, US industrialisation relied on the recruitment of skilled artisans from Britain, Germany and Scandinavia. In the latter part of the century, the labour-power was supplied by Irish immigrants; before and after the First World War, by Italians and Poles and Southern migrant blacks; and after the Second World War, by Chicanos and Puerto Ricans.

Gutman (1976) divides US industrialisation in the years to 1919 into three distinct periods - 1815-43, 1843-93, and 1893-1919.

Although each of these periods signify different structurations of the US as an industrial society, Gutman argues that the responses to factory labour of the first general immigrants in these periods, though they were from diverse cultural backgrounds and experiences, were remarkably similar. Gutman also points to the considerable absenteeism of skilled British artisans as well as to that of the unskilled Italian immigrants before the First World War. Similarly, worker mobility, when economic conditions allowed, was a major form which the resistance of the successive waves of first-generation immigrants took. By 1918, with unemployment down to 1.4 per cent, annual worker mobility rates of 1,600-2,000 per cent were not unusual (Montgomery 1974: 514). Though there seems to have been no systematic sabotage of the Luddite variety, first-generation US workers in all three periods seem to have engaged in sporadic sabotage of product, if not of machine (Gutman 1976; Brown 1977).

Resistance to factory labour, like the resistance of a first generation working class the world over, stemmed as much from the US immigrants' own culture as from the labour process itself. In the context of a newly industrialising society an indigenous culture soon begins to transmute into a contra-culture, i.e. a sub-culture generated and structured by its relations of conflict with the dominant culture (Yinger 1960). Like their English compatriots in the late eighteenth and early nineteenth centuries, the first-generation US immigrants were frequently too drunk to work, particularly on pay-days and Mondays. Numerous examples can be cited of immigrants, be they British artisans in the 1830s or Italian labourers in the 1900s, adhering to traditional festivals at the expense of production (Erickson 1957; Korman 1967; Gutman 1976 Montgomery 1977). Cigar makers or coopers, for instance, apparently regularly sent a boy out for drink and food, and thus completed each day having worked only two or three hours.

The techniques adopted to habituate these successive first generation workers in the US differed from the British ones in both degree and urgency. The habituating mechanisms were firstly more systematic at an earlier period (though not necessarily more effective) than those used for their British counterparts, and secondly they were developed primarily and quite directly by the industrialists themselves.

The systematic attack on the US workers' contra-culture was initiated with the development of the monopoly trusts before the First World War. The attack, which was organised by industry and operated at the levels of both 'exterior conditioning' and 'interior determination,' for the first time in history established what has recently come to be known as the 'social factory' - in other words, the systematic extension of the relations of production into everyday life - into the realm of the employees' leisure and non-work activities.

The disintegration of the first-generation work contra-culture was effected by the development of Taylorist and Fordist production and control techniques on the one hand, and by the development of an ideological ('Americanising') and welfarist strategy on the other. The creation of the massified detail labourer (abstract labour) that was a product of the Taylorist and Fordist 'innovations' has already been mentioned. The welfarist strategy which was developed initially and most extensively by International Harvester included pension and sickness benefit schemes, profit sharing, improved working conditions, and sports and educational facilities. Like the earlier British 'industrial communities,' the strategy developed from a mixture of capitalist philanthropy and a desire to generate company loyalty and a docile labour force. Welfarism during the 'Progressive Era' went hand in hand with the physical repression of militant trade unionism, while at the same time paying lip service - via the National Civic Federation - to the ideal of (conservative) trade union recognition.[1]

It was primarily via their repressive apparatuses that the Federal and State governments assisted employers in their attempts to habituate the US working class during the decades prior to the New Deal. Working-class history of this period is strewn with examples of police attacks on strikers and militant labour organisations, from the execution of the Molly Maguires and the Haymarket anarchists, to the repression of the Wobblies and on to the sit-down strikes of the 1930s. These were the years of what Lens (1974) calls the 'labour wars,' when probably the most combative working class in history was confronted by the combined force of capital and the state, and organisationally was defeated (see also Foner 1964; Weinstein 1967; Dubofsky 1969, 1975; and Brecher 1972).

In other ways during the years prior to the New Deal, capital operated to ensure the interior determination of the relations of production. After the Young Men's Christian Association (YMCA) had initiated a language and citizenship programme ('American-isation') for immigrant workers in 1907, employers soon grasped the advantage of language training to the creation of a disciplined work-force. Language training relating directly to production needs was developed (usually with YMCA assistance) by International Harvester in 1910 and Ford in 1914. Lesson One of Harvester's (Chicago) English Instruction included these literary gems: 'I hear the whistle, I must hurry' and 'I work until the whistle blows to quit.' Lesson Two admonished 'No benefits will be paid if you are hurt while scuffling or fooling' (quoted by Korman 1967: 144-6). Ford, usually the most zealous of US capitalists at this time, made language training in his factories compulsory; this was but a part of the training his immigrant workers had to undertake to obtain citizenship.

Language training was not the only level at which US capital during this period intervened in the everyday life of workers to adjust their culture to the needs of intensified production schedules. Ford, characteristically, tied his $5-a-day pay proposal of 1914 to a cultural qualification. Not only did people have to be 'model' (i.e. disciplined) workers in the factory to qualify, but their personal and family lives were subject to the prying eyes of Ford inspectors who checked on workers' morals, drinking habits and other aspects of their lifestyles (Beynon 1973: Ch. 1).

The Federal government, though less important as an habituating agency in the US than the employers prior to the mid-1930s, did lend a hand on occasion. Most significant perhaps was the introduction of prohibition legislation, which achieved (at least for the urban working class) what the temperance movements of the nineteenth century and the British compromise of the restricted licensing laws introduced in the First World War failed to achieve, namely the (albeit temporary) elimination of one working-class habit that hindered the development of a 'reliable' labour force.

The New Deal brought to fruition cooperation between the state, monopoly capital and organised labour, which had begun in the 'Progressive Era.'[2] The failure of capital's welfarist strategy, as evidenced by the massive strike wave of 1916-19, and the failure of its 'company union' strategy, as evidenced by the growth of industrial unionism and subsequent worker militancy in the 1930s, led to state intervention to create the conditions conducive to 'point of production habituation.' The legislation which provided the conditions for the recognition of the new CIO unions (the National Industrial Recovery Act and the Wagner Act) ensured the role of industrial unions as disciplining and habituating agencies. After recognition, the development of productivity bargaining in the US and more recently in Britain was, by implication, grounded in the recognition by both sides that once the deal was struck, the unions would be able to deliver a disciplined labour force ready to tolerate the speed-ups that management inevitably introduced.

In Britain in the years up to the Second World War, the role of the habituating agencies was rather different to that in the US. This was partly a result of the different history of the relation between the state and capital accumulation and partly because the habituation tasks were somewhat different. By the turn of the century Britain had in large measure developed a working class of two or three generations' standing, and it was not until the 1950s that British capital had to confront the spectre of a first-generation working class again. Before the depression of the 1930s, British capital was rather better placed in respect of habituation problems than its US counterpart. The massification of labour typical of US monopoly capital during this period was not a significant feature in Britain until the late 1930s (Branson & Heinemann 1971). Workers in British industry remained predominantly skilled and apprentice-trained. Notions of pride-in-job and a 'fair day's work for a fair day's pay' were pervasive. The collective struggles that did develop were not typically around habituation issues, but rather were wage-related or explicitly concerned with control over the production unit. Such was the thrust for instance of the miners' strikes of 1911-12, 'Red Clydeside' of 1919, and the General Strike of 1926 (Dangerfield 1961; Kendall 1969; Renshaw 1975).

Welfarism in Britain was developed primarily by the state, though the old-style philanthropic capitalism still persisted until the Second World War (for example, at the Morris car factory in Oxford). The state was concerned in these years to assist the geographic mobility of workers (by providing labour exchanges), to provide a limited security in times of unemployment and old age, and to improve the physical capacities of workers with various health insurance schemes.

The 'social factory' in Britain was created more slowly than in the US. There were few substantial developments before the Second World War that by implication were concerned with the synchronization of working-class personal and leisure experiences with the requirements of an industrial labour force - certainly not on the scale of the cultural qualifications of Ford's $5 day. The inter-war period, however, did see the beginnings of a policy of relocating working-class families on culturally sterile, anonymous housing estates on the peripheries of the industrial cities. These 'council housing' projects were often located next to 'industrial estates' occupied by newer 'light' industries operating with massified labour processes into which the workers displaced from the stagnating primary industries (coal, steel, shipyards, textiles) were inserted.

Perhaps most significant in the state's role in habituation since 1945 has been its contribution to the development of an ideology of 'classlessness'. Though all the main political parties have propagated this ideology, the Labour Party's role has been particularly significant in that it has created a content for socialism primarily composed of extensions in welfare state benefits, a commitment to full employment, the continual improvement of living standards, and limited state intervention to harness capital accumulation for the general social good. As such it has given the legitimation of socialism to what are overtly capitalist relations of production.

Apart from the way the forging of the link between welfarism and socialism has helped legitimate general class domination (see Offe 1972), the provision of compulsory state-sponsored secondary education from 1944, and more recently, the elimination (by local and national Labour governments) of 'eleven-plus' selection has given credence to the myth of equal opportunity in a 'classless' society. If there is equal opportunity and one and one's family remain manual workers, then, or so the state-sponsored mythology goes, it is the result of some personal failure. The experience of shop-floor labour becomes the best that one deserves or can expect.

In our analysis of the mechanisms of habituation observable in early industrialising societies and in later phases of British and US capital accumulation, here and there we have referred to the significance of such social institutions as the family and community as agencies of habituation. We now need to abstract these institutions from the historical specificity we lent them in order to evaluate their individual importance in the nexus of habituation. In the course of so doing we intend to show why habituation remains as great a problem for capital as it always was.

Family and community

The locus of working-class culture in the epoch of competitive capitalism was in what Salaman (1974: 19) terms the 'occupational community.' This is a community in which 'members... build their lives on their work; their work friends are their friends outside work and their leisure interests and activities are work-based.' The structuring of culture by the work experience, by the relations of production, was as true of the skilled artisans and isolated traditional working-class communities - miners, ironworkers, shipbuilders - as it was of the unskilled labourers who sweated in the mills and foundries.

The occupational communities together with the working-class families of competitive capitalism provided the institutional and communicative contexts through which workers were able to deepen their understanding of themselves as exploited producers - through which they were able to progress towards class consciousness. The dialectic between their work and their culture was immediate and obvious and was essential to the struggles and political solidarity typical of the epoch. There was, however, a dark side to this dialectic. Family and community also operated as institutional refuges from the harshness and brutality of the factory. They were the location of the proletarian's physical and spiritual rejuvenation returning the worker each morning, more or less capable and willing to produce for another 12 or 14 hours. As such, family and community were latent components of the habituation process. Studies of the articulation of capitalist with pre-capitalist forms of production argue that the task of physical reproduction is carried out by the traditional community at an enormous saving to capital.[3] Without providing for educational, housing, or welfare needs, it

obtains cheap labour-power as and when it is required, then
extrudes workers from production, again without compensation,
when they are no longer needed. In some African communities,
traditional rites of manhood (feats of hunting or warfare) have been
replaced by a period of brutal and debilitating work in mines and
factories, the capitalist version of a *rite de passage*.

The family in Western metropolitan capitalism has, through to
the present day, carried another role significant for the habituation
process. As the Frankfurt studies of the authoritarian family suggest,
hierarchical relationships between husband and wife, parents and
children, constituted a microcosm of the relations of production.
Furthermore, as Horkheimer (1972) maintains, paternal domination
in large measure originates from the economic dependence wife and
children have upon husband and father. Just as child depends on
father for material survival, so each new generation of worker
depends on capitalist. The transition from child to worker is the
transference from parental control to the control of the factory boss.

The epoch of monopoly capitalism has seen not only the arrival of
the massified detail labourer - the so-called 'semi-skilled' worker on
a massive scale - but also the arrival of commoditised mass culture.
The increasing elimination of worker job control effected by
Taylorism and Fordism and subsequent refinements have generated
an experience of un-freedom at work. The success of monopoly
capitalism and the strength of organised class struggle within the
parameters of monopoly capital have ensured, except for the 1930s
and until the depression of the 1970s, rising proletarian living
standards. Metropolitan capital in the present epoch has been able to
construct the material context in which freedom in the realm of
consumption has been able to compensate for un-freedom in the
realm of production. Deskilling and compounded alienation has
given rise to an instrumental orientation to labour and a search for
happiness in terms of the consumption of the material fruits of
instrumental labour.

This search for freedom via consumption developed in the US
after the First World War (Alt 1976) and in Europe largely after the
Second World War. The commoditisation of culture, however, has
only been one component of a general decomposition of working-
class culture. This decomposition has generally paralleled the
extension of 'modern' (i.e. Fordist and Taylorist) production and
control techniques to more and more sectors of industry, and has
been initiated in part by housing policy and 'community planning.'

In Britain since the 1930s, the policy of slum clearance has almost
inevitably meant the relocation of working-class families on
anonymous, structurally stultifying council (i.e. public) housing
estates (one of the first of these was the town of Dagenham built by
the state to house the workers of the adjacent Ford Plant). The result

of such relocations in Britain has been the virtual elimination of the working-class extended family, the substantial reduction in kin and neighbour/friendship communication, the limitation of pre-existing institutional bases of working-class community life (pubs, clubs, snooker halls) and the consequent privatisation of cultural experience.

The classic studies of cultural decomposition, created not particularly in this case by housing policy, but rather by the constant encroachment on the artisan's control over both workplace and community life, are, of course, the studies by the Lynds (1929; 1937) of Muncie, Indiana in the 1920s and 1930s. The work of the Lynds as well as that of those who followed in their footsteps (for example, Stein 1964), points to an 'eclipse of community' in the sense of a collapse in the common identity, mutual aid and cultural control that was a feature of the life experience of both artisan and labourer (although with significant differences) in the epoch of competitive capitalism.

The degeneration of the work experience, on the one hand, and the decomposition and commoditisation of culture on the other, set up the contradiction between what Flacks (1974) calls 'making history' and 'making life.' To 'make history' meant, at least for socialists, class struggle at the point of production. Yet certainly for many massified detail labourers and increasingly for skilled workers also, work has little meaning except as a means to life - to consumption. The dialectic between work and community has been split. The institutional and communicative context in which the work experience had formerly structured the cultural, and which had been essential to the possibility of a work-based class consciousness, had all but been eliminated. Working-class people began to ground their identities more in the privatised family and - certainly in the US - in ethnic and other particularistic cultures, rather than via the institutions and comradeship of the occupational community.

If the decomposition of culture rendered problematic the cultural component essential to the possibility of class consciousness (and hence posed serious questions about the theory of consciousness and the role of the work experience in this, which many Marxists failed to come to grips with), it also reduced the effectiveness of family and community as agents of proletarian habituation. No longer were the cultural institutions refuges and regenerators in the way they had been in the previous capitalist epoch.

By seeking to organise the 'interior determination' of habituation, by seeking to organise reproduction in the realm of the cultural and the personal, by constructing the 'social factory,' capital has ensured that habituation has become not just a first-generation problem, but a problem with the younger generations of what most commentators see as a 'mature' working class.

Habituation: a continuing issue

The persistence of the problem of habituation in late capitalist societies has confounded the academic defenders of the capitalist industrial order. In a widely cited study of comparative industrialisation, Kerr and his collaborators (1960) express capital's optimistic scenario most forcibly. In their view, wildcat strikes, absenteeism, sporadic withdrawals, violence, loitering, machine breaking, thefts and the use of narcotics, were phenomena of *early* industrialisation, which progressively disappeared in mature industrial systems.

Yet, these forms of struggle - all attempts by the proletariat to resist the capitalist work ethic, are precisely those forms which are now causing concern to capitalist interests. As illustrations of this concern we might point to two examples from progressive capitalist thinking - the team-work method of car assembly used by Volvo (Sweden), and the proposals for worker participation set out by the Bullock Royal Commission in Britain. As Taylor (1976) explains, economic necessity, not high-minded altruism, impelled Volvo down the path of job reform. Volvo could not attract or hold the kind of labour needed for smooth and high productivity. In the late 1960s one in every two workers at its main Torslanda plant quit their job within a year; three in ten failed to show up in some section every day. The company was forced to employ an extra 800 workers on stand-by and to import nearly half its workers from Turkey, Yugoslavia and Greece. The attempt to create a humane working environment and the atmosphere of a small workshop is, in other words, a direct consequence of the failure to habituate workers to the demands of Taylorist and Fordist car production methods.

Whatever the outcome of the Volvo experiment, it is clear that Bullock's (1977) report on industrial democracy has ended on the UK scrap heap. Backward sections of capital, in the City and in the Confederation of British Industry, launched a savage attack on the proposals, an attack that was far from resisted by the then Labour government, anxious not to damage its electoral chances. The importance of the report, however, lies not in its possible implementation, but in the drafters' attempt to come to grips with the problem of habituation. As with nineteenth-century political representation and Keynesian consumerism, industrial democracy is now seen as a principal form of extending bourgeois 'rights' and a 'stake' in the system to working-class people. The authors of the report wished to 'release... the worker population's... energies, to provide greater satisfaction in the workplace and to assist in raising the level of productivity and efficiency in British industry.' For those who feared such a 'radical' proposal as worker directors, Bullock et al. (1977: 162) were not slow to remind them of a historical analogy:

The fears expressed in the nineteenth century in the face of proposals to give more people the right to vote did not stop short of the subversion of the constitution and the dissolution of society. Once the franchise was extended, however, the fears were forgotten and the Reform Acts were seen as essential to the country's stability and prosperity. We believe that over 100 years later, an extension of industrial democracy can produce comparable benefits.

The expressions of concern by progressive fractions of capital, as evidenced both by Volvo and the Bullock Commission, is indeed justified by the recent manifestations of worker dissent. Wage bargaining and economistic strikes which many commentators thought comprised the only remaining forms of worker struggle, have now given way to issues of worker mobility, insubordination and 'non-accidental' accidents (Baldamus 1969, 1969a). In the US, as Braverman notes, labour turnover rates in the late 1960s and 1970s at Chrysler, Ford and General Motors approached 100 per cent per annum. Another US study (Serrin 1973) notes absentee rates of 9 per cent per day and 15 per cent on Mondays and Fridays. In Britain labour turnovers in the truck and car divisions of Fords have been 40 and 50 per cent respectively, while in terms of absenteeism our own researches record daily rates of 5-10 per cent in International Harvester's assembly plant in Doncaster, England (Henderson 1976).

The historical persistence of such forms of industrial action as absenteeism, worker mobility, insubordination and sabotage, to which we point throughout this chapter, appear in Western industrial societies to be carried forward primarily by two sections of the proletariat - the young and the migrants. Even a cursory look behind the statistics on such forms of action in many countries of the late capitalist world reveals that young and migrant workers are prominent exponents of these forms of dissent. The Lordstown struggles of the early 1970s were primarily responses of young and migrant Appalachian workers. In Italy the 'Hot Autumn' of 1969 developed from the activities of young Southern migrants in Fiat's plants and, in Britain, the recent explosion in the incidence of insubordination, sabotage and absenteeism at Ford's Halewood and Dagenham plants seems to have been in large measure produced by young white and West Indian workers (Aronowitz 1973: Ch. 1; Weller 1974; Anon 1971; Beynon 1973; and Gambino 1970).

In addition to the migrants being inserted into production in advanced countries (usually in the most demanding, dangerous, lowly-paid and dirty jobs) a new proletariat of some significant size is being created in the peripheral capitalist countries. Here the task that confronts capital is first to create and control anew a stock of malleable labour-power, a task given renewed urgency by the recent tendency of capital, particularly transnational capital, to migrate to low-wage areas. The creation of export-oriented manufacturing sectors in peripheral countries (for example, Mexico, Taiwan, Mauritius, Hong Kong, Singapore and South Korea) has placed on the agenda a programme of habituation and of worker resistance, comparable to the period of early industrialisation in Britain and the US. Often the national bourgeoisie in Third World countries, which usually has a commercial or statist character, is firmly linked with international capital in an attempt to subordinate its own working classes. In their brochures advertising desirable locations for transnational capital, the ruling classes of peripheral countries compete in their complicity to hold down labour protest. The Singapore government has ruthlessly suppressed trade unions, while the Mauritian government offers 'favourable labour laws to help export industries achieve their objectives' (Mauritius 1974).

While some fractions of metropolitan capital have taken flight to low-wage areas, partly in response to the class struggles of metropolitan workers, less mobile sections of Western capital have enormously increased their reliance on imported migrant labour to cheapen the labour process and lower the costs of the reproduction of labour in the advanced countries. Migrants are held outside the organisational traditions of the indigenous proletariat by means of racism and legal restrictions on their employment, residence and familial rights (as in Germany, Switzerland, France, and increasingly in Britain). While in this way immigration can be used to render labour as flexible as capital, it is not an unproblematic development. Yet again, for the first time in decades (in Europe, but not in the US) capital is confronted with the spectre of a first-generation working class (Castles & Kosack 1973; Cohen & Harris 1977).

Although there are substantial differences in the work-cultures of the immigrant groups (in Britain, for instance, there are clear differences between West Indian and Asian workers at this level), as Berger & Mohr (1975) show, their perceptions of community, of work and play, their work and time orientations, do not resonate with the requirements of industrial production in an urban context. They display a work contra-culture (Powles 1965; Liebow 1967; and Horton 1970). Similarly in the US, a country surely more skilled in the techniques of habituation, work contra-cultures among both migrant and ghettoised racial minorities persist. Among African-Americans, at least, there is evidence to suggest that racism and unemployment have combined to deepen a work contra-culture which, though rural in origin, has been creatively adapted for survival in the urban ghetto. In Britain, there is some evidence to suggest that second-generation West Indians are maintaining contra-cultural responses to the experience of factory labour (Blauner 1972; Rainwater 1970; Gambino 1970; and Henderson 1976).

Having discussed the cases of Third World workers, both in peripheral and advanced sectors of capital, there remains finally the case of young white workers who, in many ways, have developed the major responses to the contradictions inherent in the decomposition of working-class culture, to which we have already pointed. The degradation of the work experience and the decline of 'communal space' in the community has been compensated for by the promise of private happiness rooted in commodity consumption. The attempt to overcome the inherent tendency to over-production in capitalist economies by organising the sphere of consumption (through, for example, mass advertising) has, since the Second World War, been largely directed towards the young, newly-affluent workers.

After years of trying to suppress the hedonistic component of working-class culture in the interests of productive efficiency, capital now finds it necessary to encourage *private* hedonism but collective (in the workplace) restraint. While older proletarians appear to have negotiated the schizophrenic self which these contradictory demands help generate, young workers have developed various cultural styles (for example, in Britain the Teds, Mods, Rockers, Skinheads and Punks) which incorporate a *collective* hedonism that continually threatens to engulf the workplace. Evidence abounds of shop-floor 'games' that involve both sabotage and humorous release, and of the use of narcotics at work (in the latter case particularly in the US).

The culture of young workers is not just a variety of some 'classless' youth culture. Rather the various styles and rituals of young workers represent specific articulations of a generalised working-class culture (Murdock & McCron 1976), one component of which is the search for the collective identity which cultural decomposition has undercut. That collective identity has, of course, in part been grounded in commodities - motorbikes, cars, rock music, clothes - and partly in the cafes, discos and clubs that have become the (albeit mediated) equivalents of the pubs, taverns, corner shops and pool-halls of traditional working-class culture - the institutions of 'communal space.'

Along with the resistance to privatisation has gone a resistance to authority. The crucible of this resistance has been the school. The latent function which the school system in particular perpetuates in the childhood and adolescent years, is the socialisation of failure. In a 'sponsored' education system underpinned by an elitist educational philosophy - such as in Great Britain - formal mechanisms for the communication of failure ('streaming' or 'tracking' and examinations) complement the informal, interpersonal communication of failure that derives from the relationship between teacher and student. In the US, which operates with a more populist educational philosophy, the formal communication of failure is less significant (the de-emphasis on selection) than in Britain, but the US school system is as effective in the production of failures as is any other school system in the capitalist world (Bowles & Gintis 1976).

A generalised other that constantly talks failure necessarily leads to a low self-concept, and a low self-concept means recognition on the part of the individual that she or he is only capable of, or fitted for, menial mundane employment. Failure breeds low expectations, helps legitimate inequality and assists the recognition of the 'rights' of those in authority.

Given the key role of the school in the habituation process - particularly since the Second World War - the development of a student resistance to school authority is hardly surprising. What is more significant for our purposes is that the culture of resistance developed by working-class school students seems to have begun to be transferred, in differently articulated forms, to the workplace (Willis 1977). Resistance to supervisory authority, sabotage, bad timekeeping, and absenteeism among young workers have manifested themselves strongly, even during periods of economic crisis and high unemployment.

Conclusion

We have tried to establish why habituation has persisted as a problem for the realisation of the capitalist mode of production. Changes in the labour process have often been designed to reduce worker resistance to the work ethic. But as important as the 'exterior conditioning' attempted by capital and by the state acting to maintain the common interest of capital, has been the 'interior determination' observable at the level of social institutions, culture and ideology. While we have drawn on many historical and comparative examples, we are equally concerned with the contemporary character of resistance to capitalist habituation. The dialectics of resistance and habituation are fought out at work and at the cultural level, in the sphere of production and reproduction. Capital has not yet won the battle for habituation, though progressive fractions of the dominant interest seek more and more ingenious solutions to conceal their extraction of surplus value. While resistance in several forms has been shown by all workers, particular attention should be paid to the struggles of Third World workers in peripheral and advanced countries, and to the cultural re-composition and work protests of young metropolitan workers.

At the time this chapter was drafted, Jeff Henderson was engaged on an extensive study of the labour histories of Britain and the US. His knowledge of the literature was unrivalled and we felt it would be useful to attempt a more systematic comparison, with some allusion, too, to my own knowledge of Third World situations. Our theoretical knowledge of patterns of resistance was much supplemented by the many examples Jeff's brother (then a shop steward at a multinational plant in Yorkshire) provided from his own experience and observations. A very much cut-down, popular version of the paper was issued as 'Capital and the Work Ethic' in Monthly Review 31 (6) Nov. 1979, pp. 11-26, while a full version, very close to the current text, was published in Papers in Urban and Regional Studies (Birmingham University) No. 3, 1980, pp. 3-34. Finally, a similar paper appeared under the title 'On the Reproduction of the Relations of Production' in R Forrest, et al. (eds.) Urban Political Economy and Social Theory (Aldershot, Gower, 1982, pp. 112-43).

Notes

1   The National Civic Federation was composed not only of the heads of some of the prominent monopoly trusts - such as McCormick of International Harvester - but also of federal politicians, academics (in particular, the labour historian, John Commons), and conservative trade unionists led by Samuel Gompers, President of the American Federation of Labor (see Weinstein 1968: Ch. 1).

2   The significance of the 'Progressive Era' prior to the First World War to the 'corporatism' of the New Deal is recounted by Kolko (1967) and Weinstein (1968).

3   See for instance Wolpe (1972) on South Africa. However, subsequent scholars have contended that the savings to employers are, in effect, picked up by the state - in a form of economic subsidy for the political goal of apartheid (see the discussion in Cohen 1986: 105-7).

4

The Control and Habituation
of Agricultural Workers
in the United States

Introduction

In this chapter I examine the ways in which control over migrant labourers is effected principally through the state and employers, and how migrant workers organise to resist the pressure upon them. When considering the question of control of migrants it is necessary not only to look at the complex of laws that govern the immigration of workers and their civic status, but also at the production process. Again, law and labour processes are reinforced by the ideological hegemony of the powerful image makers in society (normally the media and the politicians and the interests they serve). This ideological hegemony can, moreover, be accepted by the migrants themselves, at least to some extent.

To try to encompass these various processes of control and self-control at a theoretical level, the notions of 'exterior conditioning' and 'interior determination' suggested by Lefebvre (1976) have been adopted and modified. In Lefebvre's account, exterior conditioning comprises the overt moves by capital against labour, normally at the point of production. In the case of international migrants (particularly) it is also necessary to examine the role of the state in policing its frontiers and to look at both the state's and the employers' roles in labour recruitment. Lefebvre is followed more closely in seeing interior determination as those elements of worker culture and ideology that sustain and reproduce the forms of control generated at the exterior level.

When it is necessary to indicate that these processes of control and internalisation are continuous, unsystematic and often unconscious, the term 'habituation' rather than 'control' has been used, as the latter can sometimes suggest too conscious a management strategy directed against labour. The case study taken for the examination of the habituation of migrant labourers is that of agricultural workers in the US.

With respect to the concept of 'resistance,' a working distinction between 'overt' and 'hidden' forms of resistance has been used, which I first developed in the context of a more general article on African workers (reproduced in this volume as Chapter 6). Overt forms of worker resistance are those that are easily observed or accessible to measurement. Such forms may include the number, scope and duration of strikes, the number of 'man-days' lost, the rate of labour turnover and the extent of worker participation in union organisations, radical social movements or street demonstrations. Hidden forms, by contrast, may include desertion, revolt by pre-capitalist communities, target working, task, efficiency and time bargaining, sabotage, the creation of a counter work-culture, accidents, sickness, drug use, adherence to other-worldly solutions or theft.

The role of the government

The first point of intervention by the state is to regulate its outer frontiers through immigration policies and controls. Who is let in, in what numbers and for what purpose? Who is expelled? In so far as the state can regulate this process, it is able to activate or deactivate the outer labour reservoirs ('the proletariat at the gates') and therefore affect the bargaining position of agricultural labour within the US.

The situation facing agricultural labourers in the south-west, for example, was decisively altered in 1942 when the Bracero Program was initiated. The Program was essentially a government-to-government agreement stipulating conditions to protect the wages and living conditions of Mexican migrants. From 1942 until the period 1965-8, when the Bracero Program was officially ended but 'admitted aliens' continued to be imported under the same category, a total of 5,060,093 *braceros* were admitted into the US (Samora & Simon 1977: 140). The close connection between the demands of the growers and the flow of migrants is shown by the fact that the peak of admissions under the Program coincided with the boom years of the 1950s, sometimes leading to the displacement of local labourers not prepared to work for the pay and conditions provided for *braceros*. The usual pattern of labour-market segmentation was somewhat violated during this period, for there was a certain amount of job displacement and job competition between indigenous and foreign workers.[1]

The principal form of migrant agricultural labour to the north-east consists of contract labour from the Caribbean. A contract programme with Puerto Rico was initiated in the 1940s, but given that Puerto Ricans had had the right to travel freely to the US since 1917, many arrived under their own steam. Estimates of the number of Puerto Ricans working in agriculture in the post-war period vary between 60,000 and 200,000. Officially, over 21,000 were recruited annually in the peak years of 1967 to 1969, but by 1977 annual recruitment had dropped to only 4,191. The reasons for this drop are not difficult to find. Over the years the Commonwealth of Puerto Rico attempted to tighten employment contracts in the interests of its migrants. New contracts began to stipulate wage rates, hours of work, procedures for firing workers, housing standards, and housing and food costs. Most importantly, the contracts also included provisions against reprisals if a worker joined or assisted a labour organisation (NACLA 1977a: 22).

Even though the Puerto Rican authorities were unable to enforce many of these provisions, the growers were sufficiently alarmed by what they considered onerous contracts and a difficult work-force to turn to Jamaicans, whom they considered 'docile and diligent.' This characterisation of Jamaicans is ironical given the frequently expressed view on the island that the heritage of slave revolts and the prevalence of single-headed households have produced a particularly violent culture (Lacey 1977). The Chairman of the Farm Labor Executive Committee, representing apple growers in the ten states from Virginia to Maine, was particularly explicit: 'Over my dead body will there be any Puerto Rican workers picking apples in Wayne County' (NACLA 1977a: 33).

The US government responded by providing temporary visas for alternative labourers from the Caribbean under Section H-2 of the Immigration and Nationality Act of 1952 (also called PL 414). About 20,000 a year came in under this provision, most of whom were Jamaicans harvesting sugar in Florida and fruit in the other eastern states. In general, the growers have replaced government-to-government contracts with grower-to-government contracts, over which they have more control. Growers send recruiting teams to the Caribbean, which carefully screen potential workers, eliminate poor physical specimens, test comprehension, investigate the worker's employment background and check local police records. A US sugar corporation in Florida recruits 800 Jamaican workers a day through this screening procedure (NACLA 1977a: 10-17). If a grower is dissatisfied with a migrant's work or behaviour, he has the power to recommend deportation. The ability to deport and the fact that it is easier to house single men are the critical elements in growers preferring West Indian to domestic or Puerto Rican labour.

Behind the officially-sanctioned Bracero, Puerto Rican and West Indian programmes are large numbers of illegal aliens, many of whom enter the casual agricultural labour force. Indicators of the number of illegals in relation to *bracero* and indigenous agricultural labour are hard to come by, but some early pointers can be given. Galarza, a union organiser for the National Agricultural Workers' Union, estimates that in 1948 there were 40,000 illegals compared to the 33,288 authorised *braceros* working in California. In 1951, a confidential check by an official of the Wage Stabilization Board indicates that 60 per cent of the total labour force involved in the tomato harvest were illegals (Kushner 1975: 99; Galarza 1977: 37). These figures suggest that the immigration policies and practices of the state act only as a first crude filter. This is not, however, to argue that immigration policies do not have powerful political and psychological effects - simply that many slip through the net, partly with the connivance of employers.

Those who evade immigration controls are unprotected by the state when they find employment. Illegal workers are especially at risk but agricultural labourers in general have found themselves victims of what might be called a principle of malign neglect. Occasionally public concern surfaces, as during the movement of destitute families from the 'dust bowl' to California - a migration graphically portrayed in John Steinbeck's *The Grapes of Wrath* (1975). But Steinbeck's vision remains contained within a racially exclusive appeal to the plight of the archetypal poor white family, the Joads. Workers from other ethnic groups appear only fleetingly in his account, international migrants and illegals not at all, even though these groups constitute the bulk of the agricultural labour force.

Despite periodic congressional committees set up from 1936 onwards, presidential commissions on migratory labour established in 1950 and periodically thereafter, and numerous other cosmetic displays of political concern at Federal and state levels, legal protection against the conditions that afflict agricultural labourers remains woefully inadequate. Agricultural workers are normally excluded from unemployment insurance, employee compensation, minimum-wage legislation and collective bargaining, and have poor health and educational facilities. (The question of housing is considered later in this chapter.)

These exclusions and hardships are briefly examined in turn. First, unemployment protection. The Federal employment tax specifically does not protect migrant workers, while migrant farm workers are again excluded from state insurance programmes everywhere but Hawaii and Puerto Rico (where sugar workers are covered). In 1970 a proposed change of the Employment Security Amendments of 1970 would have extended unemployment coverage to some 40 per cent of farm workers (i.e. still excluding foreign contract workers, illegals and many others) but it was defeated in the House Ways and Means Committee (R. Marshall 1974: 168). Some recognition of the plight of agricultural workers was given by

President Ford, who signed an 'emergency' Special Unemployment Act in 1974 which permitted weekly payments of a maximum of $85 in unemployment entitlement for a maximum of 26 weeks.

Second, worker compensation. Fieldworkers have an expected life span of 46 years compared to 69 to 75 for non fieldworkers; they suffer 22 per cent of all fatalities from work accidents, despite constituting only 7 per cent of the work-force (Kushner 1975: xii). The state none the less manages to avoid paying compensation that would be compulsory for workers in other industries. The farm worker is denied disability payments, subsidised medical services and rehabilitation payments to his family in the event of death or illness. To add insult to injury, burial benefits are also not payable. Coverage under the Social Security Act came in 1951, but again the regulations favour the more stabilised farm workers; there are few benefits, and only rarely a pension, accruing to seasonal or migrant labourers or those with an irregular legal status.

As for minimum-wage legislation, coverage was nonexistent until 1966, when Congress extended the minimum wage to most of the large farms under the Fair Labor Standards Act. These farms employed about half the hired farm work-force, including two-thirds of the migrants. Employers were required to raise the minimum hourly rate by 50 cents, phased in *over three years*. This less than onerous burden on the growers was, however, as Marshall (1974: 166-7) reports, 'widely violated, sometimes outright and sometimes by various subterfuges such as the use of piece rates. Moreover, many farmers pay wages in cash and keep no records, therefore making it difficult to prove their violation of the law.'

With respect to collective bargaining, farm workers in the US are specifically excluded from the National Labor Relations Act. While this does not legally prevent trade union organisation, the lack of statutory recognition means that farm workers have to develop struggles like boycotts, pickets and publicity for their cause - precisely the forms of struggle that migrant workers are normally poorly placed to undertake.

Finally, health and educational facilities. The incidence of infections and parasitic diseases, as well as diseases of the respiratory and digestive systems, is 200 to 500 per cent higher among migrant workers than among the population at large. There is further evidence of poor diet, a high rate of infant and maternal mortality, low life expectancy, a high accident rate and enormous risks in farm workers' exposure to modern pesticides. The Federal Government has made some small efforts to address the special health needs of migrants. The Migrant Health Act of 1962, amended in 1965 and 1970, allows the Public Health Service to upgrade health services to migrants with the help of voluntary agencies. Migrant health centres were established following legislation in 1973 and

1975, but, as Dunbar & Kravitz (1976: 74) note, 'centers are not required to offer pediatric and family services, including children's eye examinations, preventive dental care, prenatal services and family planning.' As for the education of migrant children, Marshall's (1974: 57) judgment of a special programme offered in Texas can be cited. In his view, the 'migrant education project has done very little, other than changing school schedules, to gear education to the value system and experience of migrant children.'

In addition to immigration controls and lack of legislative protection, the exterior conditioning of agricultural labour by the state is also seen in the establishment of an ideological hegemony over even the construction of a demonology about alien migrants. Recent statements by politicians and the media stand in marked contrast to some of the founding principles that provided the *raison d'etre* of US nationalism. Emma Lazarus's inscription on the Statue of Liberty has only to be recalled, calling upon the nations of the world to send 'your tired, your poor, your huddled masses yearning to break free... the wretched refuse of your teeming shore.' In a less poetic counter-proposition the US Attorney-General, William B. Saxbe, demanded an increase in the expulsion of illegal migrants to one million in 1975 because of the supposed 'severe national crisis' they constituted. Not of course that 'prejudice of any kind exists,' he unctuously maintained: 'We oppose the entry of all illegal immigrants regardless of their race or country of origin' (*Los Angeles Times*, 31 October 1974).

Such revised versions of the founding principles of American democracy depend for their general acceptance on the characterisation of migrants as constituting an uncontrollable 'invasion' - a 'horde' of aliens. Numbers are exaggerated and negative individual characteristics are attributed to all migrants. Migrants are supposed to exhibit criminal traits, evade taxes, yet make exorbitant claims on welfare medical services and housing, provide a cultural threat to mainstream North American values and deprive US workers of jobs that are rightfully theirs. The stigmatisation of migrants is of course widely shared and diffused through many sections of US society - the press, some sectors of organised labour and right-wing political organisations. The state and its agencies serve both to condense the major ideological expressions of hostility and to lend them greater legitimacy. While the dominant racial ideology is directed against 'aliens' and 'illegals' in general, in so far as many migrants (and perhaps one-third of the illegals) are engaged in agricultural pursuits, the negative stereotypes, often derived from images of the rural world, have a particular impact on agricultural workers.

The very language of popular and official expression encourages the imagery of a puritan Rome being overwhelmed by a mass of barbarians. For example, Nixon's appointee as Immigration Commissioner, General Chapman (formerly a Marine Corps General in charge of urban relocation in Vietnam), in an oft-quoted phrase, warns of 'the growing silent invasion of illegal aliens... forming power groups to influence American foreign and internal policy.' The numerous readers of the *Reader's Digest* were further cautioned by Chapman that 'action must be swift, for there is no time to lose' (cited in Baird & McCaughan 1979: 156). Other press descriptions refer to 'great waves of Latin Americans,' 'a surge of immigrants,' 'a flood,' 'a human tide,' 'the war along the Mexican frontier,' 'an army of the jobless overwhelming US defenses,' 'an economic time bomb south of the Rio Grande' and 'a problem of epidemic proportions,' to quote only a small selection of phrases used in the most respectable newspapers.

The primary forms of exterior conditioning of agricultural labourers by the state can now be summarised. Immigrant policies act as a crude filter, a means of acquiring temporary seasonal labour-power, and as a way of isolating an illegal and stigmatised, but indispensable, group. The legislative provisions for agricultural labourers do not even provide a protective fig leaf to cover the bare bones of poverty and exploitation. Instead, farm workers are exposed, virtually without state mediation, to a labour market wholly dominated by employers. Their weak economic situation is compounded by the ideological drive against migrants in general and illegal Hispanic migrants in particular. Even though the charges laid against this group - its supposed criminal propensities, its claims on the social wage, its fostering of a 'dollar drain,' its threat to US jobs and to the hegemony of Anglo culture - are only marginally sustained by evidence, the effect of negative stereotyping none the less acts as a powerful habituating mechanism. Non-native agricultural workers are thereby isolated and find it difficult to escape the image of a parasitic pariah group.

The role of the growers

As I have shown, employers are the dominant force in the organisation of labour markets for agricultural labour. They were successful in pushing through the Bracero Program, in blocking any attempts to penalise employers of illegal workers, and adeptly switched supplies within the Caribbean reservoir when their control over the conditions of work for Puerto Rican labourers was mildly challenged. Employers have also been able to use their economic muscle to ward off attempts by the state and the unions to limit their exploitation of foreign and illegal workers. The organisation of the recruitment of workers, the forms of housing provided and the direction of other elements of the labour process all illustrate the powerful position of the employers.

In the 1920s growers evolved a system of recruitment that used 'crew leaders' or 'labour contractors' as intermediaries between themselves and the labour force. Friedland & Nelkin (1971: 51) describe the role of crew leaders supplying labourers to the north-east as follows:

> The crew leader establishes contracts with northern employers and assembles the crew. He must schedule the movement of his crew and arrange for their transportation to the north. Upon arrival in the north the crew leader becomes a camp manager, responsible for the direction and control of the crew in the camp. He is provider of food, tobacco, alcohol and a variety of auxiliary services, including transportation. He brings the crew to the work site, where he acts as supervisor, allocating tasks, directing work in the field, monitoring inspection procedures, and often managing all aspects of the operation until the produce is delivered to the packing house.

Until 1963, when the Farm Labor Contractor Act provided that anyone who recruited ten or more farm workers had to be certified by the Department of Labor, there was very little regulation of the powers of crew leaders. Though crew leaders were enjoined to ensure that their vehicles were insured and were instructed to give statements of earnings to their workers and to keep employment records, the fine for non-compliance was modest ($500 for 'wilful violation') and only about 2,000 of the estimated 5,000 labour contractors bothered to register. The law was strengthened in 1974, but non-registration remained the norm - first, because the compliance officers were thin on the ground (of the 950 relevant inspectors, none was specifically assigned to agriculture); second, because the law only covered inter-state recruitment; and third, because an offending labour contractor was able to continue in business by simply sub-contracting parts of the operation (Dunbar & Kravitz 1976: 88-9). One such operator was Jesus Ayala, a labour contractor who had been convicted of a number of violations of state regulations and one of whose buses with insecurely fixed seats overturned, killing 19 lettuce pickers. Though Ayala was under contract to High and Mighty Farms to provide teamster workers, the foreman of the farm was disinterested in whether the workers were receiving union rates or were even union members: 'The workers on that bus? Hell, I don't even know who they are. I don't know if they were Teamsters or what because I don't know anything about them. I pay Ayala to take care of that' (cited in Dunbar & Kravitz 1976: 90).

The initial source of worker dependence rests on the labour contractor's control of transport, which severely restricts worker mobility. When and where to start work, how to reach the fields, when to knock off, how to gain access to entertainment or shops - all are dependent on the goodwill of the contractor. Some of the smaller crew leaders may dispense their favours with a degree of paternalism and thus work through a limited form of consensus, but most use their monopoly of transport to enforce labour discipline. For the grower, using contractors for exterior conditioning has the benefit of deflecting grievances, thus limiting the terrain of protest for agricultural workers and allowing the employer to distance himself from particularly onerous practices when protests do occur.

One source of possible protest is the issue of housing for agricultural workers. It is difficult to provide a single typical description of housing conditions as the units vary from single-sex barracks, to cardboard shacks, tenant houses, trailers, cabins or (rarely) well-constructed family housing subsidised by family grants. Normally the grower (or a group of growers) provides housing for the period of the cropping - between one and five months. One of the students in a participant observation study of migrant agricultural workers (in Friedland & Nelkin 1971: 37) describes his camp like this:

> My camp is a two-storey wood frame house on a dirt road a mile from the nearest phone and grocery store. The house is heated by a Franklin wood stove and has no window on the first floor. The rooms are created by paste-board partitions.... When I first arrived in the camp early in the season before it was crowded there were not many flies. But when people increased so did flies. Now when you sit down, your body literally became covered by them.

The lack of privacy, combined with the isolation of the migrant camps, leaves workers with little alternative but to accept the existing rents, the common practice of selling food prepared by the labour contractor's wife and the sale of beer and wine at marked-up prices. By undermining the capacity of the workers to exercise any choice in their living arrangements, growers are combining two aspects of habituation - at the point of production and at the point of reproduction. Mining compounds, plantations and company towns represent more complete versions of the fusion of work and residence in so far as employer control over residence is more continuous. None the less, the growers' camps represent a severe restriction on worker mobility and on the consequent capacity to challenge poor conditions by withdrawal or the search for an alternative job.

For the allocation of work the crew-leader system is again the dominant form of mediation between employer and migrant. On a small farm the employer might directly hire and personally supervise six or eight workers. But in the great majority of cases, as Harper, Mills & Parris (1974: 284) show, 'the grower has relinquished his management of the work-force to the contractor; he typically does not care how the work-force is managed, as long as his crops are harvested.' These authors provide (1974: 285) a pen portrait of the *modus operandi* of 'Ernie,' a labour contractor operating in the north-east. Ernie was big enough to employ two foremen to supervise the workers in the fields and orchards, and he kept records of worker productivity. Favoured workers were given jobs as yard men and truck drivers. Others assembled after breakfast for the assignment of their tasks, which were paid on a piece-work basis. Ernie himself, however, was paid on a lump-sum basis for a whole crop, thus obviating the need for the employer to keep a separate tally. (In another system the grower pays the contractor an 'override' for each hamper picked over an agreed amount.) In the fields each worker's productivity was recorded in terms of crates, hampers or boxes by the field foremen. Pay-day was Saturday, when Ernie, complying with Federal regulations, gave each worker a list of his earnings, with deductions for rent, social security, meals (cooked by Ernie's wife) and items purchased on credit. Typical pay envelopes would record $60, $70 or $80 a week, but contain $10, $15 or $20 after deductions.

The habituating mechanisms used by Ernie and other labour contractors rested primarily on the provision of apparently arbitrary pay envelopes and the close supervision of the work task. But there were a number of subsidiary mechanisms too. Contractors purchased candy, soft drinks, liquor, beer, gloves and other items and sold them to workers, frequently at double their retail value. By extending credit for these items, contractors secured a convenient state of indebtedness and were able to discriminate between workers by withholding or granting further credit. Meals were also withdrawn from recalcitrant workers and a limited amount of breakfast provided to encourage early starters.

The exterior conditioning of the workers by the growers, in sum, can be seen in terms of the dominance growers have over the labour market, the control they derive from having their work-force housed at the point of production in debilitated and isolated conditions and their use of crew bosses to manage and discipline the labourers. The crew bosses derive their credibility with employers by exacting a strict regime and by delivering the right amount of labour-power at the right time to pick a ripening crop. In his day-to-day contact with the workers, the crew boss is thus the effective agent of exterior conditioning carried out indirectly at the behest of the growers.

Interior determination

Unlike exterior conditioning, which refers to the leverage the state and the employer exercise over the worker, interior determination refers to the elements of a proletarian culture that internalise, transmit or even generate ideologies or forms of behaviour conducive to the worker's own continued exploitation. It is necessary, however, to place some careful qualifications around the notion of interior determination. In one sense evidence of interior determination indicates successful socialisation (to use a related and more conventional term) carried out at the behest of capital. Alternatively it can be regarded as another version of a 'culture of poverty,' to use Oscar Lewis's much debated term (see Valentine 1968). In the popular use of Lewis's concept, what one is talking about are the forms of adaptation, or even more fundamentally acceptance, of the capitalist world view.

The expression 'interior determination' is intended to suggest a more complex mediation between ideology and observed behaviour. First, while consciousness in work-related contexts often reflects and refracts elements of the dominant ideology, this does not constitute the worker's whole being - what happens after work, or after a return from seasonal labour, or what is clandestinely thought, felt or acted out. Where deviant behaviour is conscious, dissimulation is the basis of apparent compliance. Second, there is a complex relationship between forms of adaptation and forms of resistance. The very indices of an acceptance of adverse conditions may provide the means to assemble an ideology of resistance: a subculture becomes a contra-culture. Some examples of this process are provided later in the chapter when I discuss patterns of resistance amongst migrant miners in southern Africa. For the moment, however, I shall concentrate on two aspects of interior determination observable in US agricultural workers. The first concerns the internalisation of the ascribed and heavily-promoted attribute of being an 'alien.' The second concerns varying manifestations of psychological disturbance and disorientation in the migrant labour camps and at work.

Being an alien is not generally a comfortable state, though the Hungarian humorist George Mikes (1946) managed to ameliorate his own alien status by poking fun at England and the English. The acceptance of his observations, however, depended on a certain cosy consensus going something like this: 'Poke your fun, but poke it gently and we will treat you not as a foreign threat, but as a quaint curiosity.' Patronising as such an attitude is, it is preferable to the expression of xenophobic fears and hostility when confronted with an outsider. Many migrants to the US have had to face just such hostility. One common reaction is to wish to appear invisible so as to deflect the more brutal manifestations of racism. Bisharat's (1975: 23) characterisation of the typical Yemeni farmworker in California shows evidence of this reaction:

> He is shy, definitely wary, hesitant to make any disclosure. He is Moslem. Though he does not observe the fast of Ramadan because of the arduous nature of his work, he does pray five times a day in the field and attend mosque whenever possible. He is married. His wife and children are in Yemen. He speaks no English and makes no attempt to

learn it formally. He can read and write Arabic, we were told. He is seclusive and associates with few people outside the circle of his fellow workers. He avoids drinking, smoking and public entertainments. He is sure to avoid any situation that might cause trouble and to this end he polices his friends.

The effects of an alien status are clearly visible in this portrait and it is a status that applies to a high proportion of US agricultural workers. The inability to speak English is especially important, for many Hispanic migrants are forced to accept the word of the labour recruiter, the employer or the crew boss. Workers are unable to communicate effectively with social workers, or with US Department of Labor inspectors, and have little access to information about their civic rights, even where these obtain. In one case, where the US Department of Labor set out contractual rights in Spanish, officialdom used the opportunity to stress what a great favour was being granted to migrants by the US state and employers. In translation, the *Guia para los Trabajadores Agricolas Mexicanas* states:

> You are here because you are needed to help us grow and harvest crops on the farms of the United States.... When our farmers cannot find all the workers they need in this country, they are permitted to hire agricultural workers from Mexico.... Should domestic workers become available, however, they have a prior right to jobs held by foreign workers.

On no less than ten occasions the guide reminds workers to consult their *employers* if they are dissatisfied; *thereafter* workers are advised to consult their Consul or a representative of the Department of Labor (US Dept of Labor 1959: 227-31).

Disillusionment with an employer or the authorities is often a shattering experience to migrants who have internalised at least some elements of the 'American Dream.' An autobiographical account by an *indocumentado*, 'Pablo Cruz,' provides an interesting insight into the experiential and psychological traumas of a Mexican worker. Despite growing up to think 'the United States was real bad because of what it had done to Mexico,' Pablo Cruz was 'always dreaming to be inside the Statue of Liberty and [wanted to] walk through the arm to the hand holding the torch, the fire, just to get the feeling of America.' He recalls, 'I saw movies that disturbed my mind real strong. It was the *Egg and I.* And I thought if I could go to the United States, I could do something to become rich like the man in the movie story.' Pablo Cruz's aspirant identification was, however, rudely challenged. In his first illegal crossing he was picked up and deported after two days. Among his initial jobs was one in which the farmer paid-off Pablo and his co-workers unusually early in the week. The more experienced workers were immediately suspicious but Pablo stayed on, only to find himself roughly bundled into a car at three in the morning and taken to the border. The penny had dropped. As Pablo Cruz ruefully recollects, 'this is the way they work in Indio [the US], you see. The Immigration and the farmers have a deal. The farmer can pick up and work the *alambres* [thin people] if he agrees to turn them in to the Immigration when he is finished with them' (Nelson 1975: 37, 38, 77).

As a consequence of their low and often illegal status the state and the growers are often able to widen a cultural and social rift between Mexicans and Chicanos. As Pablo Cruz put it: 'If a person is born in Mexico a Mexican-American laughs at you and calls you a dumb person, because you come from a dumb country. There is a lot of discord you see. We don't look like brothers. We are not united. We don't feel the brotherhood. Everybody is real hard and tries to take advantage of everybody else' (Nelson 1975: 168). This sense of social distance is amplified by the intra-class competition fostered by the hiring practices of the growers, who typically switch between different ethnic sections of the work-force.

The disabilities engendered by an illegal status and a minority language are compounded by the casual, intermittent and short-term nature of agricultural employment. According to a Harvard psychiatrist, this leads to the development of a migrant subculture characterised by social isolation, extreme poverty, cultural deprivation and social fragmentation:

> The uprootedness which characterises their lives, falls not suddenly upon them (as it does upon the observer who tries to comprehend their manner of survival) but is a constant fact of life from birth to death, summarizing therefore, a whole life style, a full range of adaptive manoeuvres. [Workers have] a tendency to feel not only weak and hard-pressed, but responsible for their fate (cited in Marshall 1974: 52-3).

The experiential data collected in migrant labour camps also reflects the consequences of impermanence, disorganisation and other dislocative elements in personal and inter-personal behaviour. For example, with respect to sexual behaviour:

> Women are disdained as nothing more than 'pussy' and virility is constantly reaffirmed. Discussions about sex are highly ritualized and repetitive and accompanied by much sexual license. At the same time, there is a high tolerance of sexual deviance; with most crews there were one or two homosexuals... they are accepted with affectionate contempt (Friedland & Nelkin 1971: 100).

Popular psychology would interpret the reported constant obsession with the size of men's penises as evidence of anxiety, while the existence of homosexual practices is commonly reported in the literature on closed institutions.

But there may well be deeper structural determinants that underpin these behaviour patterns and derive from a particular historic division of agricultural labour. There still remain strong vestiges of the feudal peon system which operated in Mexico and the south-west. In the classical system, the women (and children) were not only an instrument of labour-power of the patron, but a possession of their fathers and husbands. Elements of this subordinate relationship remain when a 'family wage' is paid to the male head of the family to include the labour-power of the women and children. Gonsalez, who makes this argument, further adduces (1977: 49, 50) that even where single male labour-power is dominant, 'the practices and ideology of capitalism have encouraged the retention of feudal patriarchal attitudes in Mexican-American communities. Sexism is thus common in migrant labour camps and serves to divide the agricultural working class into two subordinate sections.'

The filthy and debilitating conditions of the camps also encourage an attitude of self-neglect, fatalism and anti-social behaviour. One researcher reports the following friendly greeting: 'Joe, get your ass up. You've been drunk all the God damn day and all night, and you shitted right on the floor here.' As Friedland & Nelkin explain (1971: 105, 108), 'as a recognised object of taboo, faeces "out of place" is considered by some to represent a desire to create anxiety. Such behaviour, reminiscent of Gulliver urinating on Queen Mab's castle, is a pungent symbol of contempt and defiance of order.' The labour process itself also encourages a degree of intra-class conflict. Harper, Mills & Parris (1974: 288) quote a fieldworker to this effect:

> It's each man for 'isself. One day we're packing tomatoes. You pick a basket and leave it by the row. When you finish a row you call Stamp [the foreman]. Well, I was pickin' like shit and once't I looked behind me and there's ole Jack, who don't pick so good, taking one of my baskets and puttin' it in his row. You can't trust nobody.

Medical and religious practices equally show evidence of deviant conduct that inhibits the growth of collective consciousness. Where access to conventional medicine is in any case limited, great store is set on the efficacy of 'roots' and other home-brewed remedies. Religious observance rarely conforms to the practice of the organised churches. Instead, the dominance of a single 'preacher' tends to encourage a sharp distinction between the secular world (which is marked by an absence of control over one's fate),and the spiritual world (which has to be attained through absolute conviction and a belief that God works in mysterious ways). In one case, a preacher strongly criticised Martin Luther King for allowing people to believe that *social power* was relevant to their lives and the attempt to find 'the living God' (Friedland & Nelkin 1971: 120).

Habituation and resistance

So far it has been shown, both at the levels of exterior conditioning and of interior determination, how the cards are stacked against US agricultural labourers and held largely by the state and agricultural capital. But, by concentrating attention on the habituating mechanisms effected by the state and the growers, the points of conflict and tension have also been highlighted. State and capital are never able to effect a total hegemony over labour, nor do they always achieve a total congruence of purpose. Such is the dialectic of habituation and resistance that each point of pressure against migrant agricultural workers is also a point of leverage and movement against the state and capital.

Without attempting a complete analysis of the forms of resistance practised by agricultural workers, let me illustrate the connection I have made between control and resistance. While the state uses tough immigration controls to regulate the flow of external and subordinate sections of the agricultural proletariat, its manifest inability to close the frontiers effectively exposes the authorities to ridicule and reveals the contradictory interests of the state and the growers. The attempt to deny foreign workers civic rights has activated the government of Mexico and the Commonwealth of Puerto Rico to intervene on behalf of their citizens. Dividing off the racially different and unorganised section of the agricultural work-force from the stabilised indigenous workers has led some sections of organised labour to argue for the extension of bargaining and other rights to migrant workers (for examples, see Baird & McCaughan 1979: 167-70). Racial stigmatisation has served to generate affirmative national concepts like 'the Atzlan nation' and 'La Raza' to create communal bonds of solidarity. Again, weaknessess of bargaining power at the point of production have been somewhat offset by consumer-based protests and boycotts carried out particularly by the United Farm Workers and its supporters.

Finally, at the level of interior determination, while many agricultural workers internalise negative stereotypes derived from their cultural marginality and illegal status, most are not so mesmerised by their circumstances so as actually to prefer farm work. In one survey 77 per cent of a sample of Michigan migrants explicitly stated they would leave farm work if they could, while only 5 per cent wanted their children to work on farms (cited in Dunbar & Kravitz 1976: 89). Attitudes do not, of course, always translate into action. It is important not to exaggerate the possibilities of protest amongst agricultural workers in the face of the debilitating conditions described. On the other hand, there is a history of determined farm worker protest in the US which should not be overlooked (see, for examples, Kushner 1975; McWilliams 1971; Foner 1964; Galarza 1977; Kiser & Kiser 1979; Levy 1975; and Majka 1980). The struggles described in these sources demonstrate that the state or capital should not be accorded a degree of rationality and hegemony that they intrinsically do not possess and are unable totally to effect.

A summer school job in California in 1972 and a lengthier stay in Mexico in 1978 gave me an opportunity to observe agricultural labour in the US at first-hand. What I had only previously known through novels like Steinbeck's The Grapes of Wrath, was now supplemented by direct observation and interviews. The most striking perception I gained as an outsider was of the limited extent to which middle class, respectable, US citizens were aware of the vast underbelly of subject labour which sustained the benefits they enjoyed. In this respect, the reactions to the plight of US agricultural workers reminded me of the reactions of many white householders to black workers in South Africa. Of course, in the US the situation was much ameliorated, at least psychologically, by the 'log cabin to White House' myth. By officially adopting caste-like barriers in the period of classical apartheid (1948-73), the South African regime denied to itself this important level of vicarious mobility. In a recent book (Cohen 1987: Ch. 7), from which parts of this chapter are extracted, I compare the possibilities of mobility among US agricultural workers with those of black miners in South Africa. No doubt my respectable US friends would be shocked by my argument that, through unionisation and political advancement, black South African miners are more likely to achieve political integration than US farmworkers. (The comparison would be less advantageous in the case of South African farmworkers.)

Note

1   This phrase is deliberately vague as I do not want to get too deeply into the complicated argument about the existence, or otherwise, of a 'dual labour market' - a theme I have discussed elsewhere (Cohen 1987). The broad comment I can make here is that a strict belief in dual labour market theory tends to suit two very different groups in the US. First, those who are political liberals in immigration matters, who can therefore hold the view that immigrants do not in any circumstances create job competition with indigenous workers. Second, those who employ migrants, whose interests may be served *either* by paying lower wages, *or* by covertly denting the militancy of better-organised workers. The degree of job competition, at certain historical periods may, therefore, be underestimated by employers or liberal adherents of the theory. One the other hand, the level of job competition is vastly exaggerated in the popular consciousness, particularly bearing in mind that many immigrant groups become small proprietors whose economic activities are likely to *generate* employment.

5

Peasants to Workers and Peasant-Workers in Africa

Introduction

Though much of the central argument of this chapter remains unchanged since its original publication (Cohen 1976), it has proved necessary to alter the introductory section and to include some important new theoretical material on the character of peasant production, which affects some of the underlying themes of the argument.

In the original version I spent some time defending the use of the terms 'peasant' and 'worker' in the African context, indicating that there was still some scholarly resistance to utilising such a vocabulary. This is now largely a dead issue. The pages of journals are no longer littered with contention over whether a 'rural cultivator,' 'subsistence farmer' or 'peasant' is an appropriate designation: the last has passed into general usage. Even the term 'worker' and its cognate, but more definitely Marxist-oriented term 'proletariat,' has gained widespread acceptability, though here and there a bastion is constructed questioning the use of such a notion (Lloyd 1982).

The generally more favourable climate of acceptance in the use of class concepts has a liberating function in that some hitherto necessary stridency can be replaced by some currently necessary subtlety in examining issues of stratification among subordinated African classes. For example, one line of argument that it is easier to challenge is that propounded by 'essentialists' on each side of what is seen as the peasant/proletarian divide. Thus it seems to me to be an error to appropriate all migrants (who may have been in mining or industrial employment for many years) to the 'essentially peasant' category because of the existence of family land, a family in the rural area or a set of peasant values (Shanin 1978). Equally, it may be in error to deem a neophyte worker 'essentially proletarian' the moment the factory gate is crossed and without reference to his/her culture, values, or the retention of rural ties (Peace 1979: 141-2). It is now possible to accept the existence of a large group of individuals who are *both* peasants and proletarians (see, for one formulation, First 1983). This argument was presaged in the work of the social anthropologists working on the Copperbelt (see Epstein 1958) whose writings were cited in the first version of this chapter. But *they* were essentially trying to resolve a psychological ambiguity and saw 'peasanthood' or 'workerhood' as states of mind that could be alternated and reselected as the social context demanded. The notion First and others have now constructed suggests a single, but fixed category - people who are both peasants *and* workers simultaneously, who are 'peasant/workers' or even more adventurously members of a 'peasantariat,' a designation used by a prominent scholar of Botswana (Parson 1987).

This interest in categorisation signifies (as in all scientific enquiry) a deeper unease with conventional frameworks of explanation. Class structures do not simply appear in a different context like old wine in a new bottle. Instead, as I argue, they have to be seen as living, changing outcomes that derive from specific forms of historical processes. The two interrelated social processes that are treated here are those of peasantisation and proletarianisation. Peasantisation refers essentially to the widening and depersonalisation of market relations consequent on the introduction of a pervasive cash economy and a colonial state. But the close connection that I shall seek to establish between the processes of peasantisation and proletarianisation suggests that there are more general dynamic forces (specified, for the moment, simply as the introduction and spread of capitalist social relations) which set *both* processes in train more or less simultaneously.

The problem under review is thus conceived not as a continuum from an original condition of 'peasanthood' to one which contains a fully-fledged proletariat, but, on the contrary, as a dynamic form of social change impelled partly from internal factors, but largely from homonomic external factors which propel each ongoing chain of processes. The 'chains' of proletarianisation and peasantisation - like breeding chains in a nuclear reactor - proceed at differential rates, with differing degrees of intensity and completeness and with a greater or lesser level of internal differentiation. Proletarianisation is, however, immanent in peasantisation in that the former represents a branch or side chain originating in the displacement and undermining of precapitalist modes of production (see the later discussion of 'peasants as proletarians').

Further amplification of the notions just outlined is provided below: here I wish merely to note the continuing elements of interconnectedness between the two major chains, seen, for example, in the development of a small rural proletariat and, *par excellence*, in the persistence of migrant labour even in the areas of the most intensive capitalist development like the South African mines.

The emergence of wage labour

The creation of a stable wage-labour force in Africa is essentially a product of white settlement and the establishment of European colonial administrations. Yet, as Sandbrook & Cohen (1975) argue, the organised expropriation of labour power had also been widespread in indigenous societies. Various forms of chattel and domestic slavery existed in many precolonial states; customary family labour was common, while itinerant groups of workers, like the *aro* age groups of Yorubaland or the *ankofone* of Sierra Leone, engaged in house building or heavy farming on an essentially contractual basis (ILO 1962: 65-6). In contemporary West Africa, and perhaps elsewhere too, this type of labour survives in the following form. A group of young men tour the farms of the wealthier peasants when heavy brush needs to be cleared, the land tilled, seeds sown, or the crop harvested. In earlier days the toilers would be content with a generous feast provided by the farmers, plus a token payment in cash or kind. Nowadays the labourers are hired in advance, the cost of their transport met and an agreed payment made. In essence, this was a localised relationship that became both more structured and more institutionalised as the mode of payment moved in harmony with shifts in the means of exchange. Equally, however, with the introduction of a pervasive cash economy, large movements of seasonal labour over vast distances became common - for example, in groundnut harvesting in West Africa. Here again piece-work payments (plus shelter and food) developed as a norm, but this time between employer and employees with no interpersonal or consanguinial relationship.

Within precolonial cities, craft traditions and guilds were well established, most of them involving the use of apprentice labour. In Liberia too, the Americo-Liberian settlers used 'apprentices' as cheap farm labour. In 1887 it was estimated that every Americo-Liberian had six to eight youths in service, while the president of the republic alone employed 120 'apprentices.'

In short, the idea of precolonial African societies comprising a set of autarchic communities, 'primitive communalist' if you will, is very misleading. None the less, the colonial administrators in the early years of colonial rule found it difficult to displace surplus labour and to recruit sufficient labourers with the qualities they wanted and at the price they were willing to pay. Of course some colonial authorities did not attempt to introduce a free labour market and developed instead brutal policies of forced labour (notoriously so in

German South West Africa, Oubangui-Shari, and the Belgian Congo). The French did not abolish *prestation*, a labour tax which compelled adult males to work for a number of days a year, until 1946, while the British, although far less culpable in this respect, none the less used unfree labour in the production of essential war supplies, like Nigerian tin during the Second World War.

Where the buying and selling of labour did take place, administrators (Governors McCallan and Lugard of Lagos are examples) were wont to complain about the supposed idleness and cost of African labour, particularly in comparison to Indian labour. As a consequence, several schemes were either contemplated or undertaken to introduce labour from outside the continent. The Indian indentured labourers on the Natal sugar plantations were the largest group of imported labourers, but Chinese constituted 27 per cent of the labour force in the South African gold mines in 1905, while small groups of workers from the Caribbean were also contracted, particularly for work on the railways. Neither forced labour nor recruitment from abroad could, however, meet the demand for labour in the long term. Africans therefore had to be induced by force or persuasion to sell their own labour power. Conquest and the dispossession of land rights, notably in Kenya, southern Africa, and the Rhodesias, began the process; the imposition more generally of hut and poll taxes completed it.

The chains of proletarianisation and peasantisation are rooted essentially in these policies. Those Africans who remained on the land gradually became incorporated into the mercantilist system and then, later, into more complex international divisions of labour. In some places African farmers were initially able to respond successfully to the new commercial opportunities and wider internal markets that were opened up by white settlement: African farmers around the Witwatersrand area, for example, took the lion's share of food production in the nineteenth century supplied to the white *Uitlanders*, until they were forced out by political discrimination (Bundy 1979). But, for the most part incorporation into the world capitalist market produced a set of 'greenhouse' economies. Regional monocultures, determined by the needs of the colonial system, became common; production was oriented to the external market; and the appropriation of the surplus (in the form of export dues and the differences between the local price paid and the price commanded on the world market) was controlled by the colonial authorities and foreign enterprises. The process by which the commercialisation of agriculture took place both concentrated agricultural production on a limited number of products and disrupted the capacity of indigenous economies to absorb labour.

It was the creation of a landless group of rural dwellers, a group which also could no longer meet the cash demands of the colonial administration, that provided the making of an embryonic proletariat. A continuous and stable labour supply none the less remained a problem for the colonial state until the 1930s, for one major reason - colonial governments refused to pay unskilled labourers at a sufficiently attractive rate. Virtually from their inception, government wage rates in British West Africa remained unchanged until the late 1930s, while in South Africa real wages in agriculture and in the mines actually fell from 1890 to 1970, when agitation by black miners finally forced an increase. The failure to recruit unskilled labour up to the 1930s had little or nothing to do with the Africans' unfamiliarity with wage labour or their lack of commitment: rather, the conditions and type of work offered and the rate of remuneration were the main disincentives involved.

Colonial administrators cared little for such realities. First, they wanted labour on the cheap and they often considered that they were offering a 'just' wage. Second, many administrators operated with the now discredited theory of a backward-bending supply curve of labour - that is, the notion that demand and consumption patterns were inelastic and that the supply of labour would dry up when income targets were reached. Third, in some places where labour was being employed in the production of export crops - for example, palm oil - administrators did not want to divert agricultural labour by making government labour in the towns too attractive a prospect. Problems of labour recruitment only disappeared in the 1930s through the effects of the worldwide depression. Probably for the first time in colonial labour history, there were more men on offer than jobs to be had.

By the 1930s the chains of proletarianisation and peasantisation were considerably advanced. Within or near the cities of colonial Africa, a stabilised proletariat had come into existence - particularly on public works programmes, in the mines, in the building of roads and railways, and in the development of harbour and port facilities. Other than unskilled 'general' labour, as it was called, colonial governments had additional manpower needs in accord with their étatist character. Soldiers, clerks, court stenographers, sanitary inspectors, policemen, and messengers all serviced this need for local manpower to prop up the *pax colonica*. The urban workers evolved particular forms of social consciousness, identity and organisation about which I will comment briefly later, but it is necessary first to follow the chain of peasantisation in respect of three developments - the evolution of migrant labour, the creation of a rural proletariat and the notion of 'peasants as proletarians.'

Migrant labour

A pure system of migrant labour might be conceived as a regular and cyclical oscillation, the numbers entering wage employment corresponding to those returning to peasant production. To some degree, this pure form did obtain for seasonal workers, for those on temporary contracts, or when (as in South Africa) labour recruitment was rigorously regulated by administrative means. But over the years the general picture is that the rate of return to the rural areas declined. The reasons for this are manifold, but three factors may be suggested. First, though this process is still far from complete, production in the rural areas shifted slowly out of the hands of the community into 'middle' peasant proprietorship. Second, employment opportunities in the cities opened up as industry and administration expanded. Expansion was never sufficient to meet job demands, but social aspirations deriving partly from the expansion of education remained high, and many unemployed workers preferred to stay in the towns. Finally, the degree of impoverishment which became common in many African rural economies meant that a return to the land was in any case unfeasible for most migrants.

The contemporary patterns of in-migration to the cities are clear. Demographers have noted an upward shift in the median age of town dwellers, while many scholars have commented on the huge and growing pool of unemployed or casually employed labour in the cities and the associated growth of shanty towns and slum conditions. Such an outcome was, as I argue below, entirely consistent with the policies of labour recruitment inaugurated in the colonial period. But leaving aside this general issue for the moment, the trends of city growth noted above all suggest that the pattern of short-term migration is seriously in decay.

Only in southern Africa does an efficient and institutionalised use of migrant labour survive, and this too is showing signs of strain, particularly in response to recent political events on the subcontinent and to technological changes in the mines. For many years, however, the system was highly labour intensive. When the Chinese mine labourers were deported after the Boer War by the Liberal Government in Britain, the gold mines relied extensively on a system of private recruiting, often done by unscrupulous, so-called 'blackbirder' agents. Gradually, the mining companies combined to form a recruiting agency themselves. As the supply of suitably pliant and cheap labour from the immediate area decreased, the recruiters extended their range - into present-day Mozambique, Malawi, Lesotho, and Botswana and often further afield. It is quite fallacious to see the system of contract labour to the South African gold-fields as an anachronistic survival of a precapitalist mode of production. On the contrary, it was designed and carried out precisely according to the needs of a highly capitalised extractive industry of the type involved.[1] In its most intensive form in southern Africa, aircraft are chartered to the areas of supply, a medical inspection is carried out, and recruits are batched and labelled with names and destinations attached to their wrists. On arrival at the Witwatersrand, they are lectured in a common denominator patois on matters of safety, mining terminology, and so on and are housed in single-sex compounds. The latest version of this, outside Johannesburg, comprises a modern set of high-rise buildings, with strategically located gates, electronically controlled from a defensible strongpoint and capable of being brought into operation if unrest reaches alarming proportions. The 'compound' architecture is San Quentin penitentiary rather than traditional African. As mentioned earlier, however, this system is becoming subject to some strain as the home governments of the labourers concerned (Malawi, Botswana and Lesotho notably) have become increasingly involved in the conditions of employment of their nationals. The Frelimo government in Mozambique (which prior to 1974 supplied over one-quarter of the recruits) also embarked on the difficult task of providing alternative rural and urban employment for migrants in order to reduce their dependence on South Africa (see First 1983).

As I anticipated in the first version of this article, the post-1973 increase in the price of gold enabled the mining companies to withstand any pressures on their labour supply. I also correctly argued that mine owners were likely to show an increasing willingness to pay higher wages in order to stabilise a local work-force. What I failed to appreciate at the time was that a strange coincidence of interest would become manifest between the South African authorities, the mining companies and the surrounding African states. I saw the pressure to erode the migrant system essentially stemming from the labour supply areas. In fact, the South African government has forced the pace in this respect, having pressed on the governments of Lesotho and Botswana an agreement virtually to terminate supplies by 1985. The haste in slowing down 'foreign' labour supplies relates largely to the fact that the political benefits conferred by using such a labour supply (no citizenship rights or welfare entitlements and limited rights to bargain) can now be obtained from South Africa's own 'foreigners,' i.e. those Africans located in the nominally independent states within South Africa's frontiers. The general downturn in employment has also allowed the vast oversupply of labourers, which the mining houses prefer, to be accumulated within the internal reservoirs. Again, the development of labour-saving devices which I signalled earlier, has now taken effect and it is now much more possible to envisage many mines using men living with their families near the mining compounds. This statement needs some refinement however. It now appears that what is envisaged by Harry Oppenheimer (Anglo-American's former president) is the three-tiered system comprising (a) better paid permanent workers accompanied by their families, (b) contract workers who would have preferential rights and incentives to do another contract, (c) a much smaller male migrant labour force retained on the old system. However, whereas some of Anglo's newer mines are already working to this system, the older, less technologically efficient mines are still locked into the old system.

The owners of some South African gold-mines are thus partial converts to a policy of labour stabilisation and urban residence that the Belgian Congolese authorities adopted 50 years ago. Though the Belgians have sometimes been praised for their progressive policies on this issue, in point of fact the devastation that was wrought on the rural populations during the pacification period was so great that the Belgians were left with little alternative but to provide the means of subsistence around the areas of employment. In other parts of Africa, migrant labour was a useful source of labour supply, and its use left the rural areas just sufficiently viable to support the reproduction of labour power and the minimal welfare needs of returning labourers.

Ignoring the complexities provided by the South African case, the political economy of migration in the colonial periods hinged around the following features: (a) a pattern of ribbon development of capitalist enterprises around the loci of administration of mining areas; (b) the appropriation of surplus agricultural wealth by the state or European companies at the points of distribution and market. From the point of view of the colonial state, the ideal solution was one in which agricultural production remained sufficiently virile to produce an exportable primary product and absorb returning migrants, but not so viable that it threatened the supply of cheap unskilled labour. Such a delicate balance was impossible to achieve and may indeed be considered one of the central contradictions of the colonial political economy. Migrant labour represented a possible resolution of this contradiction but one that was incapable of solving the ultimately incompatible ends of the colonial state. The tendency is for migrant labour, as an organised system of recruitment, to be on the decline, as the reserve army of the proletariat created by colonialism increasingly prefers a precarious existence in the towns and cities to an impoverished existence in the rural areas.

The rural proletariat

Despite a drift to the towns, within the chain of peasantisation a small but growing rural proletariat emerged. This group was much larger in the Caribbean, Malaysia and parts of Latin America, where plantation economies were common. In Africa, extensive experiments with plantation agriculture were, however, for the most part unsuccessful (A.G. Hopkins 1973: 211-12). Some exceptions to this overall failure should none the less be noted. The use of indentured Indian labour on the Natal sugar plantations has been mentioned. In Liberia, rubber plantations of one million acres, leased for 99 years by the Firestone Rubber Company, became operative in 1926. Employment of rural workers was also considerable in the Tanzanian sisal plantations, until adverse world prices for the crop forced the closure of many plantations. A considerable problem of rural unemployment has resulted. Lastly, in the Ivory Coast the local plantation interests were sufficiently important to produce a political party (the PDCI) organised to represent their interests. From the late 1960s French commercial interests in the Ivory Coast began to grow citrus destined for the French market on a large scale.

Despite the absence of large numbers of plantation workers in Africa there has recently been a largely undocumented growth of a rural labour force working wholly or largely for wages. In Kenya, for example, the indigenous takeover of the so-called white highlands after independence did not foster a return to smaller units of production. If anything, the commercialisation of agriculture, often undertaken by Kenyans prominent in business and industry, has produced a further stage in the growth of capitalist social relations - namely, an absentee landlord, employing an on-the-site manager who in turn supervises the farm labour. This pattern is as yet fairly rare in Africa, at least on a large farm basis, though several observers have noted that senior civil servants in West African countries are shifting their investable capital from speculative urban property to land and poultry farming. In more general terms, the degree of social differentiation already present in the countryside has been carefully explored by Hill (1963, 1970). Though hostile to the concept of peasantisation (she prefers instead to talk of 'farmers' and 'rural capitalists') her work is outstanding in shattering, to use one of her own phrases, 'the myth of the amorphous peasantry.' The term 'peasant' may, in short, conceal the vast differences in wealth, incomes, and power in the countryside. Many of the richer peasants and farmers are fast moving into the position of becoming small employers of rural labour, and it is in this area, rather than in plantations, that rural proletarianisation will grow.

Peasants as proletarians?

I indicated that one of the major theoretical debates which now requires some attention is the notion, argued in its strongest version (Roseberry 1978), that peasants are, in effect, if not in name, being transformed into proletarians. This notion has nothing to do with prior discussions of labour migration, urbanisation or the creation of a wage earning rural proletariat. Rather, it starts from a re-examination of the nature of peasant production itself. Three critical elements are involved:

(a) The process of *commoditisation* in the countryside. The basic argument is that so enmeshed is the peasant household in producing goods and crops for sale that the very condition of the household's continued existence is predicated on entering commodity relations. Put in another way, producing for sale is not additional or incidental to producing for subsistence. Rather a 'reproduction squeeze' occurs forcing the peasantry to intensify commodity production or face starvation (see Bernstein 1977).

(b) The related question of the formal versus real *subsumption* of labour by capital. This question opens a large theoretical Pandora's box, but here it can simply be noted that a number of writers have questioned whether it is necessary to the dominance of capital to assume complete commodity production and the creation of free wage labourers. Is is not possible, they argue, to find that in reality capital has subordinated the countryside informally through a 'concealed' wage relationship in which surplus value is none the less realised? (Banaji 1977; Goodman & Redclift 1981)

(c) Finally, the issue of the control of *labour time* has been raised with respect to the increasing direction of the conditions of production by capital (and the agencies acting on its behalf) and the post-colonial state (and *its* agencies). The growth of marketing boards, state-directed cooperatives, agricultural credit agencies, extension services and centralised control over the provision of seeds, fertilizers and pesticides, all challenge the notion that the individual peasant proprietor is in some way autonomously engaged in production and marketing decisions. In short, the labour time of the peasantry, in this view, has been commandeered and organised by the state and capital.

The effect of these theoretical interventions is to predicate that peasants are (as it were) outdoor proletarians. The physical structure of the factory is absent, as is the gang boss or foreman, but the impelling necessity to work for capital is constructed by other institutional means. It is an attractive argument and one that has wide-ranging implications for traditional analyses which firmly separate the peasantry from the wage labourer. My own view is a somewhat cautious one: welcoming this debate, seeing it as an exciting opening to a more empirical discussion of the implications of 'modes of production theorists,' yet wishing to point out, with Bernstein, that peasants are still not wage labourers (with all that implies about the separation of home from work, collective organisation and forms of consequent consciousness). As Bernstein states, unlike wage labourers, peasant producers 'are not yet fully expropriated nor dependent for their reproduction on the sale of labour power through the wage-form' (Bernstein 1977: 73). At most, therefore, peasants are 'wage labour equivalents' not wage labourers.

The unskilled urban worker

While the peasant-as-worker debate is at an embryonic, but potentially rewarding stage, the growth and character of the urban worker proper is a subject that has already generated extensive discussion. A common approach in this area has been to move away from the self-interested concerns of white administrators in problems of labour productivity, recruitment and supply, and toward an actor-directed perspective of a group groping for self-expression and the creation of a corporate identity.

Once the labour history of the continent is approached in this manner - from below rather than from above - case after case of action undertaken to defend class interests appear. Workers, in other words, are, seen as active agents in the creation of their own group solidarity, consciousness and action. As E.P. Thompson remarks of the English working class, the African working class 'made itself as much as it was made.'

Here I can do no more than indicate some of the lines of research pursued. Some authors concentrate on describing early manifestations of strike action. Railwaymen and dockers are usually at the forefront of such events, but Hopkins (1966) describes the case of the Lagos strike of 1897, when PWD workers were the main element involved (see also Hughes & Cohen 1971; and chapters by Iliffe, Turner and Allen in Sandbrook & Cohen 1975). More often than not strikes in the early years of colonial rule were short-lived affairs generated in the heat of the moment and, though frequently involving large numbers of workers across several occupational ranges, left little in the way of an organisational imprint. The degree to which the workers concerned were aware of their class position, in itself and in relation to the dominant authority and class structure of the colonial period, cannot easily be discerned. For the most part the degree of class consciousness involved is simply inferred from the nature of class action, but Gutkind (1974) forcibly argues that, even in the pre-Second World War period, there is sufficient evidence in workers' petitions and in the observations of colonial officers to argue that a working-class consciousness had emerged. Naturally, an argument along such lines should not be overstated. The social universe that was comprehended was often the workplace for a localised employer-employee relationship; rarely did workers express, in the early period of colonial rule, a national, let alone an international, solidarity. Other mitigating factors included a fairly sharp division of status between unskilled workers and members of a more respectable white-collar salariat, and the persistence in many areas of ethnic forms of identity and interaction. Where, in rare cases, the employer was an indigenous private entrepreneur, patron-client links reinforced ethnic ties and damaged the capacity of workers to organise along class lines.

The degree to which ethnicity replaced or undercut forms of social interaction based on class lines is still a contentious issue, and one which cannot fully be explored here. Suffice to say that the new studies of labour history referred to are unanimous in showing that the work relationship was a far more determinate experience than a picture of African societies divided rigidly along ethnic lines of competition can possibly allow for. For the sociologists and social anthropologists working on the Copperbelt (for example, Epstein 1958), the diversity of the social worlds that African workers entered into and came from could be encompassed in a set of alternating models of social interaction. Basically, the theory proposed was that a worker shifted or changed his identity as new social fields or networks were encountered. But a working-class identity could shift back into ethnic forms of consciousness once the stimuli or environment of industrial employment assumed a permanent character, both in the lifetime of any one individual and as an irremovable mode of production; the forms of social consciousness and organisation that grew up had to move more or less in harness with the changing economic realities.

The chain of proletarianisation has been discussed in relation to the growth of class consciousness and in relation to class action. The third necessary component is that of organisation. It is clear that strike action has to have a degree of organisation behind it, but it is less clear that workers were able prior to 1945 to organise bodies - i.e. trade unions - to defend or promote their interests in a sustained fashion. Though it has been customary to argue that an organisational hiatus existed in most African countries prior to 1945, this view has to be somewhat modified. In Nigeria and Ghana, an examination of archival and newspaper evidence reveals the existence of many worker organisations, some of them, to be sure, being moribund or ineffective for much of their existence (Hughes & Cohen 1971). In South Africa the Industrial and Commercial Union, organised in the inter-war period, mobilised large numbers of African workers until its demise.

After 1945 the pace of proletarianisation advanced considerably. Absolute numbers of workers engaged in full-time employment increased dramatically and their struggles to increase their pay or ameliorate the conditions of their employment became enmeshed in a more general anti-colonial movement. There is considerable controversy in the literature as to how involved the trade unions were in the nationalist movements or the degree to which they were able to maintain an organisational independence apart from the elite-controlled political parties. Such questions are only of interest in this context in two respects. First, in so far as the unions were able to mobilise a popular base in the post-war period outside the confines of their membership, this base was insufficiently strong to challenge the basis of legitimacy to which the parties laid claim. Proletarianisation had not, in other words, proceeded so totally as to allow the proletariat to act as the 'general representatives' of the society at large. Second, and this is the other side of the coin, the trade unions had just enough organisational coherence and popularity not to be ignored by the nationalist politicians.

In a sense, the period from 1945 until the independence of most black African territories was one in which a temporary and often fitful class alliance was forged between the indigenous bourgeoisies and the organised working class. This cooperation rarely penetrated beneath the formalised structures (parties and unions) that organised each class, except on occasions, such as elections and rallies, when the politicians needed a suitable display of mass support or acquiescence to use in their negotiations with the colonial authorities and in their construction of a neo-colonial state. None the less a substratum of worker radicalism, particularly at the rank-and-file level, survived throughout this period and was to resurrect itself dramatically in the post-colonial period.

Managers, professionals and bureaucrats

Lest anyone be misled into thinking that all those who sell their labour power in African societies can be considered as part of an exploited working class, some comments can be made on those in the higher echelons of salaried employment.

In this category I include members of the civil service in senior staff positions, those who work in private industry or public corporations on the managerial side and those, like government doctors and university lecturers, who are employed on the public purse (I exclude professionals like lawyers and private doctors who work on an individual contractual basis). Though not normally discussed in descriptions of African labour issues, this group does merit some comment in its own right, for three reasons.

First, civil servants, in particular, are often well organised, especially in Francophone African countries. In Dahomey, for example, civil servants were able to effect upward salary increases during successive military and civilian regimes which amounted at one point to two-thirds of the national budget.

Second, the salariat is often in a situation in which its skills can be bought or sold internationally. Its reference groups tend, therefore, to be located outside the country in which it lives. (Nigerian university lecturers, for example, went on strike in 1973 and used United Kingdom university pay scales in pursuit of their demands.) If successful, such pay claims serve to widen further the normally high wage differentials. They may then produce a demonstration effect downwards in the form of a felt sense of relative deprivation by other workers in the society, a deprivation that it may not be easy to satisfy within the framework of a post-colonial state.

Third, the social and political role of the group identified can be seen as parasitical on other segments of the society and instrumental in serving the ends of neo-imperialism, either as direct employees of the state or as auxiliaries of the external estate (the foreign powers and interests that dominate most African countries and are located at the metropole). The groups concerned are often trained in metropolitan institutions imbued with Western tastes and prejudices, or in local institutions heavily penetrated by the influences of the external estate. They are, in short, a true labour aristocracy, a term which has been misleadingly applied (Arrighi & Saul 1973) to all workers engaged in selling their labour power above the level of what they call a semi-proletarianised peasantry. I would myself resist such a blanket dismissal of the African working class (but, for a modified position, see Saul in Sandbrook & Cohen 1975). On the other hand, there is no doubt that there does exist a reactionary element in the top echelons of those in employment, who are so close to the occupiers of the seats of power that they are virtually indistinguishable from them.

Other urban migrants

If a common thread of organisational endeavour, class consciousness and class action can be traced throughout the colonial period in the case of wage labourers, the same cannot be said of other dispossessed segments of the urban social structure. Once the chains of proletarianisation and peasantisation became fully operative, many Africans migrating to the cities found themselves either without employment of any kind or in a situation in which what few opportunities existed were incommensurate with their aspirations or job expectations. Some accommodated themselves to a socially disapproved existence as pimps, touts, prostitutes or thieves, living often at the margins of subsistence or preying, like parasites, on what few pickings a capital city of an impoverished country can offer. Others swelled the ranks of those who staff the industries, small trades and services that blanket the landscape of any African city. Workshops run by masters and apprentices cover every possible small-scale need - from photography to making farmers' machetes and low-cost furniture, or tyre-retreading. This sector of the urban economy, often described nowadays as the 'informal sector,' in fact accounts for a considerable degree of urban employment. Several writers, notably Keith Hart (1973), have demonstrated how useful and important the informal sector is to the national economy. It operates without the government subsidies, tax concessions, low-interest loans or other government incentives to attract foreign capital and industrial investment. It also provides on-the-job training in a wide range of skills for a minimal cost. But while a good deal can be said for the economic advantages that derive from the operation of a healthy informal sector, it is worth remembering that the conditions of employment can be extremely harsh. For three or four years apprentices are bound to their masters in a condition resembling that of servitude. A space on the workshop floor is living accommodation, and pocket money barely covers the means of survival, while the eldorado to the apprentice, namely a workshop of his own, is difficult to finance and may indeed never materialise. The exploitative character of the work relationship in such a context can rarely be personalised, for the master himself, in a buyers' market for his goods, usually ekes out a precarious existence and has to turn away more young migrants than he can employ.

Finally, there exists a group of genuinely unemployed workers, 'job applicants' by self-description, but in fact a lumpenproletariat proper. The origins of this group go back to the contradiction in the colonial political economy outlined earlier. As Gutkind (1974: 17, 22) puts it:

> Recruitment policies were designed to create a readily available labour reservoir, yet the consequences resulting from policies establishing a stabilised labour force were thought to be undesirable economically and especially politically.... [And later] administrators... needed cheap and readily available labour.... However, they were reluctant to support the establishment of a stable, urban, resident labour force by means of good wages and adequate urban facilities.

The consequences of this ambivalence were already observable in colonial times. The most dramatic growth of an urban lumpen-proletariat occurred, not without coincidence, in the areas of white settlement - where land-grabbing and the breakup of rural, particularly pastoral, economies had occurred most ruthlessly. In Kenya, influx control measures in the form of the notorious *kipande* (work certificate) provided much of the incendiary material that fuelled the Mau Mau rebellion. The pass system in South Africa, indeed the whole construction of apartheid as a systematic ideology, can also be considered as an attempt to meet the dilemma that white settlement and conquest generated. For the white South African regime to turn back the flow of urban migrants, let alone resettle those who have been urbanised for generations, it has to revitalise rural economies which previous white regimes systematically succeeded in underdeveloping and emasculating. Yet the chains of proletarianisation and forced peasantisation have gone too far to be reversed, even assuming that the South African government had the ability and the white electorate the willingness to countenance the massive redistribution of resources that would be necessary to achieve such an objective.

Conclusion

For the bulk of African countries the measures employed in colonial Kenya or white South Africa to arrest migration to the cities are politically unfeasible. The growing numbers of shanty-town dwellers and unemployed workers represent a formidable, and probably intractable, social problem. To what degree they represent a political threat is a moot point. I am myself inclined to the view that the degree of normlessness and disorientation manifested in this group, its incapacity, in contrast to the working class, to evince a collective consciousness and organisation, and the possibility that its loyalties can be bought by repressive agents mean that the lumpenproletariat, acting alone, is a minimal political threat to the ruling classes in African societies. On the other hand, Worsley (1972) argues that the very opprobrium that attaches to the lumpenproletariat in traditional Marxist writings itself conditions the view that it is incapable of revolutionary action. He maintains that the subproletariat (the term he prefers) can indeed be mobilised provided there is some revolutionary leadership and organisation.

Where a certain amount of consensus is emerging is in the view that it may be possible to effect a degree of political collaboration across several segments of the urban poor - the unskilled wage labourers, the unemployed, those employed in the informal sector, petty traders and the like. Some evidence of such links having been forged in the past is provided in descriptions of strike action in Sekondi-Takoradi in 1961 (see chapters by Jeffries and Peace in Sandbrook & Cohen 1975). What this represents in essence is a form of urban populism, not the manipulative 'Peronist' brand orchestrated from above, but rather the evolution of a set of demands and grievances common to the urban dispossessed, but articulated by its most active elements. But, as Sandbrook (1982) argues, populism is 'a vague and limited ideology.' He continues:

> It does not reject the dominant value system, but merely demands that this be respected in practice. It thus fosters only protest against a corrupt, nepotistic and self-interested political class, not concerted action to control or reshape institutions. Its long term political import is further reduced by the characteristically spasmodic and localised nature of populist protest. Given these features, regimes can normally quell the poorly coordinated unrest by means of repression, concessions and verbal acceptance of populist rhetoric. Populist rebellions do

occasionally unseat governments, but then power passes to the only institution ready to exercise it, namely the military.

Sandbrook's cautious summary of the limits of popular protest is instructive. With the exception of those countries where liberation movements have succeeded in spreading political consciousness to the humblest rural dweller, there is little evidence as yet to suggest that urban protest, however radical in rhetoric, has been able to channel rural discontent into a national political form. And without liberation from the rural indebtedness and wretchedness produced by the satellitisation of the agricultural economy during the colonial period, and the generalisation of commodity relations, a revolution led by urban workers can only be partial and incomplete.

This chapter was first published under the title 'From Peasants to Workers in Africa' in a highly successful collection edited by Peter Gutkind and Immanuel Wallerstein, The Political Economy of Contemporary Africa *(Beverly Hills, Sage, 1976, pp. 155-68). The book went into several printings and reproduction of my chapter here could therefore be thought to be unnecessary. However, judging from the royalty statements, the book was particularly successful as a course text in the US, and was not that readily accessible in Europe and Africa. In addition to reaching a non-US readership, I am particularly concerned that the idea of a linear historical progression from peasant to worker, which was reflected in the original title, is much more firmly challenged here. Even in 1976 I was sceptical of the notion of an inevitable* debouchement *from peasant to worker. But I have now been aided by the interesting work of Roseberry, Bernstein and others (cited in the present version) who write on the proletarianisation of rural social relations. One author, whose work on Botswana is alluded to in this chapter and who coined the suggestive term 'peasantariat,' is Jack Parson, who is engaged on a major study of the evolution of this intermediate social category in Botswana. A considerable advance on the debate can be expected in the wake of such recent and impending publications.*

Note

1   That the use of migrants is not simply a survival of an anachronistic
    mode may incidentally be seen in Europe, where the very exemplars of
    successful capitalism, Germany and Switzerland, rely considerably on
    migrant labour from Turkey, Italy and other poorer areas of southern
    Europe. One effect of the collapse of state socialism in Eastern Europe
    during the course of 1989 will be to make all these countries available as
    a gigantic labour reservoir available to the countries of Western Europe,
    a process already far advanced in the case of Yugoslavia, according to a
    forthcoming study by Schierup.

6

Resistance and Hidden Forms of Consciousness amongst African Workers

At dusk, two Mauritian sugar-cane cutters carefully cut off the long central stem of an aloe plant. They discussed briefly the appropriate length, then determined on a piece about 15 inches long. One end was carefully hollowed out and stuffed with nearly two boxes of tightly packed matchsticks. This incendiary device, with the slow-burning pith of the aloe acting as a fuse, was strategically placed to catch the strong gusts of wind coming in from the sea, while the matchsticks were covered with a handful of wilted strippings from the cane. Back at the village the two men drank quietly with their companions in the local store. When the dull glow appeared on the hillside, they walked home. Work tomorrow. The estate-owner, one of the score of Franco-Mauritians who owned the sugar industry, had laid off many of his workers the previous day. Too much cane had been cut and there was a log jam at the estate mill. Now the burnt field had to be cut within 48 hours if anything was to be rescued. The sirdar would be rounding up the labourers in the morning.
—Field Notes: Mauritius, 1976.

A pungent odour streamed from one corner of Mokola market. An old woman was selling newspaper wraps of dried 'Indian Hemp' for one shilling a piece. Labourers, mainly from the Public Works' Department, squatted at the side of the road and sucked deeply on their joints. 'It is our reward for a day's work', they said.
—Field Notes, Ibadan, 1968.

Initially the workers' conflict with the technical manager (of a Hausa-owned textile firm in Northern Nigeria) concerned allocation of time for prayer. Some time during 1961, a worker was caught praying without permission and was penalized by a seven-day suspension from work. He was able to arouse support for his position among fellow-workers, so that an appeal was made to the Emir resulting in the worker's reinstatement along with the provision for proper prayer breaks. The Union Secretary recalled ... 'I told them that we should not agree to this ruining of our

91

religion by the company.'
—Lubeck in Sandbrook & Cohen 1975: 146.

Retiring workers would inform those in the villages of their experiences and this would in turn affect the labour flows in subsequent seasons.... Parties who left the rural areas with some knowledge looked forward to gathering more recent information along the route... returning parties took considerable care to warn new workers of bad employers and in case they missed anybody making their way to Rhodesia, they took the precaution of pegging notices to various trees en route. Sometimes written in Swahili, these notes, addressed to Africans in general or individual workers in particular, warned of mines to be especially avoided. For the illiterate, a system of signs carved on trees served the same useful purpose.... The African names (for mines) were (also) rich in meaning... most helpful of all to the prospective workers were those names which gave ready insight into management policies and practices.... The total absence of generosity in food and wages at the Ayrshine mine was reflected in the name chimpadzi - meaning small portion.... And while Chayamataka - 'hit on the buttocks' - was hardly a name to make the Masterpiece mine popular, the fact that the Celtic mine was known as Sigebenga (a murderer or cruel person) made certain that the manager there was never plagued with work-seekers.
—van Onselen 1976: 234, 235.

Introduction

The opening quotes are designed to highlight forms of labour protest in Africa that are 'hidden' or 'covert' - forming part of the everyday forms of consciousness and action by the African proletariat, but rarely systematically considered in the literature on workers and trade unions in Africa. It is in fact only recently that studies of everyday forms of resistance by American and British workers have led to a drastic reappraisal of the often-repeated conventional wisdom that workers in these countries lack 'class consciousness' (Sennet & Cobb 1977; Gutman 1976; Beynon 1973). The major impediment to the study of working-class consciousness in whatever country has been the lack of theoretical elaboration of the concept itself, particularly by those of a narrowly orthodox Marxist persuasion. Working with a set of formula dichotomies (false vs true consciousness, economistic vs revolutionary consciousness, a class-in-itself vs a class-for-itself) cannot encompass the levels and variety of class consciousness, its fluid and mercurial character, its infusion with, and relationship to, the more general categories of a working-class 'culture', 'sub-culture' or 'contra-culture' (for an elaboration of these terms see Yinger 1960). While it is tempting to follow the conceptual trails laid by such terms as 'contra-culture', the limited number and character of ethnographic studies on African workers dictates that the discussion must be confined to more randomised examples of the theory and practice of everyday resistance by African workers, both within the confines of their work situation and in the wider labour process.

The previous literature on African labour protest has for the most part been confined to those indices of worker dissent that are easily observed, or accessible to measurement. The number, scope and duration of strikes, the number of man-days lost, the rate of labour turnover, the extent of worker participation in union organisations, radical social movements and street demonstrations - all these are, quite rightly, considered as evidence of labour protest. Within the factory, pro-management studies of the 'human relations' school employ indices such as worker productivity, job satisfaction and the rate of absenteeism to test the extent of habituation to the industrial ethnic. Worker resistance is seen as an impediment to be subdued or manipulated - through job incentive schemes, productivity deals, the sponsoring of house unions, consultative committees, and the like. As to studies of the more overt forms of protest (predominantly strikes, unionisation and overt political activity), these have secured, in recent years, a wider scholarly attention (see Sandbrook & Cohen 1975). This book, covering the work of some 18 scholars working in a dozen countries, can be seen as representative of the conceptions prevalent in the late 1960s and early 1970s. The concentration on obvious forms of dissent is explicable in terms of the dialectic that several of this group of scholars established with the earlier literature in the field. They sought to define the characteristics of an African proletariat where others had denied its existence, to show the extent of self-organisation of workers where others had insisted that beneficent colonial labour officers or metropolitan parties had brought unions into existence; they insisted that workers were engaged in various forms of political bargaining where others sought to restrict the workers' political role to a formal alliance between a party and a central union. To be sure, several scholars (Stichter, Iliffe, Lubeck, Peace and Jeffries) represented in the Sandbrook/Cohen volume envisage a more pervasive picture of the relation of the worker qua worker to the labour process, but none were interested in the social relations of production *per se*. What little interest had previously been shown in this subject was by way of an occasional anthropological account (for example, Epstein 1958) or paternalist concern about the poor conditions under which African labourers toiled (for example, Davis 1967). A more detailed and specialised account of the social relationships of African workers in an Indian-owned factory in Zambia appeared in Kapferer (1972), but the author is so preoccupied with spinning the complex webs of exchange and network theory that few clear findings emerge. It is virtually entirely in the context of 'closed institutions', i.e. the mining compounds of southern Africa, that the most directly relevant work has been undertaken. The most recent account was made possible through the unlikely circumstance that the author was a personnel officer in a Namibian mine as well as being a doctoral student at the University of Illinois and a sympathetic observer of the workers in the mining compound (Gordon 1977). But while providing good ethnographic information, the more theoretically satisfying is the work of an economic historian of the Rhodesian mines (van Onselen 1976). In the concluding chapter of his book van Onselen maps out what he considers are the special features of labour protest in the 'labour coercive' economy he surveys, which is that of the Rhodesian mines. His comments can, however, be widened in applicability and seen as laying the groundwork for a richer approach for the study of African labour protest. He writes:

> In a labour-coercive economy... worker ideologies and organisations should be viewed essentially as the high water marks of protest; they should not be allowed to dominate our understanding of the way in which the economic system worked, or of the African miners' responses to it. At least as important, if not more so, were the less dramatic, silent and often unorganized responses, and it is this latter set of responses, which occurred on a day-to-day basis, that reveal most about the functioning of the system, and forward the woof and warp of worker consciousness. Likewise it was unarticulated, unorganized protest and resistance which the employers and the state found most difficult to detect or suppress.

To discern the 'silent' and 'unorganised' responses of African workers in the face of the limited number of ethnographies and social histories that are available is no mean task, but it is possible to widen the range of our sources beyond the area normally considered to be part of 'labour history' or 'labour studies' by shifting the problematic, that is to say by decomposing older paradigms and recomposing known data into a new paradigm. To do this it is necessary to provide a generalised model of the labour process and the pattern of worker responses within which our categories of discussion can be organised.

The labour process and worker responses

In specifying a new problematic it is first necessary to isolate some generic features of a capitalist labour process before identifying characteristic worker responses and their particular African manifestations. It is postulated here that the labour process under capitalism involves both the creation of a working class and its habituation to industrial production in five major ways:

—The potential worker is forced to abandon his own forms of subsistence or income (landholding, petty trade, craft-production) and to rely, increasingly fully, on wages. This, in the language of industrial relations experts, is known as 'labour-commitment' - a notion which typically misconceives the problem by presenting it as if it were a matter of psychological choice for the worker. In fact, of course, there is more typically a high element of compulsion in what is more accurately perceived as the creation and control of a stock of labour-power (for short, *Enforced Proletarianisation*).

—Once at work, the worker has to accept the unequal authority structure of the workplace - with directors, managers, gang-bosses, foremen and supervisors installed in a relationship of superordination (*Managerial Control*).

—The worker has to adapt to the physical and psychological conditions of employment that obtain in the workplace (*Psychological Adjustment*).

—The worker has to accept an unequal distribution of reward for the labour-power extended (*Differential Reward*).

—The worker is forced to recognise the overall political and juridical structure that permits, or encourages, the growth and establishment of capitalist social relations (*Political Control*).

Even within the most advanced capitalist modes of production not all elements of the labour process are fully commandeered by 'capital'. In the case of Africa one would anticipate that the element of control would be much reduced in view of the incomplete character of capitalist penetration, and the remaining (though drastically reducing) possibilities Africans have for producing a wage supplement. It is important to emphasise, as do the editors of a volume on African labour history, that 'the spread of capitalism even to a peripheral zone detaches man from his product, man from his habitual environment, man from the right to dispose of his labour-power and his agricultural goods in his own right. It is in the scale and intensity of this dislocation and decomposition of domestic modes of production, distribution and exchange, that the colonial presence manifests itself' (Gutkind, Cohen & Copans 1979). The opposite side of the coin, the face that shows incomplete capitalist penetration, would suggest that workers are not always able to mount an effective challenge to all elements of the labour process. None the less, historically and experientially, African workers have (and do) resist incorporation into capitalist production in many ways. Before citing the African data directly it is necessary to tabulate and group these responses and show their relationship to the five elements of the labour process previously specified.

Figure 6.1: Workers' Responses to the Labour Process

Enforced Proletarianisation
  - a.   Desertion
  - b.   Community withdrawal/revolt
  - c.   Target working

Managerial Control
  - d.   Task & time bargaining
  - e.   Sabotage
  - f.   Creation of 'work-culture'

Psychological Adjustment
  - g.   Accidents and sickness
  - h.   Drug use
  - i.   Belief in other-worldly solutions

Differential Reward
  - j.   Theft
  - k.   Unionisation
  - l.   Economistic strikes

Political Control
  - m.   Participation in rallies, riots, demonstrations
  - n.   Support of anti-status quo parties
  - o.   Political strikes

Note: Responses a-j are singled out for subsequent discussion in this chapter;
  I do not thereby discount the importance of responses k-o.

Even a superficial examination of Figure 6.1 will help to ground
further the initial distinction between hidden and overt forms of
worker protest: categories a-j comprising the former; categories k-o,
the latter. In the first set, we need to establish and draw together
existing African data; in the second the literature is already in a
much more theoretically elaborated and empirically demonstrated
state. But the distinction between the two sets of categories and
between individual categories should not belie the fact that real
events are not always containable within the confines of a single
form of response and often show a mixed and even paradoxical
character. Here Mauritian workers are committing sabotage, not as
in the normal case to delay production and evade work, but

precisely to ensure that they would be permitted to work. How is this to be explained? Given the destruction or emasculation of all prior modes of production on the island, the indentured Indian labourers and freed African slaves had perforce to adapt to the capitalist mode. A few ex-slaves became fishermen (*not* their previous occupational specialisation) in an attempt to escape work on the estates, but nearly all the remaining workers had little alternative but to sell their labour-power merely to survive. The estate-owners, for their part, neither wanted nor needed a stable labour force - far better to rely on a seasonally employed and unorganised group, with a large reserve army hovering in the wings. (Though this was in essence the estate-owners' strategy, it also had its problems: for example, reproduction costs had to be met by estate housing and by permitting a small planter class to develop.) In such circumstances worker protest needed to be directed towards fostering stabilisation, a strategy which elsewhere has been fought under the slogan 'A Right to Work'. In other contexts, workers, far from demanding that their surplus values be expropriated from them, may well be engaged in leading the revolt against work.

The combined and paradoxical (i.e. dialectical) character of nearly all of the stated categories could *pari passu* be demonstrated. To continue this exercise in full would lead to too complex a theoretical elaboration: suffice it to remind the reader that the dialectical character of each category of worker response in Africa should be borne in mind in the following examples, which are organised simply by discussing the identified responses a-j in sequence.

Worker responses in Africa

(a) Desertion

This was a common means of escaping habituation into the capitalist mode all over Africa. Stichter (in Sandbrook & Cohen 1975) regards desertion as the 'chief mode of protest' once labour recruitment in Kenya had begun. One report from Nyanza, in 1907, said that railway workers were 'extremely apt to throw down their tools and run away on the slightest pretext'. Another from the Kikuyu area complained: 'no man can run a farm with monthly relays of raw natives: labour of this kind is always capricious and liable to desert'. In 1909, 31 out of the 48 complaints received by the Nairobi Labour Office concerned cases of desertion. A year earlier, on the other side of the continent, the British were attempting to push through the Baro-Kano railway line in northern Nigeria. According to Mason, 'resistance spread and became more determined'. Mr Gill, a political officer on the railway in southern Zaria province, reported 300 desertions from the line while another officer complained of 800. The Acting High Commissioner counselled caution but not, of course, the abandonment of the enterprise: 'It is madness to take large levies during the farming season from pure agriculturalists like the Gwaris, far better go slow till dry weather' (Mason in Gutkind, Cohen & Copans 1979). Desertion of soldiers from colonial armies, often used as 'labour brigades', was also common, as were cases of self-mutilation to escape conscription. Both these forms of protest are extensively documented in the case of French West Africa (Echenberg 1975). In the case of southern Africa, a similar structure exists. Van Onselen quotes the lament of Mashonaland mineowners: 'The police use every possible effort, but the fact remains that whole gangs can, and do, abscond and are never traced or heard of again'. He goes on to show that where total contraction out of the wage-labour system was not possible, workers deserted in one mine after another to try to secure better wages and working conditions.

Colonial governments and mineowners alike responded to the high rates of desertion by attempts to control and supervise both the recruitment and mobility of workers. In the French colonies highly supervised forced labour was used until the 1930s. In the British colonies, Masters and Servants' Ordinances and other legislation (registration bureaux and work certificates like *kipande*) were all designed to criminalise worker mobility and reduce the rate of desertion. In the armies of the two principal colonial powers it was a clearly recognised principle of service that a private recruited in one place should, where possible, serve out his time in another colony. As well as reducing the possibilities for flight, this strategy conferred the incidental benefit that the stranger troops fired with less hesitation in the event of riot or public disturbance. In the case of a Namibian mining compound, Gordon argues that the company's control over the workers' income and expenditure 'attempts to subject the worker totally to the goals of the organisation for the duration of his employment by minimizing the worker's commitments to his outside world'.

The rate of desertion depends on the degree of control exercised, but also, more saliently, on the degree of viability that remains to the pre-capitalist mode of production. Herein, as has previously been argued, lay a contradiction for the underdeveloped form of capitalism prevalent in Africa. 'The ideal solution... was one in which agricultural production remained sufficiently virile to produce an exportable primary product and absorb return migrants, but not so viable that it threatened the supply of cheap unskilled labour. Such a delicate balance was impossible to achieve and may indeed be considered one of the central contradictions of the colonial political economy' (Cohen 1976: 161 and Chapter 5 in this volume).

(b) Community withdrawal or revolt

This, *par excellence*, is a category where there is an enormous weight of historical evidence to reinterpret. Most of the colonial historical sources have rich and bloodthirsty descriptions of the early wars of 'pacification'. Usually, of course, some higher purpose is adduced such as destroying 'barbarity', 'spreading the light' or preventing 'tribal wars'. The reasons for such adventures may not be totally reducible to the need for the fledgling colonial states to create a reservoir of cheap and available labour (the colonial authorities did need to reaffirm their political hegemony internally and against their metropolitan rivals), but this was clearly a motivating factor and was certainly the major effect of colonial wars. The necessity for the colonial authorities - especially in the areas of white settlement - to create and control a substantial quantum of labour-power, is further demonstrated by the constant repetition in colonial sources that such and such a chief or headman needed to be deposed or killed for failing to honour his treaty commitments to provide labour. The local communities had two alternatives: to withdraw into regions so inhospitable that the blackbirder (labour recruiter) or raiding party could not reach them (for example, the Pygmies or many nomadic peoples) or to organise a communal revolt against the authority of the colonial state, its agents or its local collaborators. Examples of these forms of protest are legion, but the degree to which a protest against forced labour was the core of a communal protest has not always been emphasised. Witness, however, van der Post's (1958: 48) account of the withdrawal of Bushmen into the Kalahari:

> Everywhere they (the Bushmen children) were in great demand as slaves because, when they survived captivity, they grew up into the most intelligent, adroit and loyal of all the former servants. Even long after slavery was abolished and until the supply was dried up their service was exacted under a system of forced labour. From the earliest days, all along the frontier, the more desperate and adventurous characters among my countryside added to their living by kidnapping Bushman children and selling them to labour-hungry farmers. Hardly a commando came back from an expedition without some children.... Many tried to escape and if recaptured, were flogged heavily for their pains. Others... would try furtively to signal by fires to their own people... and move stealthily ever deeper into the interior.

As to evidence of communal revolt, a recent history of the Igbo documents is a not untypical story. The people of Udi, who had given only a token resistance when the British first came, took advantage of the outbreak of the First World War to rise in rebellion. According to Elizabeth Isichei (1976: 134, 136), 'it was a protest against forced labour on the roads... where the unpaid workers, who were expected to feed themselves, often went hungry - sometimes they used to eat leaves. The survey of the railway line seemed to threaten their ownership of land, and herald more forced labour'. When the revolt was brutally crushed the peace terms included the supplying of 2,000 unpaid workers for the railway. After 1915 they were forced to work in the mines as well.

In Kenya and Giriama the revolt of 1913/14, which resulted in the deaths of 400 Giriama, was a direct result of the government's attempt to use Giriama labour on the European and Arab sisal, cotton, rice and coconut plantations. Again in Kenya, millenarian cults, like the Mumbo cult, whose believers refused to pay tax or labour for the administration, grew up precisely amongst those groups, like the Gusii, which had their first exposure to labour demands on a large scale (Stichter in Sandbrook & Cohen 1975). European depredations of African land were associated with European demands for African labour and it was for control of their own land and labour-power that such well-known revolts as Maji-Maji (1905-7) and Mau-Mau occurred. In short, there was a high element of labour protest in events that had been interpreted by colonial historians as wars of pacification and by the post-1950s Africanist historians as 'proto-nationalism'.

(c) Target working

This rather old-fashioned and now discredited notion was first used by colonial officers to justify the payment of low wages. New workers, they argued, preferred 'leisure' to income, once they had reached a certain 'target' commensurate with their desire to purchase certain established consumer goods. A backward-bending supply curve was thought to result - the supply of labour drying up, and the return to the country speeding up, as wage levels increased. With other commentators, I have criticised this notion arguing that, 'in fact the targets that workers set themselves were much more elastic than the colonial administrators realised (or were prepared to admit), and there appears to be solid evidence to support the view that wage-earners responded favourably to monetary incentives once these were offered' (Cohen 1974: 189).

This 'liberal' critique (the African as 'economic man') needs to be supplemented by the more plausible argument that elastic targets are ultimately determined less by choice than by the increasingly limited possibilities for a return to rural life. The subjectivist element in the notion of target working can, however, be usefully refashioned to explain the undoubted fact that many urban workers perceive their employment as temporary, not because they can now hope to return to the land, but because they hope to become petty entrepreneurs and independent craftsmen. These petty-bourgeois aspirations are thought by Lloyd to inhibit class consciousness:

'Rather than identify with wage employment, the migrant aspires to be his real master; he sees society as a ladder up which individuals have risen to various levels of success; he does not see an irreconcilable antagonism between rich and poor'. Target working is thus an important element of what has been called the 'ego-centred cognitive map' of workers. But a sociologist cannot explain the world simply in terms of people's intentions and decisions. In practice, there is a crucial difference between young single workers who are seeking to establish themselves by converting their savings to independent proprietorship, and the bulk of workers with family commitments confronting a situation of rises in rent, transport and the general cost of living. For such workers, the mythology of successful petty entrepreneurship has replaced the rural idyll as an object for escapism. Subjectively, such fantasies are part of a worker's resistance to the objective reality that most of them will have no choice but to sell their labour-power, be it in the public sector, in modern industry or in the open-air sweatshops of African cities (euphemistically now designated the informal sector).

To summarise this first set of forms of resistance: to implant capitalist social relations in an area previously characterised by pre-capitalist modes, it is necessary to create and control a stock of labour-power. In Africa, this was achieved particularly violently, through wars of pacification, the imposition of hut and poll taxes, the use of forced labour, and the application of a legal code equating worker mobility with criminality. Africans responded by desertion, by withdrawal or by revolt. But acquiescence of the loss of control over labour-power and its product was inevitable, even where symbolic escape was possible. Equally, one might have to accept the fact of wage-labour without accepting the conditions under which labour-power is utilised. It is to these forms of resistance that attention is now directed.

(d) Task, efficiency and time bargaining

What is meant by task bargaining? Here a worker deliberately seeks either to restore his traditional skill or craft in the face of management attempts to detail, deskill and massify the productive process, or (more commonly) he seeks to reduce his exploitation by adhering overstrictly to job specifications and rules detailing his work. A 'work to rule' and job-demarcation dispute are typical examples of this form of protest - often triggered off by the managerial redefinition. Witness, for example, the indignation of an African tailor in an Indian-owned factory in Zambia who was accused of stitching a pair of trousers badly: 'If you continue to treat us like animals you will find your work in this factory becoming very difficult. I have been a tailor with Narayan Brothers for over seven years and have never during this time sewn short trousers like that pair we are talking about now'. His co-workers supported him - 'If you (the foremen) do not stop treating us like learner tailors we will walk out. Now! Now!' (Kapferer 1972: 243). Time/Efficiency bargaining is a closely related form of resistance and may be seen in the workers' characteristic and frequently successful attempts to bamboozle the time and motion men, the planner and the job-setter. The collective solidarity ('Brotherhood') in time/efficiency bargaining on a Namibian mine is well described by Gordon:

> White supervisors attribute quota restrictions by the workers to 'laziness' and point out that in terms of cash earning it is illogical behaviour since it cuts into the underground workers' bonus. Thus, it is felt that laziness must be inherent. But quota restriction, from the workers' perspective, has a logic of its own. It enables them to avoid fatigue by allowing them to work at a comfortable pace. They are thus able to establish a degree of control over their own work targets.... Quota restriction prevents competition at the workplace which would disturb established interpersonal relationships and protects slower Brothers thus alleviating white pressure because it is believed that if one worker works harder, the white will also expect other workers to put more effort into their tasks... walk offs were quite frequent and entailed considerable Brotherhood solidarity.

As well as for the reasons adduced by Gordon, go-slows may reflect the difference between rhythms of work derived from agriculture, craft production and seasonal employment and those conducive to industrial production or office routine. In his discussion of the prolonged disputes that led to the workers' seizure of the Mount Carmel Rubber Factory in Tanzania, Pascal Mihyo (1975) shows how the employer tried unsuccessfully to use the workers' committee to discipline the workers and secure greater efficiency. They responded by 'a perpetual go-slow'.

(e) Sabotage

As a form of resistance this carries time/efficiency and task bargaining to a more extreme conclusion. Sabotage is, in other words, rationally based in the determination of workers to slow down the production process and to prevent redundancies occasioned by the introduction of labour-saving machinery. Sabotage can also be seen as a means of levelling down profits to reduce inequality rather than, as in a wage demand, attempting to reduce inequality by levelling-up. A series of incidents witnessed in a Lagos plastics factory by the author (December 1968) demonstrated this clearly. After a wage demand had been refused, the workers systematically jinxed the machinery, the vats, the moulds and the firm's transport. Subsequently, when the workers' consciousness escalated and they decided to occupy the factory and sell the goods themselves, they regretted their earlier enthusiasm; but there is no doubt that the initial outburst was directed against what workers perceived as excessive managerial profits. Sabotage therefore is linked with the other forms of resistance to the differential reward inherent in a capitalist labour process.

(f) Creation of a 'work-culture'

The structure of workplace authority is also frequently undermined by the deliberate creation or amplification of social distance between the worker and manager. Frequently the creation of a contra-culture is subtle and difficult to assess even after long participant observation. In-jokes, private linguistic codes, wall slogans and the like are most common, but the creation of a work-culture takes many forms. In the Namibian mine Gordon was employed in, workers had four or five names, including a 'white' name, used mainly for interaction with the management. The proliferation of names obstructed the whites. If a 'name' was sought, the confusion gave the worker an opportunity to start an investigative relationship; if trouble loomed, the 'name' could disappear. On the other hand some workers stuck to their indigenous names. If the name was difficult for the white foremen to remember or pronounce then the worker could be anonymous and immune from singling out. In East Africa, Grillo (1973) points out that within the East African Railways an *esprit de corps* or 'corporate ethos' evolved around the use of Swahili: 'Railwaymen whatever their national background, were willing and able to use Swahili as a means of communication - even Ganda, who in Kampala tried to ignore other languages except English'. Work-songs to break the monotony of the labour and to mock the gang-boss, dances, drinking patterns all take on the character of a distinct moral universe, a private culture where, as Gordon notes, blacks can 'be themselves' and be masters of their 'own' actions. The dialectic between 'resistance' and 'adaptation', an issue that is discussed in the concluding section of this chapter, is seen most clearly in the case of a work-culture, which can act either as an insulative force or a set of symbols to mobilise the hunger of workers. A sensitive study by Ranger (1975) of the Beni dance societies, for example, shows how the symbols of white power (hierarchy, discipline, barracks, uniforms) were combined with an African-based language and music to create a new and vibrant art form which spread over much of East and southern Africa. Van Onselen surmises that the organisation of the early mutual-aid societies in Rhodesian mine compounds among workers owed much to the influence of the Beni dance societies. At another point van Onselen shows how mine dancing was generally approved of by the management as a means of social control and as a reinforcement for their beliefs in happy tribesmen, and only evoked disapprobation when the dancing took on an inter-tribal character and the dance organisers began to look more like an embryonic strike committee.

The control that managers attempt to effect in the workplace is challenged, in sum, by four principal means: (a) attempting to repossess the definition of the task; (b) evading management or deluding it as to the level of possible 'productivity'; (c) engaging in sabotage; and (d) amplifying social distance and creating a work-culture. The degree to which many of these actions can be considered a serious challenge to the managerial authority depends on the local circumstances. Some may be no more than pin-pricks; others, particularly cultural manifestations like mine dancing, may be sanctioned by management as a form of repressive tolerance. The work-culture created is, however, of fundamental importance in providing the organising symbols around which a grievance located elsewhere may be galvanised (i.e. given appropriate leadership, organisation, or an 'issue').

(g) Accidents and sickness

The next set of responses are those which are normally conceived of as having little relation to the labour process itself and are often thought of as extraneous to the relations of production, even by workers themselves. A closer examination will, however, reveal that, while there may be an element of unconscious reaction involved, these forms of behaviour do indeed constitute forms of worker resistance and adaptation. Take first the question of sickness and accidents. The distribution and the incidence of illnesses and 'accidents' are, despite the verbal paradox, neither fortuitous nor random. The type of industry, the track speed-ups by management, the particular time of the day and time of the week; if all these factors are taken into account, accidents are far from being accidental. In like manner, morbidity is closely related to housing conditions, conditions at work, and the distribution of health care. Accidents and illness are, like Durkheim's Suicide, social facts: facts to which workers are expected to adjust. In the South African gold mines, Wilson (1972: 21) reports that in 'the period 1936-66 no less than 19,000 men, 93 per cent of them black, died as a result of accidents'. The white death rate was 0.97 per 1,000 men, the black death rate 1.62 per 1,000 men. By 1967, medical compensation for miners was paid at the rate of R10 million a year, but two-thirds of the total went to black workers. Beri Beri (heart failure due to lack of thiamine), for example, first extensively documented amongst young able-bodied Chinese working in Malaya, was found largely among male hostel workers in the Johannesburg mines - and barely among other workers (*South African Medical Journal* 1972, cited by Wilson 1972a: 186). The disease is caused by bad food and heavy drinking, particularly of the 'Bantu Beer' produced by the Johannesburg municipality - which lacks the traditional ingredient sorghum, which contains thiamine. Municipal beerhalls were the first targets of the 1976 Soweto rioters. Far from destroying their social facilities workers were smashing the very symbol of social control and (less consciously) destroying what, it transpires, is a positively lethal form of 'nutrition'.

With regard to reported sickness, what for managers constitutes 'malingering' may for workers constitute an attempt to deny their labour-power to the employer while coping with debilitating conditions the employer has provided. Equally, accidents are deliberately (or even unconsciously) used to evade work or slow it down. The self-mutilation by army recruits mentioned earlier in the case of French West Africa, is obviously an act of volition; but accidents such as clothing caught in moving machinery, eye grit, fainting and muscular injuries have the effect of acts of resistance even where they are not consciously so directed.

(h) Drug use

Almost invariably this represents a form of psychological resistance but social quiescence by workers. Drugs tend to be used as means of 'ironing out' emotional peaks and troughs. Some stimulants, for example, the widely used West African kola nut, are taken as food substitutes and simply to keep going, but more often 'downers' like alcohol and cannabis are simply used as a means of relaxation and enjoyment - a form of compensation for an unrewarding work experience. Worker-initiated drug use as illustrated by the opening vignette from Mokola market should, however, be distinguished from managerial and public provision of drug centres as in the large beer-drinking facilities in mining compounds and townships of southern Africa. Alcohol was sometimes provided in a company store operation, but more often it was designed to prevent the recreation hours of workers being used for anything more harmful. Van Onselen recounts an interesting managerial variation; a beer brewing monopoly was granted to favoured workers as a bonus. As van Onselen points out, this increased productivity, while the reward was financed by the workers themselves (van Onselen 1976: 169). A second example can be cited. Partly under the pressure of local wine interests, the sale of alcohol other than beer was permitted in South Africa in the early 1960s. This had the anticipated effect. During the period 1963-71 the Cape Town City Council bottle stores recorded an increase in sales of over 500 per cent (Wilson 1972a: 180). Despite the undoubtedly quiescent effects of alcohol consumption (violence being predominantly intra-, not inter-class directed), there is no doubt that it can also provide a form of companionship and solidarity. Gordon observes that drinking together is one of the most important rituals of friendship in a Namibian mine. Friendly relations and mutual trust are engendered by drinking together from a common pot in a context where tales of poisoned beer abound. 'Everyone, young and old, sits within conversational range around the beer bins, which emphasises the egalitarian basis of compound society'.

(i) Belief in other-worldly solutions

A common form of psychological resistance to work is the adoption of religion or other-worldly beliefs, particularly those that stress relief from suffering in the next world. Often this might not be a coherent set of religious doctrines but simply a belief in chance, fate, a lucky break or the evil machinations of some other person whose actions are wholly beyond control - all forms of withdrawal which Lloyd records in Yoruba society. Yet, while undoubtedly an opiate for most workers, religious belief and practice might also provide some elements in the construction of a workers' ideology (asceticism, solidarity, retribution) and some practical experience of organisation. Because many African workers followed Islam or African Christian sects, employers were often suspicious of 'nativism' or 'Ethiopianism' being fanned by religious practices. This was undoubtedly the reason why at first all the independent churches were outlawed in the Rhodesian mine compounds (van Onselen 1976). That the colonial authorities and employers did not misapprehend the danger from independent religious movements is confirmed by Hodgkin's remarks in his classical study, *Nationalism in Colonial Africa*. According to Hodgkin (1956: 82), the main achievement of the independent churches was 'to diffuse certain new and fruitful ideas, in however confused a form, among the African mass, the peasants in the countryside and the semi-proletarianised peasants in the towns for the most part: the idea of the historical importance of Africans; of an alternative to total submission to the European power'.

When discussing forms of psychological resistance to the labour process, it is difficult to disentangle motive and intention from unconscious or dimly apprehended action and reaction. But the question of volition is less important than the capacity of workers to create some private domains and psychological 'space' free of the insistent pressures of the capitalist labour process.

(j) Theft

The last of the categories of 'hidden responses' considered here is that of theft. Many large industrial concerns calculate on a given proportion of raw materials, tools and product losses and simply pass on the increased prices to the customer. Worker theft can be usefully considered as a wage-supplement, which varies in volume with the rise or fall in real wages. To take one example from the Rhodesian mines, it appears that 'the volume of illegal gold trade increased as the wages of black miners fell' (van Onselen). Besides keeping the gold amalgam that was caught on large canvas strips under the mill, or by running a finger-nail across the copper plate over which the crushed gold passed, workers were engaged in many other 'crimes':

> Daily, hundreds of petty crimes were committed on the mining properties with the specific objective of rectifying the balance between employees and their employers. African workers constantly pilfered small items of mine stores - such as candles - or helped themselves to substantial quantities of detonators and dynamite which they used for fishing. Wage rates were altered on documents and hundreds of work and 'skoff' tickets were forged by miners who sought to gain compensations for what they had been denied through the system.

In the much larger and more valuable diamond mining areas of South Africa and Namibia it is deemed necessary to have daily screenings of employees including anal searches and X-rays in order to reduce the numerous occasions when diamonds have been secreted in strange places or swallowed. In white settler societies any clubroom conversation will reveal the elaborate charades domestic workers play with their employers - watering down the gin, moving the mark on the bottle, or putting flour into the sugar and rice. Theft has here been interpreted not as a legal or moral offence, but as a form of labour protest which has the effect of reducing the rate of exploitation of the workers by an informal wage supplement. Seen in this view 'theft' becomes an act of recovering some 'surplus value', which would otherwise be appropriated by the employer.

Hidden and overt forms

A quick glance at Figure 6.1 will reveal that the sequential discussion of worker responses stops abruptly before category k, the subsequent categories being those that are both better argued and documented in the existing literature and that represent more obvious forms of class consciousness and action. By way of conclusion it is now necessary to relate the hidden to the overt forms of consciousness. Three theoretical positions can be briefly considered.

(a) The hidden forms are both more pervasive and more important, they are a 'bedrock', 'grassroots', 'genuine' sort of consciousness. Van Onselen seems to be inclined to this view, though by limiting his theoretical elaboration to a 'labour coercive economy' (for a discussion of this concept, see Trapido 1971), that of a mining compound, it is easy to reply that in that context only the hidden forms were possible. Certainly, those disillusioned with the iron law of oligarchy, and shall we say the copper law of co-optation of trade union leaders, might well find some attraction in the 'grassroots' view. It is a view, however, that would tend to the romanticisation of everyday events that by their very nature cannot but be often disconnected, spontaneous, individualistic and with short-term effect. There is no sense here in which workers can combine for a sustained long-term programme, or seize the instruments of production or govern themselves, let alone establish themselves as what Marx called 'the general representatives' of their society.

(b) The hidden forms are at a lower level of consciousness but can be seen as part of an incremental chain of consciousness leading towards a 'higher', more politicised, form of consciousness. This seems a somewhat more plausible position, though any incremental process cannot be viewed deterministically. In the absence of leadership, organisation and a galvanising issue (and in the presence of a repressive state or employer), there is little reason to assume that the process cannot be sidetracked or aborted. If protest can be kept on a sporadic and informal basis, it can ultimately be seen as a form of adaptation to the conditions of capitalist production. None the less, those informal acts that do involve collective solidarity (for example, feigning illness) can lay the basis for an organisation and leadership, if not a consistent ideology.

(c) The idea of a step-by-step consciousness is often now challenged by Marxists who, following Lukacs, press for a theory of 'dual consciousness' (*New Left Review* 52, 1968). The dualism is derived from Marx's contrast in *The Holy Family* between, on the one hand, what any proletariat or even the whole proletariat *imagines* to be its aim and, on the other, what the proletariat *is* and what it *consequently* is compelled to do (full citation in Mann 1973: 45).

Marx's dualism is instructive in exposing the generally weak versions of subjectivism (attitude surveys) which some sociologists advance as a 'refutation' of class consciousness. But it is unsatisfactory in its underplaying of volunteristic forms of social action. Suppose, however, we reconstitute a 'dual consciousness' theory in another, related, sense. Overt forms can represent an extant, readily observed consciousness - (which may be revolutionary or conservative to any degree between the two), whereas the forms of resistance described above can represent a latent and subterranean reservoir of consciousness. Workers can transcend the prosaic limits of everyday actions and reactions in given circumstances, and with a leadership that is able to amplify and galvanise forms of dissent that have not previously gained a conventional expression.

To prescribe the manner in which such a transition might take place - from latent to 'becoming' to actual consciousness - would take us beyond the realm of an academic chapter into the world of practical politics. None the less, one might conclude by arguing that the variety of responses and tenacity of purpose shown by African workers in their attempt to resist the capitalist labour process have thus far exceeded the capacity of African trade unions and revolutionary parties to channel such dissent for progressive or revolutionary ends.

I had some hesitation in reprinting this contribution again as it probably has had more exposure than any of the other chapters in this book. It started first as a paper entitled 'Forms and Characteristics of Labour Protest' given to a small conference organised by the US Social Science Research Council in New York State in 1976. The conference was entitled 'Inequality and the Poor in Africa' and was held at the former home of the Heinz family (they of the 57 Varieties) at Mount Kisco: this was now a conference centre for one of the Ivy League universities, I think Yale. The contrast between the theme of the conference and our surroundings could not have been greater. We dined sumptuously and jogged to and fro from the marbled indoor swimming pool in the gowns and slippers provided by the establishment. Added to contrast was irony. The waiters serving the Africanist and African guests were white colonists from Mozambique who had fled to the US as FRELIMO's struggle was triumphing. The paper was, I am almost certain, issued in a mimeographed form by the Faculty of Commerce and Social Science at the University of Birmingham at about the same time, but I cannot now find a copy of this version or an exact reference. In 1980, it was published under the present title in the Review of African Political Economy *No. 19, Sept.-Dec. pp. 8-22. Two years later, extracts of the piece were published in a collection edited by two of my colleagues on the Editorial Working Group of the Review in G. Williams & C.H. Allen (eds.)* The Sociology of Developing Societies: Sub-Saharan Africa *(Basingstoke, Macmillan, 1982). A more popular, but somewhat truncated, version appeared in an Open University set book edited by H. Johnson & H. Bernstein,* Third World Lives of Struggle *(London, Heinemann, 1982, pp. 244-58). It was a great pleasure to give some seminars on the chapter to student groups in this remarkable institution - the most innovative and worthy legacy left by the Wilson government in the UK. Finally, a French translation appeared in M. Agier et al. (eds.)* Classes ouvrières d'Afrique Noire *(Paris, Karthala, 1987, pp. 113-36). Despite the strong prior interest in this chapter, I felt it was so intrinsic to the purposes of this book that I could not bring myself to leave it out. Additionally, a corrective purpose may be served by reprinting it in this volume: namely setting the role of 'hidden' resistance within a wider political and sociological context. This piece has been wrongly cited several times to imply that I ascribe a fundamentalist primacy to covert forms of protest. It should be apparent from the concluding sections of the chapter that this is not the case. However, the discussion of the relationship between hidden and overt forms, and their relative primacy, is necessarily brief and I therefore hope that the argument provided in other parts of this book (particularly in Chapters 3 and 4) will make my views more evident.*

7

The Revolutionary Potential of the Lumpenproletariat: a Sceptical View from Africa

with David Michael

... the deserter, the mutineer, the primitive rebel, the rural bandit, the market rioter, the urban criminal, the pickpocket, and the village prophet have been taken in as honoured, pampered members of Senior Common Rooms. A promotion so rapid may well be premature, for the subject itself is far more intractable than it would appear at first sight
—Cobb 1970.

There has recently been much concern expressed among professional developmentalists about the level of unemployment in underdeveloped countries. The Director-General of the ILO, for example, has given expression to what is now widely felt to be a matter of overriding importance to governments and developers alike, namely the 'increasing numbers of young people who have left school and are unable to find jobs, [and who] roam about the streets in lawless bands' (Morse 1970: 1). In like manner, the editor of the *Bulletin of the Institute of Development Studies*,[1] while warning against 'unemployment becoming a new kind of shibboleth which united all those who were for virtue and against sin' (Anon 1970: 2, 4), carries an article (by Dudley Seers) which argues that development strategy demands that 'the growth of employment has to be a more important target than the growth of income.'

Other writers of a more radical bent see in the development of large unemployed or unemployable strata, whether in Latin American slums or in the interstices of African cities, the beginnings of a potentially revolutionary class. The term 'lumpenproletariat' is rejected by this group of scholars[2] as not only being opprobrious, but conditioning the view that the unemployed are incapable of revolutionary struggle. Ideological validation for the elevation of the

111

lumpenproletariat to the forefront of world history is provided *inter alia* by the Fanonist belief that the lumpenproletariat could provide the urban spearhead and second base for a revolutionary struggle waged by the peasantry, by the use of certain elements of the lumpenproletariat by Amilcar Cabral's PAIGC in its war against the Portuguese, and by the experience of such groups as the Black Panthers in the northern cities of the US.

The new vision of the lumpenproletariat, while being superficially attractive, appears to have the character of ascription rather than achievement. We rather fear, to paraphrase Richard Cobb, that in the case of Africa at least, the promotion of the lumpenproletariat has been too rapid. Its elevation seems in part to be an expression of disappointed hopes in the performance of other social classes. The independence ruling elites of Africa appear quite incapable of fostering a national bourgeois revolution (who but the ever believed that anyway?); the working class is thought (wrongly in our view) to have lapsed into an 'economist' deviation; the extent of peasant activism is more than adequately matched by the persistence of peasant passivity - so by a process of arithmetic elimination, if not entirely by dialectic purity, we arrive at the urban outcasts.

Marxists, above all other social analysts, should be wary of ideological shifts conditioned by fashion, and by the concerns of bourgeois social scientists wishing to find managerial solutions to underdevelopment. In this respect it is perhaps worthwhile to point out that ideologues of the capitalist order have always expressed, and continue to display, fear and revulsion at the sight of 'the poor' or 'the masses' haunting the central core and fringes of their citadels of power. But even if Marxists should recognise that such concerns may shape social reality by influencing bourgeois policy-makers, they do not necessarily encompass reality.

Before 'Fanonists' let their aspirations run away with them, we should be a little clearer about the real political capacity of the lumpenproletariat. On what sort of evidence and on what sort of suppositions is an appreciation of their political potential based? What are the factors that prevent or inhibit independent class action by this group? At the moment we seem to have little else but programmatic statements and self-assured predictions. As an example of the first we may take Fanon's (1967: 103) key statement that:

> The lumpenproletariat, that horde of starving men, uprooted from their tribe, and from their clan, constitutes one of the most spontaneous and most radically revolutionary forces of a colonised people.... It is within this mass of humanity, this people of the shanty towns... that the revolution will find its urban spearhead.

Peter Gutkind also seems certain that the 'unemployed will stand in the forefront of the political arena' despite the fact that he allows that there is as yet little evidence of a developing class consciousness, or of organised collective action and leadership (Gutkind 1967). Gutkind's caution is instructive, for where is the evidence? Africa has not yet experienced its equivalents of the rampaging food rioters of West Bengal. It has of course seen numerous examples of urban discontent and peasant-based revolts spilling into the cities.

But if the very evocations of the names 'Sharpeville' or 'the Kwilu rebellion' are thought sufficient to demonstrate the centrality of the lumpenproletariat, in fact they do no such thing. The inhabitants of Sharpeville were all, or nearly all, employed in wage labour. Indeed the 'location' was established precisely to house workers in the Vereeniging area - the rigid pass laws and system of work permits largely excluded the unemployed. Again, in the most reliable account of the Kwilu rebellion that we have, the authors specifically discount newspaper stories that the bulk of Mulelists were unemployed adolescents. 'Actually,' Fox and her colleagues (1965/6: 101) say, 'the followers and members of the Mulele movement in the Kwilu seem to have come from wide and diverse social backgrounds, even from social situations and statuses that would not be defined by Mulelism as disadvantaged or oppressed. And the rebels do not seem to be largely "abandoned youth" as has been suggested.'[3]

That the lumpenproletariat has participated in collective expressions of dissent is not in question. One may cite popular demonstrations in support of strikers, tax riots in Western Nigeria, or celebrations after the downfall of an unpopular government. In no case that we know of, however, have the lumpenproletariat played a major, let alone initiatory, role.

But even ignoring the general lack of action of the lumpenproletariat *for* itself, can we see the beginnings of group consciousness and group organisation? Here again the African data is extremely thin. We have nothing, for example, like the series of questionnaires and taped interviews based on participant observation, collection of genealogies, psychological tests and family case studies that Oscar Lewis (1967) was able to gather in his study of the urban poor of San Juan, Puerto Rico, and which together allowed him to develop his controversial notion of a 'culture of poverty.' Lewis is unequivocal in saying that his case studies did 'not support the generalisations of Fanon' (ibid.). Instead we have fragmentary reports of two associations of the unemployed in Lagos and a 'Society of Loafers in Zambia' by Peter Gutkind (1967, 1968), which, though helpful, tell us virtually nothing about how many members these associations had, how long they lasted or what difficulties of organisation and leadership were encountered. Some degree of social cohesion and group action was also apparently manifested by slum dwellers living on the fringes of Nairobi, though this seems to have largely depended on the sympathetic goodwill of a Kenyan Member of Parliament (Gutkind 1967).

It should be pointed out, however, that this type of self-generated fringe slum development, which is common in Latin America, is much less common in Africa. Though such sprawls might be expected to foster radical political sentiments, most of the literature on Latin American *favelas* and shanty towns does not provide evidence of 'urban breakdown,' 'disorientation' or 'marginality.' Rather, it suggests a strong retention of familial ties and a tendency to convert slums into respectable working-class neighbourhoods (see, for examples, Hauser 1961; Mangin 1970). Despite this comparative data, the degree to which marginality, perceived or objectively defined, exists in the African lumpenproletariat (our principal focus) is a crucial datum, and one to which we will return at a number of points.

For Marxists, a rebuttal couched merely in terms of the absence of behavioural manifestations is not enough - for latent development, the process of becoming and the intervention of the human agency are all important in testing the potential of a class for revolutionary struggle. In this respect, following Fanon, there has been a regrettable and we believe largely fallacious tendency to see a number of classes as equally manipulable, all clay to be moulded by the revolutionary's fervour. Of course individuals, including members of the lumpenproletariat, *can* forge a revolutionary consciousness through personal experience, intense commitment and constant struggle - we need mention only George Jackson, Eldridge Cleaver and Malcolm X. But this is rather different from maintaining that a whole group (whose parameters are particularly uncertain) is prone to revolutionary sentiment. At the group level there may be significant factors that inhibit class identity and prevent the ideologues' message from getting through. We shall discuss these retarding factors in turn, following the listing of a number of critical questions.

Marginality?

Initially we would argue that the extent of the privilege of full-time wage-earners in the African setting has been vastly exaggerated. Many have experienced no appreciable rise in real wages for generations and continue to live in conditions of penury, not least because a large part of their income is disposed of to a whole collection of spongers, hangers-on, relatives and kinsmen (Pfeffermann 1968: 170).[4]

A reserve army of the proletariat looms in the background certainly, but it is one that is still intimately tied to the proletariat by blood and situational bonds. A convincing demonstration of the extent of these ties can be seen in the context of a long strike where, lacking strike funds, the worker falls back into what precarious security his kinsmen can afford to give him.[5] The *quid pro quo*, and one which the jobless member of the kin group may recognise and rationally calculate, is that the breadwinner will continue to redistribute his income when times are better. The affinity between members of the proletariat and the lumpenproletariat is reinforced also by physical and geographical contiguity (Lux 1969). Family houses and compounds, often located in the heart of an African city, continue to provide a poly-class locale which narrows the perceived social distance not only between jobless and employed, but also between these two groups and members of the elite. Quite often too there is a degree of 'hidden' wealth existing behind the apparent dilapidated and disordered exterior. Of course in the context of the overall problem we are discussing such instances may not be numerically all that significant, but what we seek to demonstrate is that it is not always true that the unemployed 'have nothing' - some may have a stake in the major prop of bourgeois power, namely property.

Romanticisation

The new vision of the lumpenproletariat appears to have parallels in a rather older literary and political tradition that romanticises the thief and the outsider. Genet and Bakunin are among the progenitors of this tradition, and it is one that finds contemporary expression in theorists of deviance who see little distinction between socially-defined 'criminality' and political dissent. We do not particularly wish to question this perspective here - but rather to point out that labelling deviance can also lead to an overstatement of the political implications of lumpenproletariat activity. The state machinery and media are adept at redefining political action as lumpenproletariat criminality, thus serving to hide dissent stemming from what are felt to be more threatening quarters. Equally there may be bureaucratic interests at work that themselves support this process of redefinition. In the context of the French Revolution, for example, Cobb (1970) suggests that because the police, being creatures of habit, failed to comprehend new social forces, they used old labels for the new people. He demonstrates how the police contrived to arrest innocent transients as scapegoats for civil disturbances.

Coherence

The extent of social differentiation within the lumpenproletariat, on closer examination, is considerable, and it may be a mistake to impose a researchers' taxonomy that regards this group as one social category rather than many. Though their definitions leave something to be desired, Marx and Engels did not themselves make the mistake of seeing the lumpenproletariat as an undifferentiated mass. Engels, for example, refers at least once to a transitional group which 'vegetates in the borderland between the working class and the lumpenproletariat' (cited in Jones 1971).

Once one breaks up the category, certain hard questions follow. Without wishing to be disrespectful or obscene, we must ask who is to storm the barricades - the beggars, the religious ascetics and prophets, the physically disabled, the insane? In the absence of basic welfare services in most African countries, these constitute a very visible part of the urban poor and comprise a considerable part of the lumpenproletariat that has been cast out onto the streets of the cities.[6] Within other sections of the lumpenproletariat distinctions need to be drawn between those who, though once employed, have been fired; those who are intermittently employed; those who have given up all hope of securing employment; those who still seek jobs; and those who have accommodated themselves to a socially disapproved of livelihood as thieves, pimps or prostitutes. We hold no special brief for these categories, no doubt individuals can shift from one state to another, but it needs to be borne in mind that the degree of politicisation that can be expected will vary considerably within the various component sections of the urban poor.

Identification of class enemy

Where common organisation, interdependence and close working relationships do not obtain (as they do, say, in a factory situation), there may be a good deal of internalised, unfocused violence. Thus, even though the objective reason for the condition of the lumpenproletariat may be rooted in the structure of a neo-colonial economy, it is not always possible for the dispossessed groups to see this, rationalise it and delineate their 'real' enemy. The next bowl of food, the stealing or begging of a few pence, the fighting over a cigarette, a joint or a piece of territory on the pavement may assume a much more immediate and practical reality.

'False consciousness'

Internalised violence is but one expression of false consciousness (we can ignore for our purposes the difficulties attached to this term, and merely assume a working definition that false consciousness expresses faulty ascription of causality and a lack of congruence between possibility and reality).[7] The avenues of social mobility are increasingly blocked in African societies, in contrast to the brief period of high opportunity accompanying the achievement of independence, but the ideological residue of this period has survived into post-colonial times. The large number of Samuel Smiles-type texts that abound in the market-places, the frantic attempts at self-improvement and the demand for formal education that persists, are ample testament to this. Field researchers are also finding that many urban Africans have high expectations that their children will be better off than themselves. There is, too, a persistent belief in the 'lucky break' as the obsession with filling out football coupons indicates, as well as a degree of genuflection towards the powerful, rich and ostentatious which has its psychological explanation in the vicarious enjoyment that the immobile derive from the 'big men' who have made it. (Pelé lives also in Africa![8])

Another crucial aspect of false consciousness is located in the growth of various chiliastic religions in African cities which are both deeply rooted and increasing in numbers. Here the Brazilian experience has something to offer. *Umbanda* spiritualist and Protestant Pentecostal sects provide a forum within which a '*symbolic* subversion of the traditional order' takes place (Willems 1969: 209). Amongst *Umbanda* initiates, religious power produces trance states in which black and Indian ancestors are exalted while slave-masters are seen to wallow in perdition. Similarly, in South Africa it is reported that the theology of the African Zionist churches includes a 'reversed colour-bar' that is said to operate in Heaven (Sundkler 1971: 260).

In sum, we would argue that political involvement of any kind may be the least likely option of a number of alternative accommodations to poverty, poor education and despair.

The political dimension

We have questioned the degree to which Africa's lumpenproletariat is a marginal group, argued that social differentiation within the group is an important datum and suggested that a number of avenues of self-expression, other than revolutionary consciousness, exist. It remains true none the less that elements of the lumpenproletariat have provided supportive action in revolutionary struggles, and concrete attempts have been made to politicise members of this group.

All the experience of practising revolutionaries seems, however, to confirm the unreliability, volatility and danger of using this group as an ally. Mao Zedong (1967: 17), for example, wrote in 1926: 'One of China's difficult problems is how to handle these people. Brave fighters, but apt to be destructive, they can become a revolutionary force if given proper guidance.' Subsequently he appended a footnote to indicate that they were used also by local landlords and tyrants and by Chiang Kai-Shek in his destruction of the urban proletariat movement in the 1927 *coup d'état*. Similar comments are to be found in Trotsky's account of the Russian revolution.

Within the African continent itself, the experience of the liberation struggle in Portuguese Guinea, which is often thought of as confirming a revolutionary status on the lumpenproletariat, is not borne out by the views of one sympathetic observer. According to Gérard Chaliand (1969: 20), 'the experience of the PAIGC struggle has shown that this category [the lumpenproletariat] is often reactionary. The PIDE [Portuguese secret police] has many informers and other agents in this class and does not seem to have much trouble in recruiting reinforcements.' Chaliand makes a clear distinction between the lumpenproletariat and the 'city youth' who are a 'temporary proletariat with a lower-middle-class-mentality' and amongst whom the revolution has gained considerable success. Interestingly enough, a similar distinction between 'youth' and lumpenproletariat has been drawn by participants in the political struggle in Congo Brazzaville. Whereas the Youth of the National Revolutionary Movement gained an honoured place in the struggle, the Political Commissar of the National People's Army had this to say about the lumpenproletariat (cited in Cleaver 1971: 41):

> The means of struggle must be to the advantage of the lumpen... when the revolutionaries take away their means of struggle, they kill the revolutionaries. These are very terrible things, but without being idealistic or dogmatic you have to recognise that the lumpenproletariat are absolutely unstable and go with those who provide the livelihood.

The Commissar also stressed that the lumpenproletariat was on occasions useful to the revolution - for example, it looted the Catholic press on instructions from the Party, anxious at the time to keep its claim to legality - but it is notable that, in each case we have mentioned, no more valiant role has been assigned to the lumpenproletariat than as instruments, and instruments that had to be kept on a very tight leash lest they switch their loyalties to the other side. One reason for this is that the lumpenproletariat may not have any particular stake in a revolutionary outcome. It may indeed suffer from a thorough-going revolution through the loss of political patronage, stricter control over crime and the punitive moral climate usually associated with post-revolutionary situations.

Conclusion

In view of the paucity of evidence to support the 'Fanonist' thesis, the major onus to provide the necessary data collection lies with its exponents. The field is obviously one that will bear considerable intellectual fruit, but if the challenge is accepted, much difficult research faces social scientists before we can confidently claim to be thoroughly *au courant* with 'the low life.'

We would be the last to suggest that the urban class formations confronting Marx and Engels are faithfully reproduced in today's underdeveloped societies. Yet, for the present at least, we feel reluctant to accept any major revision of their views on the political potentiality of the lumpenproletariat. When Marx and Engels wrote in the Manifesto that 'here and there [the lumpenproletariat might] be swept into the movement by a proletarian revolution; its conditions of life, however, prepare it far more for the part of a bribed tool of reactionary intrigue,' their comments must be seen as a political statement by those who knew and strongly felt the defeats and betrayals of the proletariat. 'Fanonists' may take umbrage at this and similarly derogatory statements by Marx and Engels, but when concrete struggles in African cities develop we rather think we will be asking the question, 'Was not Marx right after all?'

This paper was first published some 18 years ago, yet was to occasion such acrimonious and unpleasant responses from a few fellow academics that the memory of their reaction still stays with me. The paper was commissioned by the editor of the Bulletin *of the* Institute of Development Studies *after he had heard me give a paper on a similar theme. I subsequently added the first paragraph alluding to the previous themes covered in the journal, with the intention of linking David Michael's and my own interests to those of the journal. This turned out to be a disastrous, though innocent, error. The late Dudley Seers, the distinguished economist and then Director of his love-child, the Institute of Development Studies at the University of Sussex, apparently took umbrage at the reference to him. I did not myself see that the reference in the first paragraph was either controversial or offensive. But what apparently attracted his eye was not only this, but later phrases referring to 'bourgeois social scientists' and 'ideologues of the capitalist order,' (phrases which had already formed part of the presented paper). These crude labels, which I would hesitate to use today, were part of the rhetoric of the time. But Seers falsely assumed that David Michael and I wished to apply them especially to him. Unguent, then increasingly angry, voices from two or three of his colleagues came down the telephone lines. 'Dudley was upset'; I had to withdraw the article; it wasn't commissioned by the* Bulletin *(I produced the letter); it was commissioned, but the editor had no right; the offending phrases had to be struck out; it was not very good anyway, therefore could I not just forget it? For some reason, this last jibe irritated me and I replied with false bravado that I had just spoken to one of my caller's colleagues who said it was the best thing ever to be considered for the* Bulletin. *Oddly enough, this utter lie, of which I am now deeply ashamed, was taken as the truth - and a veritable witch-hunt ensued at the Institute. David and I refused to bow to our callers' demands, reasoning that academic freedom was now at stake. We demanded publication, as previously agreed, without changes of any kind. This finally went ahead and Seers replied to the article in a subsequent issue of the journal. I cannot now trace this rather obscure correspondence, but I remember his reply as oddly inappropriate - he thought, for example, that we were writing about the lumpenbourgeoisie (a term just then popularised by André Gunder Frank) and he was dubious about the political potential of the poor (a point we thought we were making). More sensibly, he ticked us off for substituting orthodoxies for original thought. I have some regard for Seers's work and I do not think it would besmirch his memory to say now that I doubt he had read the article with any attention. Rather, his attentive and obsequious minders at the Institute were probably more concerned than he was and wanted to protect him from bothersome gnats. At any event, within the Institute's circle I was seen to have blot-*

ted my copy book with a mulish stance in defence of what David and I had written. It was many years before I received a friendly invitation from the Institute. One further comment is perhaps in order - indicating that not all academics are quite so self-protective. As can readily be seen, the primary targets for our attack were the 'Fanonists' (not the 'developmentalists') and it should be recorded that the opposite reaction came from them. Peter Worsley, then at Manchester, wrote in friendly terms and subsequently was a warm colleague, while Peter Gutkind, then at McGill, became a close collaborator on African labour studies and one of my firmest friends.

Notes

1   For which this article was commissioned and where it first appeared (see endbox above).

2   Without wishing to impose an artificial unity on a disparate group of writers, we none the less feel that an identifiable 'Fanonist tradition' has been established by Peter Worsley (1972), Peter Gutkind, and others. More than anything else, they have in common a marked antagonism toward classical Marxist statements on the lumpenproletariat. It is, however, arguable that they have overstated the consistency of Fanon's views and his enthusiasm for 'the horde of starving men.' Fanon qualifies his fervour for the lumpenproletariat in a number of places. Stressing their unreliability, he instances their counter-revolutionary role in Algeria, Congo and Angola and is careful to note the necessity that they be 'urged on from behind' by other revolutionary agents (Fanon 1967: 109, 103). Oscar Lewis, while somewhat romanticising the urban poor in common with the Fanonists, does not support their political conclusions.

3   Note also how in the face of disorganisation and a lack of leadership, the political component of what lumpenproletariat support there was for the rebellion collapsed in Kalemie (Crawford 1970).

4   The idea that workers in Africa constituted a 'labour aristocracy' was subsequently taken up by John Saul and Giovanni Arrighi. The challenge to this thesis formed the underlying theme of an edited collection by Sandbrook & Cohen (1975).

5   A graphic description of this phenomenon can be found in Ousmane's (1969) fictional recreation of a Senegalese railway strike but there are other more contemporary examples.

6   Of those sleeping out on the main street in Bathurst, The Gambia, an average over four nights of observation gave the figure of 58 per cent who could be so categorised. (Field notes, 1971, R.C.)

7   Reading this sentence some 17 years after it was drafted, made me react 'how glib.' I would now not abolish the problem of false consciousness so easily and would be much more inclined to accept the common sociological observation that all consciousness is 'real' in its consequences. Similarly I would reduce to only a residual issue the Marxist distinction between 'real' and 'false' consciousness.

8   In case this reference is now obscure to a newer generation of readers, Pelé was the great Brazilian football star who had risen from the slums. He was lionised by the regime and the media, his career being used to demonstrate the possibility of upward social mobility by poor black Brazilians.

8

The 'New' International Division of Labour: a Conceptual, Historical and Empirical Critique

In essence what we people in the Western Hemisphere really need is a more efficient division of labour among us. The division of labour is one of the tried and true economic principles that will be as valid in 1976 as it was in 1776 when it was first spelled out by Adam Smith.... The less developed countries would also gain. With abundant supplies of labour and wage levels well below those of the US, they could export processed food, textiles, apparel, footwear and other light manufactures.
—Rockefeller 1963: 102-3

Capital today has two ways available to it of reconstructing the industrial army: on the one hand the intensification of capital exports and the systematic suffocation of investments at home, i.e. sending capital where there is still excess labour-power, instead of bringing labour-power to excess capital; on the other, the intensification of automation, or in other words the concentration of investments to set free as much living labour as possible.
—Mandel 1978: 182

When the leading living capitalist and the leading living Trotskyist agree on the best prescription for the survival of capitalism, albeit in somewhat different language, it is perhaps time for the rest of us to defer to their joint wisdom. Certainly, there is no doubt that the processes anticipated by Rockefeller and suggested by Mandel have become part of our contemporary world economy. The casual traveller to the four 'golden economies' of Asia - Hong Kong, Taiwan, Singapore and Korea - cannot fail to be impressed by the sudden evidence of modernity and industrialisation. Even using the appellation 'Third World' of such places sounds absurd, particularly when one is conscious of the transformation of great sections of the old industrial boom cities - like Cleveland, Detroit, Birmingham or Liverpool - into depressed slums and economic wastelands. Clearly, an economic transformation of some magnitude is taking place, as investment patterns alter and industrial plant becomes spatially redistributed.

The global shifts in the location of manufacturing enterprises have been recognised in a number of largely discrete academic debates which still require more synoptic vision to bring them together. One line of argument has stemmed from a critique of Latin American dependency (or 'underdevelopment') theory, which, in the popularised versions offered in Frank's early works (1967, 1969), came to dominate much thinking about the non-European and non-North American countries. The model Frank suggests as characteristic of relations between rich and poor countries is a chain of 'metropole-satellite' connections with the stronger partner being parasitic on the weaker. As Roxborough (1979: 45) notices, the image is graphically rendered by Swift's verse:

> So, naturalists observe, a flea
> Hath smaller fleas that on him prey;
> And these have smaller fleas to bite 'em,
> And so proceed ad infinitum.

The problem with this model is that it allows very little room for alterations in the fleas' existing preying order. It is difficult to explain how, for example, Brazil became more powerful than Portugal, or the US than its former coloniser, Britain. Class relations within and between countries also remain obscure because the theory largely relies on aggregate trade and investment data which intrinsically cannot illuminate some of the social structural relationships that were held fundamental to the exercise.

With respect to the growth of industrialisation in Third World countries, the left-wing economist Warren (1980: 166, 193-8) denounces dependency theory as 'nationalist mythology,' arguing that 'it may be that the greater the previous experience of imperialist penetration, the greater the subsequent ability to respond to the world market.' He shows statistically that the growth rates of many of the less developed countries compared favourably to those of the developed market economies in the period 1960-73. Though Frank (1981: 96-101) subsequently sought to derogate the extent and meaning of this development in less developed countries, the substance of Warren's critique stands - in that any student of development has to recognise a more complex picture of growth at different, and in terms of dependency theory unpredictable, points in the global economy.

Recognition of tendencies towards the uneven distribution of global development sites in the contemporary period also comes from those working with a 'world system' perspective (Hopkins 1977, 1979; Wallerstein 1979) who allow switches in fortune between peripheral and 'semi-peripheral' states; from those who see the multinationals as leading a new phase of capital accumulation and expanding their global reach (Barnet & Müller 1974; Hymer 1979); and from those who seek to rework the classical Marxist texts on imperialism despite the force of Warren's (1980: 114-15) acid comment that, 'the quality of post-war literature has naturally suffered from ascribing rising significance to a phenomenon of declining importance.' (But, for exceptional accounts see Amin 1974; and Magdoff 1978.) More recently, a thriving and self-critical group of 'urban and regional' scholars have prefigured a 'political economy of space' that attempts to contextualise the new class and economic relations arising from the redistribution of production sites (Castells 1977; Harloe 1977; Harloe & Lebas 1981). On the side of the world from which capital and jobs appear to be departing, more alarmist and in tone nationalist studies talk of the 'collapse of work' or the 'deindustrialisation' of the US (Jenkins & Sherman 1979; Bluestone & Harrison 1982).

Some of the threads of these debates, though by no means all, are woven together in the work of a number of German scholars who coined the expression 'the new international division of labour' (NIDL) (Fröbel et al. 1980; Ernst 1980). Without overt intellectual debt, the NIDL theorists basically followed the line of analysis suggested by Warren's critique of dependency theory and, to a lesser degree, by the depiction of 'peripheral capitalism' suggested by Amin (1974). Taking over the vocabulary of world systems theory, they argued that industrial capital from the core was moving to the periphery as 'world-market factories' were established producing manufactured goods destined *for export*. The strategy of export-oriented manufacturing from newly-industrialising countries (NICs) was also adopted as an alternative to import-substitution strategies of development, which were held to have failed Third World countries. The movement of capital away from the core industrial countries was, in turn, necessitated by the difficulties in securing and realising high profits - as industrial conflict, the increased reproduction costs and the growing organisation of migrant communities prevented the attainment of high levels of exploitation. These difficulties were particularly evident in European countries, where, at the beginning of the 1970s, the initial economic advantages that accrued to employers by importing large numbers of migrant workers rapidly began to erode. On the one hand, many Third World countries had large supplies of cheap, unorganised labour. The oversupply of labour-power had occurred with the commoditisation of agriculture (accelerated by technological innovations like the 'green revolution'). As the rural poor were pushed off the land, unemployment, underemployment and, for some, the process of full proletarianisation had resulted. The NIDL theorists further observed that technical and managerial developments in the labour process now allowed the effective use of peripheral labour-power. The increasingly minute division of labour permitted the reorganisation of unskilled and semi-skilled tasks. With a minimal level of training, levels of productivity soon matched or exceeded metropolitan levels.

The movement of manufacturing capital to parts of the periphery was also accelerated by an investment climate made more attractive by government policies. A number of governments in the Third World passed laws restricting the organisation and bargaining power of the unions. They provided freedom from planning and environmental controls, poor and therefore cheap health and safety standards, permission to repatriate profits without restriction, tax holidays and in some cases, like Singapore, a powerful paternal state, which appeared to guarantee political stability. At the level of transport and communications, international facilities had dramatically improved in the form of containerised shipping, cheap air cargo, and computer, telex and satellite links. Especially in the case of low-bulk, high-value goods, with a high value added at the point of production, it was often no longer necessary for the site of production to be near the end-market. Examples of goods of this kind include electrical or electronic goods, toys, shoes and clothes - virtually the same list Rockefeller had identified in the early 1960s. Finally, the world-market factories could be staffed predominantly by young women, who were particularly prone to exploitation given the difficulties of organising a group characteristically under patriarchal dominance and with a limited commitment to life-time wage labour. (see Fröbel et al. 1980; Elson & Pearson 1981; Henderson & Cohen 1982; Henderson 1985.)

In short, it looks very much as if metropolitan employers, having been frustrated in their countries in fully exploiting imported migrant labour, had alighted on another cohort of exploitable workers in the periphery, whom they would now be able to deploy directly rather than by importing their labour-power. Moreover, it was a labour force that presented few of the demands for social and political rights that even the South African government and companies are slowly having to recognise. The empirical demonstration of the thesis was supported by some convincing data (Fröbel et al. 1980: 275, 276-90) from Federal Germany. After 1959, when restrictions on German companies investing abroad were lifted, a steep increase in the amount of direct foreign investment began to occur - from DM 3,291 million in 1961, to DM 19,932 million in 1971, to DM 47,048 million in 1976. However, this investment did not, in general, represent a net expansion of German capitalist development on a world scale, but rather the integration of new sites and the relocation of certain manufacturing processes previously reserved for domestic manufacturing. Within Germany, this was bound to have consequences for the number of jobs available. A small rise over the period 1967 to 1973 was followed by a sudden drop of nearly a million jobs over the next three years. However, this loss of domestic jobs coincided with an *increase* in turnover and profit for key German firms. Simultaneously, an estimate for the number of jobs created abroad by German manufacturing firms by 1976 was 1.5 million. Fröbel and his colleagues (ibid: 287) are properly cautious in saying that these figures alone 'do not allow us to deduce the extent to which employment abroad has replaced employment in Germany,' but the inference is none the less there for all to read. By the pattern of imports of manufactured goods, by the statements of the companies themselves and through an examination of the free production zones in Third World countries, we are led ineluctably to the conclusion that capital has migrated in search of its own comparative advantage, especially in respect of labour-power costs, and at the expense of domestic and imported workers, whose job chances have been correspondingly diminished.

The picture presented by the NIDL theorists seemed to confirm observable reality in the NICs and also presented a far superior explanation for industrial decline in the old centres than that currently preferred by 'monetarists' and right-wing demagogues. Consequently, part of the work undertaken by Henderson and this author (1982) on international restructuring was a replication study using the British data. Again, the basic contours of the German experience were evident. As is shown in Table 8.1, if the rate of overseas investment by British capital is compared to the rate of investment within Britain (as measured by net domestic fixed capital formation), 'overseas' starts at three times the rate of 'domestic' investment and accelerates to nearly four times the rate towards the end of the period surveyed.

Again, although it is difficult to separate out the many factors producing unemployment (including government policy, automation, the loss of international competitiveness and underinvestment), there is some evidence to suggest that in Britain, as in Germany, key firms are adding to their payroll overseas and cutting their workforce in Britain. Thus, an ILO report (1981: 82), surveying the operations of 118 major British firms, shows that over the period 1971-5, they added 150,000 employees to their payrolls abroad compared to only 80,000 in the UK. As the study concludes, 'employment-wise they were clearly growing much faster abroad than at home, both in absolute and relative terms.' The US also reveals a similar picture. Bluestone & Harrison find that between 1968 and 1976 there was a loss of approximately 15 million jobs as a result of plant closures. The closures partly resulted from technological changes but managers also saw the transfer of production abroad as an attractive alternative to production at home, for risk was diversified, greater control over labour was achieved and they could take advantage of large international wage differentials (see Nash & Fernandez-Kelly 1983: ix).

Table 8.1: Domestic and Foreign Investment from Britain, 1969-80

Year	Domestic (£ mil)	Overseas (£ mil)
1969	4,233	13,950
1970	4,754	14,400
1971	4,911	15,180
1972	5,488	19,170
1973	6,859	19,500
1974	7,906	19,224
1975	9,603	23,415
1976	9,844	30,401
1977	9,628	30,573
1978	10,908	35,328
1979	11,483	41,024
1980	11,483	48,439

Source: Henderson & Cohen (1982) citing Government Blue and Pink Books.

From the discussion and data so far presented, it would seem that NIDL theory provides a major key to understanding some of the processes of capital accumulation in the modern world order. While not wishing to deny its powerful explanatory value and the important contribution made by the NIDL theorists, there are none the less some major limitations and omissions that inhere in the theory. I will concentrate my critique of NIDL theory on three aspects, taking the opportunity also to develop some alternative formulations. First, *conceptual problems* - where I shall argue that the variety of meanings attaching to the phrase 'division of labour' makes it difficult to understand what precise phenomena are under investigation. This uncertainty can in turn lead to differing political and practical conclusions for those committed to the theory. Second, *historical gaps* - where I maintain that NIDL theorists have ignored or misconceived the historical evolution and successive phases of the international division of labour. And third, *empirical omissions* - where I shall show that NIDL theory tends to concentrate attention exclusively on the growth of the manufacturing sector in the periphery at the expense of other growth points in the global economy, which are better reflected by measuring movements of labour, rather than movements of capital.

Conceptual problems

When trying to understand the phrase 'the new international division of labour,' it is necessary first to unscramble the good deal of ambiguity arising in the prior expression 'the division of labour.' The notion has been used very differently to explain different phenomena. In its earliest usage it was often pressed into service to distinguish what are now described as sectoral divisions in the economy - divisions, for example, between industry, agriculture and services. It was used also to define the occupational and skill structure of the labour force and the differences between skilled and unskilled labourers, masters and apprentices, craftsmen and production workers. Additionally, the division of labour referred to the organisation of tasks, characteristically dictated by the management, in the work place - who is on the line, who is in the office, who minds the machines and who sweeps the floors? As Braverman's (1974) contribution on the process of 'deskilling' testifies, though related to skill and occupational structure, the detailed specification of tasks is by no means coincidental with skill.

To these three original meanings of 'the division of labour' have been added others of more recent vintage. First, the gender or racial division of labour - indicating the new sensitivity to the ethnic composition of the labour force and to the role of women in production and reproduction (Pahl 1984: 254-76). Second, the spatial division of production and product (an aspect of the division of labour which, I shall argue, is far from 'new'). And third, perhaps the latest meaning attaching to the notion, the contracting out of some elements of the production processes to well outside the factory gates - into domestic, peasant or household units.

The changing definitions and meanings of the phrase 'division of labour' impel different discussions and have different implications of a more practical and political nature. For example, if it is argued that the putting-out system has now revived on an international scale and constitutes an important new feature of capitalist production, feminists who argue for a politics of the home and of reproduction would have a strong case against those who argue for a politics of the factory - from which production would be putatively or potentially disappearing. Equally, if the manufacturing sector in Third World countries is as significant a feature of contemporary capitalism as the NIDL theorists argue, the whole structure of workers' resistance to capital will have to undergo a massive lateral shift if it is to succeed. This is particularly so when the question of international solidarity is considered. Metropolitan workers are confronted with two diametrically opposed strategies. On the one hand, a more nationalist posture would argue for the preservation of jobs at home by the erection of high tariff walls and import duties designed to keep out Third World manufactures. On the other hand, an internationalist position would dictate that bonds of solidarity should be effected between metropolitan workers and Third World workers already employed in branch plants so as to restrict the manoeuvrability of mulitnational capital and spread the benefits of employment equally between the participant partners. For Third World workers, other dilemmas present themselves. Any significant growth of trade union activity by any one national working class in the Third World can result in footloose capital moving to another territory. Thus, the interests of Third World workers may lie in effecting labour solidarity between Third World sites rather than between themselves and metropolitan workers, where wage differentials are bound to create major divisions of interest. Even mentioning the difficulties of labour solidarity in this causal way raises complications enough. However, one can add to such dilemmas questions such as whether organisationally it is preferable to link workers by sector (pharmaceuticals, toys, textiles) or by firm (Phillips, IBM, Shell). And this ignores the problems of transcending the major divisions within an international trade union movement separated on cold-war lines.

In short, even only taking two possible meanings of 'the division of labour' we end up with strongly differing pictures of the changing battle lines between the old contestants 'capital' and 'labour.' There is, of course, no need logically to admit only one meaning of the division of labour as valid, but even if one accepts that a variety of meanings has now legitimately accrued to a particular label, this raises the posterior question of the relative weight, or significance, of the different phenomena grouped under this particular label. The last question is superficially one amenable to empirical enquiry - but behind the empirical question lies a paradox which inheres in the measurements so far characteristically deployed to evaluate changes in the international division of labour. The NIDL theorists use as their predominant data, aggregate trade and investment figures - i.e. they use measures of the migration of *capital* to measure changes in the division of *labour*. This method can lead to some very misleading impressions. For example, it is likely that changes in the location of manufacturing enterprises are far less important in terms of employment (and in terms of profit) than changes between sectors (in particular the movement from industry and agriculture, to services and information) within the metropolitan economies. The possibilities for the deployment of subordinate and migrant sections of the metropolitan labour force in the service sector would thereby be easily and misleadingly missed. There does appear therefore to be a case, on empirical as well as conceptual grounds, for using measurements of the movement of *labour* to indicate changes in the division of *labour*. In the empirical section below I point to two additional sectors (in the oil-rich countries and in the service and sweatshop sectors of 'world cities') where significant employment of subordinate labour-power has taken place without this being able to be easily accommodated in NIDL theory.

The empirical question therefore is linked umbilically to the prior theoretical questions of how we group and rank the different conceptions of the division of labour. As Garnsey (1981) points out, the first three meanings of the term division of labour (by skill, by sector and by task) were united in classical political economy. In the nineteenth-century economic theory was interwoven with what is now called industrial and occupational sociology. This original conflation of meaning was lost in the late nineteenth century in what Garnsey describes as an 'intellectual putsch' against the division of labour by the growth of the two separate disciplines of sociology and economics. In economics, the putsch was effected by an increasing focus on the laws of choice in economic situations and on scarcity as the basis for value in exchange. Under such a debased notion of value, wages and profits could be analysed without reference to the social and political relations between employers, investors and wage earners. The only important issues were the aggregate transactions determined by considerations of scarcity and consumer preference. Such considerations left no place for the division of labour. In sociology, the notion was not abandoned - rather it was given more specialised meanings. In Weber, the emphasis was on the social relations that the division of labour engendered, rather than on how it created different patterns of economic and social development. (Weber focused on religion as the factor associated with these patterns.) In Durkheim, on the other hand, the emphasis is on both the structurally disruptive and cohesive tendencies in the division of labour, which ultimately give rise to social integration through the process that Durkheim calls organic solidarity. Modern sociological interest in the division of labour by age, race and sex tend to follow the inheritance of Weber, whereas the meaning attributed to the phrase by Durkheim has largely been lost in modern sociological discourse.

Does the revival of the phrase by the NIDL theorists, though this time with an international focus, signify the possibility that the two great social science disciplines, sociology and economics, will once again be able to unite on a common intellectual staging ground? In one sense the NIDL theorists have prefigured just such a possibility by consciously echoing back to classical nineteenth century political economy. Thus they list as their progenitors Adam Smith (who also gets an honourable mention from Nelson D. Rockefeller), Charles Babbage and Andrew Ure (Fröbel et al. 1980: 37-44). In addition to these three figures, NIDL theorists depend on another classical theory to underpin their argument - namely, Ricardo's basic law of comparative advantage. Ricardo's law can be simply stated as follows: the pattern of international trade is dependent on the principle of comparative labour costs 'which states that if two countries, A and B, entered into trade relations, each capable of producing commodities X and Y, A would sell the commodity in which its relative (rather than absolute) cost was lower and correspondingly B would sell the commodity in which its own comparative cost is low' (Bagchi 1982: 16).

This conceptual dependence on classical political economy raises the positive prospect of the reunification between sociology and economics, but also unfortunately brings in its baggage train the limits of the classical tradition. In the nineteenth century, the state was not a significant actor on the industrial scene, and again in NIDL theory it virtually disappears - except in the Third World case, where it appears only as a bourgeoisie *manqué* having to kowtow to the overwhelming power of metropolitan capital. In the nineteenth century, with the major exception of Marx, the rising power of the working class was ignored in economic theory. Again, this feature of the classical tradition reproduces itself in NIDL theory, with the social and political relations that surround the production process being almost wholly neglected in favour of discussion of aggregate trade and investment transactions, which reflect the power of capital. All that happens can, in such a view, be explained by the logic of capital without seriously taking into account independent institutional forces, the contradictions between merchants, national capitalists, transnationals and governments, or the political and social protests by those who fall victim to the logic of capital. Inter- and intra-class conflict within and between metropolitan and Third World societies hardly make an appearance. Instead in their reliance on trade and investment flows to demonstrate their thesis, NIDL theorists show an interesting correspondence with both world systems theory and dependency theory in their common display of excessive 'economism.'

To summarise, NIDL theory provides only a partial answer to the need for a synoptic vision of the contemporary global capitalist world order. Except implicitly, it provides no guide through the variety of meanings attaching to the term 'division of labour,' nor even if a plurality of meanings is intended, any means, empirically or conceptually, to rank one manifestation above another. Though potentially a powerful tool to reunite economic and sociological theory, the theory shows too many of the economistic features of its nineteenth-century origin to provide a wholly convincing and rounded picture of the workings of modern capitalism. The rather curious conceptual leap from nineteenth-century classical political economy to the late twentieth century also reveals an odd insensitivity to the evolution of the capitalist world order - almost as if nothing of any great moment has happened over the last 100 years. This empty historical box needs some filling.

Historical gaps

How new is the 'new' international division of labour? There is no way of determining this from the theory itself, as no historical comparisons with other international divisions of labour are provided. It is as if the NIDL theorists boarded a time machine in the mid-nineteenth century to arrive at Hong Kong and Singapore late last night, without bothering to land at any of the intermediate airports - notably those marked on the historical maps as 'Imperialism' and 'Colonialism.' On *prima facie* grounds, it would seem appropriate to assume that imperialism and colonialism had something to do with the evolution of the present-day international division of labour. Indeed, I intend to make a further assertion - that the historical patterns established by prior international divisions of labour are so much part of our contemporary reality that the distinction between the 'new' and 'old' international division of labour is not a very useful one. For this reason I prefer to use the expression 'the *changing* international division of labour.'

How then do I classify and periodise successive phases in the changing international division of labour? From the point of view of the form of capital hegemonic in each phase, four sequential phases can be identified - the mercantile, industrial, imperial and transnational divisions of labour. This is a convenient classification in that these labels are readily identifiable in historical writings and although not previously used to describe phases in the international division of labour, do refer to readily understood historical periods. On the other hand, using labels deriving from the characteristic form of *capital* present may spring the same trap that I accused NIDL theorists of falling into. Should, ideally, each phase be described by its characteristic form of *labour*? Thus, should the mercantile phase be called the phase mixing free and unfree plantation labour? Should the industrial phase be signified by a label indicating the mix of free metropolitan workers and workers imported to the metropole? Should the imperial phase be deemed the phase mixing colonial peasant proprietorship, extractive mineral migrants and metropolitan wage workers? Finally, should the transnational phase be identified by its own distinctive labour mix? Unfortunately, the very clumsiness of such categories inhibits their use - and I also have cognisance of the fact that the phenomenon we describe as capitalism equally has retained its name, even in Marx's work, from the wrong side of the contestants' ring. So, although the hegemony of particular forms of capital has been granted, it is vital to recognise that inherent in each definition is the corresponding form of labour that is intrinsic to the period and helps, in its contestation with capital, to account for decline of the prior phase.

Let me start first with the *mercantile* division of labour. In this division of labour, the first element of conscious design on an international scale is revealed. A surplus of particular commodities can be generated simply through the accidents of geography and climate, the particular distribution of flora and fauna, or the spread of natural resources - be these commodities fur from Poland, blubber from northern Canada or coals from Newcastle. However, such surpluses only become important when they enter the sphere of circulation and when production methods and rhythms alter to try to replicate accidental patterns into permanent structures of advantage. The debate between the circulationists and the productionists therefore misses the obvious point that once a regular market develops with implied forward contracts, production methods are bound to adjust to meet anticipated demand. It is thus quite fallacious to assume that mercantilism implies pure exchange without any implication for the organisation of production. After all, it was under the aegis of *merchant* capital that labour was commoditised (turned into labour-power) and the beginnings of a global labour market organised. The plantation societies of the New World were established, lands were conquered, local populations decimated, eight million Africans transhipped across the Atlantic, and specialist commodities like cotton, coffee, sugar and tobacco planted, harvested and processed. Food crops like breadfruit were brought from the Pacific to the Caribbean to feed the plantation workers. There is also no doubt that institutions like the Royal Society and Kew Gardens were engaged in a systematic design in relocating such crops. For the period, the cotton ginneries, the rum distilleries and sugar mills and refineries used advanced technologies. Often small railway systems, as sophisticated as anything in the so-called metropolis, ran between the sugar canes.

This division of labour was based on the spatial relocation of production, the division of product, the reorganisation of task, and also involved a specific racial division of labour. The forms of labour characteristic of this period were, first, a combination of metropolitan free and plantation unfree labour in each regional political economy. The contrast between slave and free worker, though legally great, often was less great in practice, particularly when the exploitation of women and children in the core countries is taken into account. (Contemporaries often made the comparison.) The second feature of the labour force in the mercantile division of labour was its increasing ethnic diversity. East Indians were forced to rub shoulders with Africans in the plantations of Natal, Trinidad and Guyana; Japanese were imported to Surinam; Italians to Brazil; Dutch burghers to South Africa - each ethnic group being incorporated into the division of labour with a different status. The present-day consequences of this division of labour are ever visible in the numerous forms of ethnic and class conflict in former plantation societies. The level of plantation labour struggle against mercantile capital was, however, severely limited, as the conditions for the transhipment and deployment of labour were dominanted by the merchants and the planters. None the less, there were spectacularly successful examples of slave revolt (as in Haiti), persistent attempts to escape to the hills (as in the case of the Jamaican Maroons) and numerous instances of hidden forms of resistance, best documented for the US by Genovese (1967). The formal ending of slavery only partly reflected the strength of labour resistance on the plantation, but what also must be remembered is that the 'economic' reasons for the ending of slavery included the increased cost of supplying slaves (i.e. this factor reflected the withdrawal and organisation of resistance to the slavers by African communities).

The second phase previously identified was the *industrial* division of labour. Just as the closed circuits of trade gave way to free trade, machinofacture began to replace (but never totally superceded) the production and processing of tropical commodities. It was in Europe, the *locus classicus* of this development, that the *locus classicus* of division of labour theory developed - particularly in the work of Smith and Ricardo, but also in the work of Babbage, Fergusson, Ure, Lemontay and Say. For these writers, the argument hinged around whether a particular division of labour could produce more machinofactured goods, lower wage costs, reduce the dependence of the employers on skilled workers and craftsmen or serve to subordinate the remaining labour force to the wishes of management. The labour forces involved were at first entirely drawn from the agricultural areas surrounding the factory sites, which were in turn transformed from communal or small-farmer use to large farms. Marx (1967: 895) still provides the best summary of the consequences of this process for the English countryside:

> The spoliation of the Church's property, the fraudulent alienation of the state domains, the theft of the common lands, the usurpation of feudal and clan property and its transformation into modern private property under circumstances of ruthless terrorism, all these things were just so many idyllic methods of primitive accumulation. They conquered the field for capitalist agriculture, incorporated the soil into capital, and created for the urban industries the necessary supplies of free and rightless proletarians.

In other countries without a large agricultural population or where, as in the US, the indigenous population was nearly wiped out, industrial capitalists began to complain bitterly that the lack of labour-power inhibited the full development of their country's productive resources. Consequently, vast numbers of expropriated peasants from the decaying feudal areas in European countries (especially Poland and other Eastern European countries) were sucked into the vortex of industrial production in the US through vast transhipments. Perhaps 35 million arrived in the US alone from 1870 to 1914. This was about four times as large in scale, though achieved with less compulsion, than the Atlantic trade in labour-power organised under the aegis of mercantile capital. The industrial division of labour, as the name implies, was mainly associated with the growth in the 'mass occupations' in individual capitalist countries, occupations such as those found in iron and steel mills and related engineering activities.

However, it was also a period of great infrastructural development on an international scale - the canals in Suez and Panama, transcontinental and local railways, inland waterways, arterial roads, great civic buildings and large-scale urban housing were often conceived and financed internationally. To service these infrastructural developments, labour discarded from the plantations could be redeployed - as in the use of Jamaicans to build the Panama Canal and the northern migration of blacks from the Deep South to the north-eastern cities of the US. But such was the scale of infrastructural development that Chinese had to be imported to build the Pacific Railway across the US, while perhaps two million workers from the Celtic fringe were employed in construction works in England. The strikes and protests of the period of rapid industrialisation have entered into the heroic annals of labour history: the Paris Commune (which Marx saw as the embryo of the coming communist revolution); the protests by agricultural labourers and workers so vividly documented by Thompson (1963) and Hobsbawm (1964) for the UK; and the 'Great Upheaval' in the US (1885/6) when union membership rose to between 600,000 and 800,000 and the number of strikes more than doubled from 695 in 1885 to 1,572 the next year (Dubofsky 1983: 24, 30).

There are, of course, many explanations provided as to why such strikes and workers' upheavals failed to end the rule of the bourgeoisie in the major capitalist countries and to usher in a new socialist dawn. Rising living standards, an escape to petty bourgeois activities or the life of frontier-folk in the US, the countervailing appeals of nationalism rather than class - these and other reasons were advanced for the revolutionary hiatus. But one important explanation for the failure (or perhaps the deferment?) of Marx's prediction that industrial conflict would lead to political revolution was the successful acquisition by the European powers of non-European empires. The contradiction arising between capital and labour in the metropole could thereby be displaced to the colonies, which also returned sufficient resources and profits to the metropole to allow a modest increase in working-class living standards.

This comment serves to usher in the third phase I identified, namely, what can be called the *imperial* division of labour. The imperial idea itself (be it emanating from Germany, France, Belgium or Britain) was a racially-based ideological version of an international division of labour. The children of Ham were permitted to grow food and dig up minerals in between drawing water and hewing wood. The fruits of such labour were exported to the patriarch and his lesser offspring in the metropole. They, in turn, were permitted to continue work in the patriarch's factories, this time sending their manufactured goods not only to regional markets but to the furthest points of the empire and beyond. If we take the territorial expansion of Britain as an example, almost all aspects of her empire - its acquisition, governance and central direction from Whitehall - revealed a much more determined logic than is suggested in the often quoted phrase that 'Britain conquered and peopled half the world in a fit of absence of mind.' In fact this quote comes from the arch imperialist, Sir John Seeley, who had a very clear notion of functional and product specialisation for different parts of the empire and also saw that technical developments had fundamentally altered the material basis for international association. The anticipation of the NIDL theorists is clear. Whereas *they* pointed to the arrival of the telex, the telephone, and cheap freight, Seeley (1883) alluded to other crucial technical developments:

> Science has given to the political organism a new circulation, which is steam and a new nervous system, which is electricity. These new conditions make it necessary to reconsider the whole colonial problem.

Unfortunately for Seeley and his supporters, who included the Imperial Federation League, the *Daily Mail* (founded by Harmsworth to proclaim 'The Power, the Supremacy and Greatness of the British Empire'), and Chamberlain (the energetic Colonial Secretary), they were never able to prevent investment leakages to outside the imperial area. If we look at the period 1905-9, home investment yielded 3.61 per cent, empire investment 3.94 per cent, but foreign investment yielded 4.97 per cent. Moreover, any attempt to impose partial protectionism politically activated the colonial bourgeoisies in the white Dominions (Canada, South Africa, Australia and New Zealand) just as a similar attempt in the mercantile period propelled the colonial merchant and incipient bourgeoisie of the US to revolt. Eventually even the weak and fledgling bourgeoisies in the non-white empires heeded Adam Smith's taunt that the commercial restrictions imposed by the mother country were 'impertinent badges of slavery' and threw in their lot with the anti-colonial struggles of the peasantry and working class. In this phase the periodic use of metropolitan labour-power continued, but to this group forced labour was added in many colonies (migrant labour in the extraction industries) and, in order to service the need for cheap food, turned peasant proprietors into cash-crop producers tied into the metropolitan exchange system (Williams 1985: 144-80). Labour protests in the colonies during this phase were, for the most part, organically linked to the wider anti-colonial and national struggles, but the working class in metropolitan countries was also far from dormant, especially in the wake of the First World War and the successful Bolshevik revolution - which acted as a model for some of its militant sections. Perhaps the most extensive protest (often forgotten because of Japan's post-war image of labour quiescence) was the uprising of some ten million people in Japan in 1918 involving slum-dwellers, peasants, dockers, industrial workers and miners (Seldon 1983: 88). But elsewhere revolt flamed briefly, then died, often under the impact of brutal repression. A soviet was proclaimed in Glasgow, the American Communist and Socialist parties fell apart in internal purges in 1919/20, while the rising of the left in Germany was put down, its leaders, like Rosa Luxemburg, murdered. A relative period of quiescence through the depression years altered again with the end of the Second World War, when most European trade unions emerged as determined economic actors, even if their quest for political power had been abandoned to labour and social democratic parties acting far from perfectly in their name (Arrighi 1983: 44-8).

The final phase mentioned is the *transnational* division of labour, which I use as a category that includes the so-called NIDL, but is also much wider than that. The origins of this division of labour lie in the gradually collapsing European empires which, as early as 1880, the German economist Dietsel claimed as insufficient for 'very basic economic reasons' because (note the phrase) 'the international division of labour in trade, in the output of raw materials and in agriculture is growing at such a pace that in the long run the isolation of individual groups is no longer possible' (cited in Baumgart 1982: 71). So it proved. The humiliating defeat of the European powers in Asia during the Second World War, the strength of the anti-colonial movements and the growth of competitive capital centred in the US, and later in Japan, hastened the end of the imperial order. The transnational phase left in place some neo-colonial relationships (which the French held on to notably better than the other European powers), but also led to a major restructuring of industrial production in the metropoles (allied to the importation of migrant labour), and the further internationalisation of leading fractions of capital, particularly the oil giants, the car companies, and those producing consumer durables, electrical goods and electronic components. My empirical critique of NIDL theory (see below) includes further comments on the composition of capital in the transnational phase and refers in a more detailed way to the pattern of labour utilisation. It is therefore unnecessary to repeat a similar exercise in respect of labour as was conducted in the prior divisions of labour discussed above.

By trying to fill some of the immense historic gap left yawning by NIDL theory, I have sought to illustrate a number of major points that can be used in partial refutation of the theory. First, the supposedly novel features of the contemporary division of labour to which the NIDL theorists draw attention are not really so novel. Even in the mercantile period production sites are located abroad and elements of a global labour market created and reproduced. Second, the appellation 'new' is further misleading in that it fails to recognise the indelible heritage of the past. Thus, it is more than plausible to argue that the mercantile, industrial and imperial phases have left deep scars on the face of the global population and production facilities. That there are Africans in the Caribbean and the US, Italians in Brazil and Indians in South Africa is a more salient and determinant datum informing the workings of modern capitalism than that export-processing zones have begun to employ Third World labourers. Third, there is a sense of a logical succession between the phases mentioned. Just as conventional Marxism adduces a logical end to successive modes of production as antagonistic contradictions emerge which make a prior mode obsolete, so an analogous sequence can be found in the case of the historic phases of the international division of labour. Fourth, and again the analogy with Marxist theory holds, there is a good deal of overlap between the sequential phases. This is for the obvious reason that once populations are displaced for reasons appropriate to one phase in the international division of labour, it is near impossible to return them (like the legendary genie) to the bottle from whence they came. The forms of labour deployed in an earlier phase thus continue to operate into the next phase or phases. Fifth, I have already hinted, and I wish now to demonstrate empirically, that the current phase of the division of labour (i.e. the transnational phase) should be conceived as embracing a number of different forms of labour utilisation not adequately depicted in NIDL theory.

Empirical omissions

It is perhaps important to emphasise, in view of my other criticisms of NIDL theory, that I do recognise that it describes an important aspect of the contemporary capitalist world order - namely the growth of export-oriented manufacturing in Third World countries. But this aspect of the transnational division of labour needs contextualisation in two senses. How significant is the growth of Third World industrialisation compared to global manufacturing output? What other changes are taking place in the global utilisation and deployment of labour-power with which the use of peripheral industrial labour may be compared?

Fröbel and his colleagues (1980: 295-391) lay great emphasis on the number of countries in the Third World constructing free production zones - 36 countries in 1975, six in Africa, 15 in Latin America and 15 in Asia. This undoubtedly provides one index of the increasing scale of Third World industrialisation. However, in an oblique attempt to refute the critique of his early versions of dependency theory, Frank (1981: 96-131) seeks to deride the significance of export promotion as a strategy for the industrialisation of the Third World. Though he fails in this objective, the data he provides do allow us to gain a more balanced view of the phenomenon, neither exaggerating its extent, nor deriding it in order to resurrect an over-simplified picture of metropole-satellite relations. Between 1960 and 1975 manufacturing output increased at about 6 per cent per year in the capitalist and socialist countries, but at 7.4 per cent per year in the Third World. By 1977, the Third World's share of world manufacturing output had increased to 9 per cent from a share of 6.9 per cent 17 years earlier. According to a United Nations Industrial Development Organisation report, cited by Frank (ibid: 98), an extrapolation of recent trends would leave the Third World with 14 per cent of total manufacturing by the year 2000. However, the same organisation is cited in a recent ILO report (1984: 21) as estimating that the Third World already accounted for 13 per cent of the world share of manufacturing in 1979. Whatever the exact share, there is no dispute that it is highly concentrated in a few countries. Hong Kong, Singapore, Mexico, South Korea and Brazil provided 54 per cent of all Third World manufactures to the industrialised countries in 1972. With the oil crisis and the recession that was ushered in a year later, it becomes important not only to look at relative shares of output, but at the 'earning power' represented by these shares. While the terms of trade between developed and developing countries was stable for a while, since 1979 developing countries have watched their export prices shrinking rapidly, their import costs soaring and their debt and repayment position become critical. Two of the 'success stories' in export manufacturing, Brazil and Mexico, are also afflicted with the largest debts (ILO 1984: 5, 6). It is also unclear as yet to what extent the adoption of the strategy of export-led industrialisation is a zero-sum game, with each new participant cutting into the share of the older players. In East Asia, there is great awareness by planners of minimum wages paid elsewhere in the region and a consequent fear that footloose capital will drift down market (the minimum 1985 wages varied from US$700 in Korea to $430 in the Philippines and $100 in Bangladesh). Certain NICs, like Singapore, where the overwhelming share of employment is generated by the multinationals, have also found themselves very vulnerable to US protectionist pressures - and both Singapore and Taiwan have recorded negative or downward growth rates in 1985, the first time for many years that this has happened.

It is time also to reassert a point made earlier - that changes in the international division of labour should not only be measured in terms of changes in the circulation of capital and the distribution of production facilities, but changes in the structure and utilisation of the labour force. According to Fröbel et al. (1980: 310), by 1975 about 725,000 workers were employed in world market factories and free production zones in the Third World. A wider picture can be gleaned from the ILO (1984: 20), which claims that employment generated by the multinationals - proclaimed as the engine of growth by NIDL theorists - in *all* developing countries reached about 4 million people in 1980. The share of multinational employment in different countries varied from a low of 2 per cent in Thailand, to a high of 70 per cent in Singapore, with employment created by multinationals accounting for 20-30 per cent in countries like Korea, Brazil, Kenya and Mexico. The creation of 4 million jobs by the multinationals in Third World countries should be contrasted with their employment of 40 million workers in industrialised countries. It is possible to argue that multinational investment will create a positive spin-off in the creation of further ancillary industries, but this effect (which no doubt occurs) has to be set against the displacement effect multinational investment may have for local industry. I know of no attempt to quantify these contrasting tendencies in terms of job loss/creation.

To the quantitative estimate in employment must be added a more qualitative sense of who these workers in the NICs are. In this respect the NIDL theorists provide a good general guide to the first cohort of workers (Fröbel 1980: 344). The overwhelming majority of employees in the world market factories and free production zones are women, with an age-range of 16-25 years, unskilled or semi-skilled and employed as production workers. But a more qualitative assessment of this labour force only emerges in detailed observational studies conducted on individual work-forces. Chann and her colleagues (1984: 393, 399), for example, describe the paternal system of labour control in the Malaysian export-processing zone in these terms:

Personnel policies and factory-sponsored activities direct much of their efforts to build up the notion of the factory as a family, legitimating many of the patriarchal and authoritarian relationships and features characteristic of the (Malaysian) family.... Discipline as a form of control extends beyond work hours and the factory gates. It is regimented and controlled through management appointed houseleaders who oversee the residents' discipline and movements. Disciplinary rules and regulations or one's code of conduct and behaviour are strictly adhered to. The houseleader, who is exempt from accommodation fees, has to play the role of watchdog for the management... (there is) a stigma accorded to rural folks, coupled with a deep sense of being *malu* (shy, embarrassed, ashamed) and *takut* (afraid) should she not be able to retain her job and therefore be forced to return to the village in times of recession. This Malay attitude of *malu* and *takut* is exploited by management as a means of labour control such as when parents are informed about any infringement or belligerency on the part of the worker.

Lest we imagine that the forms of control exercised are only ideological, compare the use of traditional social sanctions in the Malaysian case with this description of the garment factories in the Philippines by Penda-Ofreneo (1984: 355):

> In addition to the breakneck speed at which they have to work, workers in garment factories labor under oppressive conditions. In some factories, they are shouted at, forbidden to rest and to talk even during breaks, and are able to go to the toilet only at certain hours. Excessive heat and noise sap their strength; when they get sick they cannot go home, and when they stay home, they are not entitled to sick leave. Not a few are subjected to sexual harassment and other forms of intimidation. The docility of female labour is considered desirable by employers, along with youth, single status and inexperience.

Switching continents, from Asia to a small Caribbean island, does not alter the basic texture of the employment relationship. In the case of the small Dutch-speaking island of Curaçao, Texas Instruments set up a small plant assembling semi-conductors, employing 1,666 workers. The government provided ten years of tax-free holidays, permission to employ women to work in night-shifts (Rockwell also moved to the island from Mexico when Mexico started honouring the night-shift prohibition for women), purpose-built factories, minimum rents and permission to pay a level of wages below the industrial minimum. Abraham-Van der Mark (1983: 381) describes the labour process as follows:

> The women work in three shifts.... Wages were the same for the three shifts, and a major disadvantage for many of the workers was that assignment to a shift was permanent, so that women in the night shift had to remain in it for years without any hope for change. Although the work was dull, extremely fatiguing on the eyes, and poorly paid, employment was highly valued, both because of the regular income and

the many social contacts at work. Headaches and eye infections were not seen as a policy issue for the company but as the personal worries of the women concerned.

Given the level of unemployment in Curaçao, it was perhaps not surprising that many women were still prepared to work at the wages paid and with the conditions on offer. But whatever the wishes of their work-force, and despite the fact that the plant's productivity was second only to another branch plant in Germany, the company decided to pull out with just two years to run on its tax-free holidays. The flight of runaway transnational capital is indicative of the casual regard it has for the labour force it hires, even if the arrival of the company gives the immediate illusion that prosperity and progress has arrived. Another study by Lin (1985: 76, 77) suggests that some of the features of the work-force are changing. While the majority is still young, an increasing number of female workers are getting older, becoming married while still working, better educated and acquiring a greater variety of work experiences within and between companies. Women are increasingly 'realising that work means being valued as productive beings,' ethnic particularities are breaking down and, according to Lin, there is a sense of having to 'build a new multi-cultural working class.'

The phenomenon of export-directed manufacturing is now perhaps sufficiently described both in terms of its quantitative significance and the character of the work-force deployed. But while the impact of this phenomenon on the employment available to global labour is not to be diminished, we must avoid not seeing the wood for the recently-sprouting trees.

There are two other major sites where cheap and subordinate labour is employed, and which are equally salient aspects of the contemporary transnational division of labour. The first site comprises the countries of the Middle East and other OPEC countries - where oil revenues, accelerated in the period after 1973 for about a decade, allowed the initiation of ambitious development plans. In Venezuela, for example, following the oil-price boom which contributed some 70 per cent of national revenue, governmental policy switched to a pro-immigration stance, which legitimised and enhanced a flow of perhaps half a million undocumented foreign migrants into Caracas in addition to the vast numbers of internal migrants. The Venezuelan Council for Human Resources planned to import another half million workers during the period 1976-80. The migrants arrived from Colombia, Argentina, Chile and Ecuador amongst Latin American countries and from Spain, Italy and Portugal amongst European countries (Sassen-Koob 1979: 455-64). Again, the Middle Eastern oil-producing countries have shown dramatic increases in imported labour-power. Workers from India, Bangladesh, Pakistan and Afghanistan poured into the oil-rich countries of the Middle East, their Muslim religion being regarded by the authorities as an important reason for permitting their import. In the mid-1970s an estimated 748,000 workers from these countries arrived in Saudi Arabia, with other large numbers going to the United Arab Emirates, Qatar and Kuwait (Halliday 1977; Birks & Sinclair 1980; Kidron & Segal 1981: 38). Some of the migration is between Arab countries (Egyptians in Libya; North Yemenis, Jordanians and Palestinians in Saudi Arabia). In other cases, the bulk of the labour force comes from outside the immediate area. For example, Sudan alone provides as many as 800,000 workers to the Arab OPEC countries (*Le Monde* 3 February 1982). In some Middle Eastern countries, the proportion of foreign workers to home workers has reached almost absurd levels: 50 per cent in Saudi Arabia, 80 per cent in Kuwait and no less than 85 per cent of the total population in the United Arab Emirates (*Times Special Report* 23 February 1981). Many of these workers became helpless pawns in the crisis in the Gulf area following Iraq's invasion of Kuwait in 1990.

If we turn next to West Africa, perhaps a million migrants from Upper Volta, Togo and other nearby countries entered Ghana during the period of its greatest prosperity in the 1950s and 1960s, though the adverse economic climate thereafter produced a strong reaction against 'the aliens' (Peil 1971). As the Ghanaian economy collapsed, workers and petty traders from that country streamed into oil-rich and development-crazy Nigeria - only in turn to be the subjects of mass expulsion orders in 1983 and 1985, harshly enforced by the Nigerian authorities. Despite the difficulties of aggregating figures collected by different authorities for different purposes, simply adding together the number of *foreign* labourers (alone) mentioned as migrating to oil-producing countries, yields a figure as great as the numbers employed in the export-processing zones.

Another part of the employment wood that has also been missed by the NIDL theorists is that part of the metropolitan economy marked by the switch of employment between different sectors. NIDL theory concentrates on the loss in employment in the manufacturing (or industrial) sector and the possible switch in these jobs from industrialised countries to Third World countries. However, as we show earlier, even if all the jobs created by the transnationals can be said to be net losses for the industrialised countries and net gains for the NICs (a highly implausible assumption), we are only talking of perhaps four to six million jobs at stake. If, on the other hand, we look at switches between different sectors within industrial economies, an OECD study finds that since 1950 the share of industrial country employment represented by 'information occupations' increased by nearly 3 per cent in each five-year period. By 1975, these occupations accounted for more than one-third of the total labour force. If we examine employment across the four sectors - agriculture, industry, services and information - we can see an anticipated shrinkage in agriculture over the period 1950 to the mid-1970s to a half or a third less people employed in France, Japan, Sweden, the United Kingdom, the US and West Germany. With respect to industry, some shrinkage also occurs in these countries over the period mentioned (as is recognised in NIDL theory). But the most significant change is a spectacular growth in all the countries mentioned of the information sector employment, and a significant growth (with the marginal exception of the United Kingdom) in the service sector (ILO 1984: 179-80).

The growth of employment demand in the service sector is a feature of a contemporary division of labour particularly highlighted in the work of Sassen-Koob (1983, 1984). She advances a theory which in important respects should be laid side by side with NIDL, arguing that the 'technological transformation of the work process, the decentralisation of manufacturing and of office work, in part made possible by the technological transformation of the work process, and the transnationalisation of the economy generally, have all contributed to the consolidation of a new kind of economic centre from where the world is managed and serviced' (1984: 140). Her analysis is concentrated on New York City and on Los Angeles, where she shows that there has been a pronounced increase in the domestic and international demand for services - which she identifies as legal, managerial, financial, technical, engineering, accounting, consulting and 'a large array of other such services.' She argues that the expansion of these advanced services is the fastest growing sector of the US economy in terms of 'its share of GNP, employment and exports.' The employment pattern and social structure characterising Los Angeles and New York City, despite the superficial differences, are moving in a similar direction - a notable expansion in the supply of very high-income jobs, a shrinking of the traditional middle-income blue and white collar jobs and an *expansion* of the low wage jobs available. It is this last characteristic that provides her most surprising and important finding in that conventional wisdom and other assumptions about restructuring and industrial decline had led many observers to assume that there would be a permanent shrinkage in the number of jobs available for the more dispossessed segments of the labour force (women, blacks, migrants). In fact Sassen-Koob argues just the opposite: 'the rates of growth of various earnings categories in the service industries from 1960 to 1975 show a 35 per cent increase in jobs in the highest two earnings classes, an 11.3 per cent increase in jobs in the medium earnings class, and a 54 per cent increase in jobs in the two lowest earnings classes.' As she points out, both New York and Los Angeles contain the largest concentrations of ethnic minorities - Hispanics and Asians in Los Angeles and Caribbean peoples in the case of New

York City. Although migration from the Caribbean and Mexico has often been explained by push factors from the recipient countries Sassen-Koob considers that demand factors in cities like New York provide an equally salient explanation for migration.

What Sassen-Koob's data as yet do not provide is some sort of global indication of this trend and it is therefore only somewhat speculative to argue that one could suggest a similar tendency occurring in other 'world cities.' These, according to some of Friedman's (1985) hypotheses, are cities integrating the world economy, providing the 'base points' for production and marketing, the sites for the accumulation and concentration of capital, the points of destination for internal and international migrants, and revealing precisely the occupational profile found in Los Angeles and New York by Sassen-Koob. Such cities are arranged in a complex spatial hierarchy, and include London, Paris, Rotterdam, Frankfurt, Zurich, Chicago and Tokyo in addition to the two fortuitously (in the sense of the world city hypothesis) examined by Sassen-Koob. Though the world city hypothesis still needs much greater empirical anchorage for its validation, the notion that there are such critical nodes in the world economy has great impressionistic appeal. These cities are where the professional and managerial classes meet, where the Inter-Continental, Sheraton and Hilton hotels are established, where frequent connecting flights by international airlines operate. The cities contain stock exchanges, theatres, sophisticated entertainment, town houses and international schools.

If it is right to suggest that Sassen-Koob's findings for New York and Los Angeles can be transposed to a world city context, we should also find a similar growth in the service industries that she describes. To generalise her argument it may be important to extend her list away from what she calls 'advanced services' into the more prosaic activities which service the needs of the world's managers, professionals, financiers and consultants. She partly hints at a wider notion in her own work, but I think it is as well to be explicit that we are talking not only of the expansion of low-wage activities directly related to advanced services, but also of the growth of ancillary occupations - the cleaners and porters in the world's airports, the waiters in the French restaurants, the prostitutes in the night clubs, the chambermaids in the hotels, the seamstresses manufacturing *haute couture* clothes in the back streets of Paris, New York or London.

If this picture rings true and can be empirically demonstrated in the majority of 'world cities,' we could then say that the transnational division of labour is characterised by the following features: a further shrinkage of agricultural employment in the advanced capitalist countries; a stabilisation or slight drop in manufacturing employment in these countries; an increase in information-related employment; and a growth in strategic world cities of service employment. The growth in service employment demand can be met either by transferring migrant labourers from the old manufacturing and public sector labour market or by triggering sufficient growth to encourage the development of further migrant employment - conceivably much of it illegal. Within Third World cities, the accelerating pace of urbanisation indicates a further shift off the land; and some of these new urbanites will find employment in transnational companies spreading their operations abroad. Others will be forced to take employment, mainly as construction workers, in the oil-rich economies. But as the price of oil drops on the world market, so this avenue of employment is declining. Illegal international migration to the industrial economies, informal activities in and around the Third World cities and, in extreme cases, the collapse into refugee status now present the major alternatives confronting many Third World peoples.

Conclusion

In developing my critique of NIDL theory, I laid emphasis on three aspects - the lack of conceptual clarity in the German theorists, the historical gaps apparent in their neglect of a century marked by colonialism and imperialism, and some empirical omissions in the contemporary period. I myself preferred a conceptual model concentrating on the 'division of labour' in respect of the different mix of labour forms apparent in each phase of the international division of labour I identified.

While clear differences exist between each period - mercantile, industrial, imperial and transnational - in the form of labour used, there is also a sense of historical continuity rather than rupture. In each phase a mix of 'free' and 'unfree' labour forms is evident. Equally, the hoary contest between capital and labour ever takes place, with the conflict being particularly acute in relation to the freer section of the labour force. Whenever the balance of advantage tilts to the side of organised labour, capitalists move from seeking to subordinate labour to seeking subordinate labourers. Elsewhere I describe this historical process of reaching out to neophyte cohorts of external proletarians in some detail (Cohen 1987).

Whereas for many Marxists, the phenomenon was perceived as unproblematic - simply the realisation of capitalism on a world scale - Luxemburg (1921) and the Austrian Marxist Bauer (discussed in Tarbuck 1972) were the first to debate the political implications of the interrupted and often partial spread of capitalism to the areas we now call the Third World. For example, Luxemburg (in Tarbuck 1972: 24) argues that:

Since the capitalist production can develop fully only with complete access to all territories and climes, it can no more confine itself to the natural resources and productive forces of the temperate zone than it can manage with white labour alone. Capital needs other races to exploit, territories where the white man cannot work. It must be able to mobilise world labour-power without restriction in order to utilise all productive forces of the globe - up to the limits imposed by a system of producing surplus value.

Despite this insight, Luxemburg lays more emphasis on the migration of European labourers to the colonies and scoffs at Bauer (and Lenin) who saw the likelihood of a movement going the other way. Again, whereas she saw the necessity for capitalism to capture non-capitalist *markets* to survive, she rather discounted the possibilities of finding large cohorts of subordinate labour-power in the colonies, having been misled by the mining companies' and settlers' cries of labour shortage. It was left to Bauer to perceive that there were huge untapped resources there for capital, once self-sustaining rural producers could be detached from the land. By failing to analyse the history and practice of imperialism the NIDL theorists have been unable to see that the phenomenon they identify is part of a much older game: one that has always had profound implications for the survival of the system itself. As Bauer (in Tarbuck 1972: 142) puts it:

Capitalism will not collapse from the mechanical impossibility of realising surplus value. It will be defeated by the rebellion to which it drives the masses. Not until then, when the last peasant and the last petty bourgeois turn into wage workers, thus no longer providing a surplus market, will capitalism disintegrate.

Theoretically, Bauer's position is still correct. There can be no socialist revolution in one country (including the countries which garland themselves with that label) because the capitalists can apparently endlessly export or displace their contradictions onto the next wave of 'helots' they alight upon, at home or abroad. But the theory is a difficult one to sustain in the ultimate sense. We can no longer comfortably make evolutionary assumptions characteristic of pre-1945 political theory, left and right. Despite the fierce denunciations of the left, capitalism does not appear too *strong* but too *weak* - in the sense that it seems unable to produce employment for all, given the exponential population growth, the unemployment time bomb and an even more potent bomb capable of destroying the globe before capitalism can realise its immanent possibilities.

As may be noticed elsewhere in this book, one of the theoretical difficulties for those interested in international labour studies is that a number of the internationalist or global perspectives are either antipathetical, or at the very least, not easily bent to our purposes. Modernisation theory, which was the common currency in the 1960s in graduate schools in the US and Britain, was all too obviously Americo-centric and conservative. It fell apart with a few well-aimed barbs by Frank - who introduced the Latin American dependency school to US and European readers. But this provided little solace - as explained in the opening sections of this chapter, the dependency school too was flawed by the inherent oversimplicity of the model and its inability to deal with discussions of intra-national, let alone international class relations. Classical Marxist theories of imperialism were often dated (therefore irrelevant) and, like modernisation theory, written from the point of view of the expansion of hegemonic capital - thus Eurocentric is a more accurate description than Americo-centric. I tentatively would turn in an 'unproven' verdict on the potency of world systems analysis, largely because much of the aggregate data collected has been trade and capital-, not labour-centred. It was therefore with considerable delight that I first read Fröbel and his colleagues' work on the New International Division of Labour. At last, a world perspective that seemed to speak more directly to us! I still believe this to be the case, or to be more exact, to be more the case than in any other form of global analysis. My critique therefore should be regarded as partly an appreciation while some of my more ferocious phrases should be understood as a sign of disappointed hopes and the frustrations wrought when something is so nearly right. At any event, I hope I have indicated enough in the chapter itself to show that I would wish the theory to be refined and extended, rather than discarded. In the hope that I might provoke our German colleagues to a counterblast, I published this article in the first issue of an Anglo-German journal which I co-edited for a couple of years with my energetic associate at Berlin, Jochen Blaschke. The article was published in Migration: a European Journal of Migration and Ethnic Relations *1 (1) July 1987 pp. 22-40 and was also reproduced in substance as Chapter 7 in Cohen (1987). So far, the proponents of NIDL theory have remained as aloof as Thomas Mann's* Magic Mountain, *but I still hope to provoke them to a scrap in the valley of ideas.*

9

Citizens, Denizens and Helots: the Politics of International Migration Flows in the Post-war World

Introduction

In a current period marked by immigration restrictions and increasingly tight definitions of nationality and citizenship, it is sometimes difficult to remember that the climate of decision-making in the immediate post-war period was far different in North America and most European countries.

In France, for example, the leading demographer at the influential *Institut National d'Études Démographiques*, Sauvy, pronounced that France needed at the minimum to import 5,290,000 permanent immigrants to renew its labour force, stabilise the skewed demographic structure arising from war-time losses and reinforce its claims to Great Power status (Freeman 1979: 69).

Across the Channel, the budding Labour Party politician, James Callaghan (later to become Prime Minister), ignored the potentially xenophobic reactions of his working-class supporters and proclaimed in the House of Commons:

> We are living in an expansionist era. Surely, this is a Socialist government committed to a policy of full employment? In a few years' time we in this country will be faced with a shortage of labour, and not with a shortage of jobs. Our birth rate is not increasing in sufficient proportion to enable us to replace ourselves... We are turning away from the shores of this country eligible and desirable young men who could be added to our strength and resources, as similar immigrants have done in the past (cited Cohen 1987: 124).

In Germany, the post-war Constitutional provision for reunification allowed millions of East Germans to cross the frontier. These expellees and refugees, together with those from the former eastern territories of the Reich and demobilised soldiers, all unprotected by the weakened labour movement, 'provided ideal conditions for capitalist expansion, and were the essential cause of the economic miracle' (Castles et al. 1984: 25). With expansion, West Germany's demand for labour increased dramatically. Though a more cautious attitude prevailed on the question of according citizenship to 'foreign' newcomers, a massive guestworker programme from Turkey and elsewhere was initiated.

In the US, in addition to the strong continued demand for migrant labour (flowing especially from the neighbouring areas of Central America and the Caribbean), temporary labour programmes, initiated to offset war-time shortages, were allowed to continue in the post-war period. For instance, the Bracero Program, designed to supply agricultural labourers to south-west agribusiness, commenced in 1942 with 4,203 recruits, peaked in 1957 with 450,422 labourers, and was only formally ended in 1965 (Samora & Simon 1977: 140).

Of all the major capitalist industrial powers, Japan was alone in not relying on the importation of large numbers of foreign labourers to fuel its post-war economy. This was not because of some general rule of Japanese exceptionalism, but because, unlike in the other industrial powers, there was still a large indigenous rural population which could be detached from the land, and a significant proportion of women who could be enjoined to enter employment for the first time. For instance, the number of Japanese women 'gainfully employed' increased from 3 million in 1950 to 12 million in 1970 (Mandel 1978: 171).

The end of the migrant labour boom

The authorised importation of labourers to the industrial economies mentioned above lasted roughly until the mid-1970s in Europe, when sharp restrictions were imposed. The US figures do not show similar absolute declines in legal immigration, but there were significant qualitative changes in the occupational and legal categories admitted - from immigrants to refugees and from agricultural and mass production workers to the professional, technical and independent proprietor categories (Keely & Elwell 1981: 192-3).

It is now no longer necessary to mount an elaborate argument listing the advantages conferred by the deployment of migrant labour by the host countries and employers in the post-war period, as there is now a remarkable unanimity of views between liberal (see Kindleberger 1967; Böhning 1972), Marxist (see Castles & Kosack 1973; Castells 1979) and official accounts. Perhaps one, remarkably frank, paper prepared by the West German government for a conference on 'The Future of Migration' organised by the

Organisation of Economic Cooperation and Development in May 1986 is sufficient to make the point. The paper (cited in Cross 1988) accepts that the German economy had gained considerable benefits with negligible costs, and continues:

> Until far into the 1960s, the employment of foreigners helped to satisfy the rising demand for labour... at a time when the labour volume was getting scarcer and scarcer.... Their considerable flexibility in the economic cycle helped to offset negative employment effects in times of recession and to avoid inflationary shortages in times of upswing. The need for infrastructural facilities, integration assistance and social benefits which followed from the employment of foreigners was almost insignificant because of the short periods of stay of the individual foreigners and the low numbers of family members who entered in the course of family reunion.

If the benefits of migrant labour were so apparent, why did the import of labour throttle off so dramatically in the mid-1970s? On this question there is no final agreement, but a number of mutually-reinforcing explanations or contingent factors may be advanced. I will briefly discuss six factors, specified below in no particular order:

The oil crisis

There is an obvious coincidence of dates in the early 1970s which may lead to a simple association between the dramatic increase in the price of oil and the end of the migrant labour boom. Certainly, the immediate wave of redundancies that followed in energy-intensive industries led to a political situation which would have made the importation of large numbers of 'alien' labourers untenable for most European governments. But, while the oil crisis can partly explain the timing of particular measures, any explanation of the end of labour migration must also be concerned with other deeper, underlying factors.

The rise of racism and xenophobia

One of the key variables, often underestimated by scholars (who frequently assumed the hegemony of 'rational' capital) and governments (who assumed their own hegemony) alike, was the rise of a virulent indigenous working-class xenophobia. This is not to argue, of course, that sentiments were only held amongst the working classes. But the opposite possibility, the belief that patterns of international class solidarity would obviate ethnic and racial allegiances, proved hopelessly idealistic.

In Britain, old protective practices, like closed shops and demarcation agreements, were used to freeze out migrant labour (Duffield 1988) while in France, a municipal Communist Party bulldozed the hostels erected for migrant workers in response to the demands of its constituents.

In short, both capital and the state were unable to continue to employ migrant workers oblivious to the countervailing racist sentiments such a policy provoked.

The organisation of migrant workers

Much Marxist theory, particularly of the 'capital logic' tendency, depicts migrants as hopeless chaff blown about by fierce economic storms - unable to respond organisationally to the market forces arraigned against them. This picture is partly correct at the earliest stages of migration, amongst those migrants with a particularly individualist ethic and in circumstances where it was difficult to effect a bond of alliance between co-religionists or those from a similar ethnic group.

Whatever the variation in activity across the different cases, there is no doubt that community associations, religious groups and political support groups were sufficiently and increasingly active - precisely at the time when issues such as repatriation, return migration, immigration restrictions and deportations were proposed by politicians, anxious to limit what were perceived as the socially divisive consequences of the untrammelled immigration period. Migrant groups were not sufficiently influential to prevent all these measures, but they were, on the whole, powerful enough to resist the pressures to mass repatriation and to press instead for the principle of family reunification to be recognised.

The rise in the cost of reproduction

The increased assertiveness of migrants not only applied to matters of immigration policy and family reunion; immigrant associations became increasingly concerned with the full range of social and employment benefits. One should not fall into the racist trap of believing that immigrant families overclaim all benefits - the evidence indeed inclines to a contrary assertion (Rex & Tomlinson 1979: 62). However, given the demographic profile and the special language needs of many migrant communities, increased costs arose in respect of child care, language training and education. Even if we assume only a broadly converging cost of reproduction between indigenous and migrant communities, the crucial advantage accruing to the host country and employer - a minimal or wholly displaced cost of reproduction - no longer obtained as migrant communities gradually reconstituted their family life and became permanent minorities.

Economic restructuring

One way of understanding the economic restructuring of the last 15 years is to argue in terms of new technology impelling a different industrial logic - away from mass production to small-batch production, away from labouring into independent proprietorship, away from manufacturing into services (Piore & Sabel 1984). The same processes also impelled a greater comparative advantage accruing to certain newly industrialising countries (for example, Hong Kong, Korea, Taiwan and Singapore), particularly in respect of low-bulk and high-value goods where the value added by the labour component was significant.

In Chapter 8 I have explored the so-called 'new international division of labour' thesis in detail, so here, by way of summary, I simply suggest that many such theories are overly technologically determinist, and can easily confuse cause and consequence. Thus, it is at least as plausible to argue that increased levels of class composition and migrant organisation made mass production methods less attractive as to assume some exogenous new technology acted as an independent force. But whatever the exact reasons for the movement to independent proprietorship and small-batch and third world production, this development obviated the need to continue to employ factory hands imported from abroad.

The 'inefficiency' of unskilled labour

In opening the paper, I allude to a remarkable uniformity of opinion between official accounts and liberal and Marxist writers on the benefits conferred by the use of migrant labour. The orthodoxy is, in my view, largely correct, but some dissent was recorded at an early date by Misham (1970).

His argument is alarmist and based on unlikely projections of large inflows of migrant labour leading to a rise in the labour-capital ratio and a consequent fall in production. While the broad thesis makes unrealistic net migration assumptions, in some sectors, for example the textile industry, it is likely that working cheap migrant labour on a 24-hour shift pattern was used as a way of holding the line against low-cost Asian textiles, thereby avoiding the inevitable day when old machinery and tracks had to be discarded.

As Reaganomics and Thatcherism began to gain ground, and unemployment levels began to rise, arguments that importing migrants was essentially an inefficient way of reducing industrial costs became more widely heard.

Labour flows since the mid-1970s

I have given an indicative, though not an exhaustive account of the explanations for the immigration restrictions of the mid-1970s. But incomplete as this picture is, it may give the false impression that international labour migration has effectively ceased. In fact it continues largely unabated - though with significant differences in the destination areas and the kinds of migrants involved.

In Europe, the post-1970s migration is largely accounted for by family reunification, refugees and to a small degree, by illegal entrants. In the US, illegals account for a much greater proportion of post-1970s migrants. Agribusiness in the south, the sweated trades in the north-east and the service sector more generally continued to deploy imported labour, both legal and illegal. But there was also a clear movement away from employees destined for the mass occupations in the auto and steel industries, towards an acceptance of political refugees (Vietnamese, Cuban and East European) and to those who could class themselves as entrepreneurs or proprietors (for example, the Koreans and Hong Kong Chinese).

Outside the US and Europe, labour migration apparently of the more well-established kind went to the Middle East and other oil-producing countries. But even in these areas important qualitative differences appear. These differences emerge in my more detailed remarks below on migration flows to the oil-rich countries, illegal migrants, refugees and project-tied contract migrants.

Migration to the oil-rich countries

While the quadrupling of oil prices deepened the climate of economic crisis and uncertainty in Europe and the US (and to a lesser extent, Japan), the same factor allowed for the massive expansion of infrastructural development programmes in the oil-rich countries.

What many oil-exporting countries in the Middle East lacked was labour-power - professional, skilled or manual. Migrant labour was recruited primarily from other Arab countries (Egypt, Jordan - including Palestinians - Morocco, Oman and the two Yemens in declining numerical order) and from the Indian sub-continent (India and Pakistan). Other significant contingents to the Middle East came from Afghanistan, Bangladesh, Somalia, Turkey, Korea, the Philippines and the Sudan. So great and so sudden was this migration that by 1975, migrant labour formed 89 per cent of the total labour force in the United Arab Emirates, 83 per cent in Qatar, 71 per cent in Kuwait and 39 per cent in Oman and Saudi Arabia (Ecevit 1981: 260). By 1980, the International Labour Office (ILO 1984: 102) cites a figure of 2,821,720 migrant workers in the oil-producing Middle Eastern countries. Although the overwhelming majority of the workers were of Muslim background, this link did not prove decisive in granting citizenship of the country of employment and many were either sent back to their countries of origin or remained without access to a new citizenship.

Other oil-rich countries, like Venezuela and Nigeria, manifested similar inward shifts of population, though of proportionately lower size to those of the Middle East. As in France during the immediate post-war period, the Venezuelan authorities, in particular the Council for Human Resources, determined on a pro-immigration stance. This encouraged a flow of about half a million undocumented migrants, the import of another half million foreign workers between 1976 and 1980 and a strong internal migration flow towards the capital, Caracas (Sassen-Koob 1979: 455-64).

Illegals

The restrictions on immigration in Europe and North America have also not strongly impeded the illegal, or as the ILO terms it, the 'irregular' flows of international migrants. Within Europe, the illegal population is estimated to be about 10 per cent of the foreign population as a whole (OECD 1987: 55) and is characterised by Marie (1983) as follows:

> Illegal migration has above all been a strategy adapted to a new institutional context... [offsetting]... the stringent restriction on the entry of low-skilled manpower by supplying workers willing to accept low-status jobs with poor working conditions and pay... recourse to illegal migrant workers may be interpreted as a movement towards replacing one category of foreigners by another contingent in a less secure position, with a view to more flexible management of the labour force.

The International Labour Office (ILO 1984: 113-14) argues forcibly that irregular migration should not be conceived as solely comprising those who cross the border fully intending to circumvent unequivocal immigration or employment law. Rather, 'irregular' migrants also include those who are permitted through administrative inefficiency or convenience to enter a country, with regularisation taking place later. Other sub-sets comprise those who enter countries (South America is cited) where few explicit immigration policies exist, or those who enter countries where laws provide contradictory signals to the intending migrant.

The last case is of particular salience to the large numbers of 'undocumented' workers entering the US from Mexico. Whereas immigration law clearly states that it is illegal to enter the US outside the procedures established in the Immigration and Nationality Act of 1952, the agribusiness lobby forced through an amendment which permitted the employment of an undocumented worker. This led to the peculiar legalism of economic interest, which lasted until a recent

change under the Reagan administration, namely - that it was
acceptable to employ an illegal, but not acceptable to be one.

The attempt by the ILO to widen the category of 'illegal' to cover
the cases of other 'irregular' and 'undocumented' workers is a useful
reminder to the authorities to avoid premature assumptions or
unjustified stigmatisation. But it is undoubtedly the case that the
illegal status attaching to irregular migrants of all kinds has
generated a fearful, wary segment of the population - largely
helpless in the face of ruthless landlords or exploitative employers,
cut off from the protection of the police and courts, and excluded
from the political life and social benefits of the society they now live
in. As argued later, they form part of a 'helot' class.

Refugees and asylum-seekers

Who is a refugee? The legal definitions derive from the 1951
international Convention which defined refugees as 'persons who
are outside their country because of a well-founded fear of
persecution for reasons of race, religion, nationality, membership of
a particular social group or political opinion.' The 1951 Convention
was drafted with the needs of the post-war displaced people of
Europe firmly in mind. The modified 1967 Protocol sought to take
account of events elsewhere in the world and was signed by nearly
100 countries.

Though the legal provisions appeared generous, in fact they still
bore the mark of their original place of drafting. Moreover, European
governments have been less than generous in applying the existing
provisions to those demanding entry as a result of the mass
displacements occurring in the Third World. As a report for the
Independent Commission on International Humanitarian Issues
(ICIHI 1986: 33) puts it:

> In the 1970s a new phenomenon emerged. Refugees from the crisis areas
> of Africa, Asia and Latin America began to move in increasing numbers
> to the industrialised countries.... The arrival of many refugees from
> geographically and culturally distant areas constituted an unprecedented
> challenge to the legal machinery and conscience of the receiving
> countries. The refugee problem, previously regarded as a factor in east-
> west relations, now had a north-south dimension added to it.

This analysis can be elaborated in three respects. First, the volume
and effects of the refugee crises were amplified as they coincided
with the reduction of aid and social investment programmes to the
Third World in response to nationalist and protectionist pressures in
the industrialised countries. These pressures became politically
effective precisely at the moment when many poor countries had
their economic and environmental resources stretched to the limit.
Increased energy costs, more expensive imports, political instability

and lower commodity prices all placed a number of Third World countries in a position where they were unable to respond effectively to the devastations wrought by famine, war and drought.

Second, the shift from a crisis of east-west relations to one defined in north-south terms can be vividly illustrated in the case of the US. Prior to 1980, when the US passed legislation paralleling the agreed international Conventions, the official US definition of a refugee referred, *inter alia*, to people 'fleeing Communist countries' or Communist-dominated countries.' The paradoxes and problems of US refugee admissions were highlighted in the summer of 1980, when two streams of refugees - the 'freedom flotilla' from Cuba and those escaping from the Duvalier regime - converged. President Carter was forced to endorse the 20-year-old policy of welcoming refugees from Communist regimes, even though many of the Cubans appeared to be less interested in the iniquities of Castro's regime than in the opportunity for some quick pickings in Miami. At the same time the Immigration and Naturalisation Service had, increasingly implausibly, to hold the line maintaining that the Haitian boat people were economic and not political migrants, even though it was apparent that many were fleeing from the violence and depredations of the US-supported regime and its armed thugs, the Ton-Ton Macoutes. (For more on this period see Cohen 1987: 148-56; Bach et al· 1981-2.)

Third, the volume of refugee migration, and potential migration, expanded to such an extent (the estimate is now 15 million refugees world wide) that many states began to argue that refugees were in effect disguised economic migrants. Zucker & Zucker (1987: xiv) seek to contradict the commonly-held official view and to develop a clear distinction between the three categories, immigrant, refugee and illegal, in the following passage:

> Refugees are neither immigrants nor illegal migrants, although, like immigrants, they have forsaken their homelands for new countries and, like illegal migrants, they may enter those new countries without permission. But a refugee is, in the end, unlike either. Both the immigrant and the illegal migrant are drawn to a country. The refugee is not drawn but driven; he seeks not to better his life but to rebuild it, to gain some part of what he has lost. The immigrant and the migrant are propelled by hope; for the refugee whatever hope there may be must arise from the ruins of tragedy. The refugee, unlike other migrants, has lost or been denied a basic human need - the legal and political protection of a government. Accompanying that loss has been the loss, as well, of culture, community, employment, shelter - all the elements that contribute to a sense of self-worth. Refugees, whatever their origins, are in need of protection.

However, such definitions depend greatly on liberal and humanist values being shared by politicians, policy-makers or immigration officials. The overall figures and the pattern of admissions do not indicate wide acceptance of such views.

In Europe, the number of refugees recognised under the 1951 and 1967 Conventions is very limited, though such individuals do gain the full protection of the host state and can be considered as holding equivalent rights to an indigenous citizen.

In the US, as Zucker & Zucker (1987) show, refugee policy and asylum decisions are governed not by the recognition of need or the volume of applications, but by whether the country of origin is currently a recognised enemy of the US government. Between 1980 and 1986 asylum was granted in 29,926 cases, but 76 per cent of these came from just three countries - Iran, Poland and Nicaragua (ibid.: 142-3). Admissions of refugees are regulated by quota and numbers exceed quotas only when an unexpected flow from a Communist country occurs or - until this no longer became fashionable - when the Cold War drum could be beaten. Even then, the exasperation of the Immigration and Naturalisation Service and many members of the public with the Cuban contingent was evident in the internment procedures effected and the lack of substantive help given in respect of settlement and employment. Many refugees or asylum-seekers remain unrecognised by the state authorities or are denied entry in the first place.

Project-tied contract workers

Foreign contract workers can be of two major kinds. Either an individual employment contract is drafted, often with an employee's existing multinational employer, or a host government or employer advertises for foreign workers in permitted categories and signs individual contracts with foreign employees. Such individually-contracted workers, often known as 'expatriates,' are likely to be in the skilled, managerial or professional category, to live in subsidised company housing, to have annual leave, child travel and education allowances, a pension arrangement and a generous salary. In short, expatriates provide a good example of privileged aliens - a group I include under the category 'denizens.'[1]

The second case is much more interesting both because it is much less known and because is has the potential of being deployed on a wide scale by governments anxious to avoid the possibilities of settlement and ethnic group formation, seen even in the case of the guestworkers to West Germany. Instead of individual contracts being issued, block visas are provided to the project contractor, who is then held legally responsible for the behaviour of the labour force and its discharge *outside* the country of work. Of course, there are many historical examples of this type of labour recruitment, but it has become a much more popular mode in recent years. Source countries often include eastern European countries anxious for the foreign exchange brought back by discharged workers. In 1982, for example, 11,335 Yugoslav, 6,914 Polish and 1,648 Hungarian project-tied workers were employed in West Germany (ILO 1984: 108).

But the masters of this trade seem to be concentrated in the Republic of Korea, where construction companies have won extensive contracts in the Middle East, Africa and Asia. (The value of such contracts was estimated as US$13,000 million in 1981.) According to the ILO (ibid.: 112-13), in the case of the Korean contractors, 'virtually every aspect of the migrant workers' daily life is under the protection and control of their employers.' Work-camps are set up in remote spots, contact with the locals is minimal, workers are forbidden to form unions, health, accommodation and safety standards are poor, medical and recreational facilities equally impoverished and work-related deaths and injuries 'high and rising.' Workers so recruited are totally under the thumbs of their employers and the host government has no interest in offering protection or succour in the event of human rights abuses or high levels of exploitation.

What's in a name?

Immigrants, guestworkers, illegals, refugees, asylum-seekers, expatriates, settlers - do these labels signify anything of importance? My argument here turns on a belief that although there are considerable similarities between international migrants of all types, the modern state has sought to differentiate the various people under its sway by including some in the body politic and according them full civic and social rights, while seeking to exclude others from entering this charmed circle.

The important role of citizenship as a means of integrating dissatisfied members of the lower orders and including them in the core society was first explicitly recognised by Marshall (1950). For him, access to citizenship allowed everyone so favoured to be given some stake in the society, at least in respect of periodic elections, protection, and access to some social benefits. With the rise of welfare and distributive states in the post-war world, the social wage - unemployment benefits, social security, housing allowances, tax credits, pensions, subsidised health care - has become a much more important symbolic and economic good. By the same token, states have sought to restrict access to the social wage by deploying workers with limited entitlements. The different statuses reflected in immigrant or guestworker categories reflect the differential access of such groups to the social wage and to the protection afforded by the agencies of law and order.

If we consider the various categories mentioned, three broad categories appear - citizens whose rights are extensive, an intermediate group (the denizens) and a group which remains a subject population akin to the ancient helots who hewed wood and toiled for the Spartans without access to democratic rights, property or protection.

Some of the typical sub-groups within the different status groups mentioned are listed below (Figure 9.1).

Figure 9.1: Sub-groups of Citizens, Denizens and Helots

Citizens
>   Nationals by birth or naturalisation
>   Established Immigrants
>   Convention Refugees

Denizens
>   Holders of one or more citizenships
>   Recognised asylum applicants
>   Special entrants (e.g. ex-Hong Kong)
>   Expatriates

Helots
>   Illegal Entrants
>   Undocumented workers
>   Asylum-seekers
>   Overstayers
>   Project-tied unskilled workers

A few remarks on each of the three major categories will perhaps help to lend greater specificity to the labels.

Citizens

This group appears as an increasingly privileged one. Many states have moved from inclusive to exclusive definitions of citizenship, abandoning the principle of *jus soli* (citizenship by being born in a territory) to *jus sanguinis* (citizenship according to the parents' nationality). In the case of the European countries that once had empires (Belgium, France, Britain, Holland), binding guarantees of citizenship to colonial subjects have frequently been ignored or circumvented by subsequent legislation. While the Dutch on the whole respected the citizenship conferred on subjects of the Netherlands, the French maintained recognition only for a small number of people in the *départements* (French Guiana, Réunion, Guadeloupe and Martinique). The British, for their part, in the Nationality Act of 1982 stripped away the rights of residents of the colony of Hong Kong (and a few other places) and created a new citizenship of 'dependent territories' which conferred no right to live or work in the UK. Under the impact of the destablising events in China in 1989, however, and its consequent effects on the colony of Hong Kong, Britain has been forced to guarantee the admission of up to 50,000 Hong Kong families. The intention of this guarantee is to stabilise the last years of British rule in the colony (it reverts to Chinese rule in 1997) by buying the loyalty of key officials and entrepreneurs with the offer of settlement and full citizenship in Britain. This will require amendment of the 1982 British Nationality Act and is likely to cause a major political crisis in Britain in the period leading up to the next general election.

Denizens

I conceive of this group as comprising privileged aliens often holding multiple citizenship, but not having the citizenship or the right to vote in the country of their residence or domicile. Hammar (forthcoming) has produced a remarkable calculation that resident non-citizens living and working in European countries include 180,000 in Belgium, 2,800,000 in France, 2,620,000 in West Germany, 400,000 in the Netherlands, 390,000 in Sweden and 700,000 in Switzerland. Many of these alien residents may be well-paid expatriates (see above) who are not particularly concerned with exercising the franchise and have compensating employment benefits - a group, in short, that can be seen as transcending the limits of the nation-state. However, the numbers involved in Hammar's calculations suggest that many residents have been systematically excluded from citizenship and its accompanying rights without any compensating benefits deriving from their employment. These form part of the helot category.

Helots

I have used the category 'helots' in a somewhat more inclusive way in Cohen (1987). Here I refer more narrowly to people who have illegally entered the country, people who have overstayed the period granted on their entry visas, asylum-seekers who have not been recognised under the international Conventions, those who are working illegally, and those who have been granted only limited rights. A good example (cited in Castles et al. 1984: 77) appears in a statement given to officials as to how to operate the 1965 West German Foreigners Law:

> Foreigners enjoy all basic rights, except the basic rights of freedom of assembly, freedom of association, freedom of movement and free choice of occupation, place of work and place of education and protection from extradition abroad.

Statements such as this reveal the powerful attempt to try to exclude, detain or deport foreigners who are regarded as disposable units of labour-power to whom the advantages of citizenship, the franchise and social welfare are denied.

Conclusion

As Marshall (1950) argues, conferring citizenship is the key indicator of integration and acceptance within a nation state. This basic symbol of inclusion is signified by the right to elect periodically a new government. But the exercise of the vote has become of rather lesser significance than the other attendant benefits of citizenship - access to national insurance systems, unemployment benefits, housing support, health care and social security. In addition to these undoubted advantages, citizens of the European nations within the European Community will soon have untrammelled rights to live, work, own property and travel within a wider Europe.

Helots and denizens are, by the same token, symbolically excluded and practically denied all the advantages just listed. In the case of the denizens, this may not be particularly burdensome - a denizen may be an employee of a multinational company with access to private medical insurance. But for a helot, the denial of citizenship is usually a traumatic and life-threatening decision. Given their vulnerability, the helots have become the key means for inducing labour flexibility and provide a target for nationalist and racist outrages.

Our trichotomy leads one to speculate that a new form of stratification has emerged which in origin has little to do with income, occupation, racial or ethnic background, gender, or a particular relationship to the means of production. Of course, there are likely to be coincidences between the different patterns of stratification. A helot is likely to be a Third World migrant, a member of a stigmatised minority, with low income, holding an unskilled occupation and having limited access to housing, education and other social benefits. Similarly, a professionally-educated, urban, middle-class salary-earner, who happens to be a foreigner, is likely to be a denizen.

Migration after the 1970s to a new country will not necessarily carry the optimistic possibilities characteristic of migration at the turn of the century. Then the 'huddled masses,' that time from Europe as well as from Asia, threw off their poverty and feudal bondage to enter the American dream as equal citizens. Equally it was perfectly possible for English and Irish convicts to become landowners and gentlemen farmers in Australia. Nowadays, one's legal or national status - whether, in my terms, a citizen, helot or denizen - will increasingly operate as indelible stigmata, determining a set of life chances, access to a particular kind of employment or any employment and other indicators of privilege and good fortune.

This chapter was first presented as a paper for the International Symposium on Cultural Changes in the Period of Transformation in the Capitalist World System, organised by the Faculty of Social Studies, Hitotsubashi University, Tokyo, 19-20 September 1988. It was also scheduled for publication in the Hitotsubashi Journal of Social Studies *in 1990, though I have not yet seen a copy. I gave the paper with some trepidation, wondering whether it would have much relevance to Japan. To my surprise, the Japanese debate about their indigenous minority and the long-standing Korean community had some parallels with my discussion. The foreign businessman ('denizen') and illegal worker - mainly from Pakistan and the Philippines - were also familiar figures. The paper was subsequently presented at the inter-sessional meeting of the Research Committee on Migration of the International Sociological Association, which met in Utrecht at Easter 1989.*

Notes

1   The term 'denizens' is derived from Hammar (forthcoming). However, he uses it to refer to all alien residents. In origin, the term referred to an alien admitted to citizenship by royal letters patent by the English crown in the 16th century. I have reserved the term 'denizen' for the more privileged alien and used the term 'helots' (cf. Cohen 1987) to refer to those non-citizens whose rights are far less extensive.

References

Abraham-Van der Mark, E E (1983) 'The Impact of Industrialisation on Women: A Caribbean Case,' in J Nash & P Fernandez-Kelly (eds.) *q.v.*

Agier, M et al. (eds.) (1987) *Classes ouvrières d'Afrique Noire*, Paris, Karthala

AKUT (1983) 'Labour and Development,' Planning document of the AKUT Group, Uppsala, *University of Uppsala* (mimeograph)

Alavi, H (1965) 'Peasants and Revolution,' *Socialist Register 1965*, London, Merlin Press

Alt, J (1976) 'Beyond Class: The Decline of Industrial Labor and Leisure,' *Telos*, no. 28, Summer

Althusser, L (1969) *For Marx*, London, New Left Books

———— (1970) *Reading Capital*, London, New Left Books (with Etienne Balibar)

Amin, S (1974) *Accumulation on a World Scale*, vols. 1 & 2, New York, Monthly Review Press

Anon. (1970) 'Editorial', *Bulletin of the Institute of Development Studies*, 2 (4), July

———— (1971) 'Organising at FIAT,' *Radical America*, September/October

Aronowitz, S (1973) *False Promises*, New York, McGraw-Hill

Arrighi, G (1983) 'The Labour Movement in Twentieth-Century Western Europe,' in I Wallerstein (ed.) *q.v.*

Arrighi, G & J Saul (1973) *Essays on the Political Economy of Africa*, New York, Monthly Review Press

Babbage, C (1832) *On the Economy of Machinery and Manufactures*, London, Knight

Bach, R L et al. (1981-2) 'The "Flotilla Entrants": Latest and Most Controversial,' *Cuban Studies*, 11 (2) & 12 (1), 30-48

Bagchi, A K (1982) *The Political Economy of Underdevelopment*, Cambridge, Cambridge University Press

Baird, P & E McCaughan (1979) *Beyond the Border*, New York, North American Congress on Latin America

Baker, J S (1978) 'Trade Union Internationalism and the Supra-National State,' *Capital and Class*, no. 5, Summer

Baldamus, W (1969) 'Alienation, Anomie and Industrial Accidents,' Faculty of Commerce and Social Science Discussion Paper, Series E, no. 12, *University of Birmingham*, June
————— (1969a) 'The Concept of Truly Accidental Accidents,' Faculty of Commerce and Social Science Discussion Paper, Series E, no. 14, University of Birmingham, October
Banaji, J (1977) 'Modes of Production in a Materialist Conception of History,' *Capital and Class*, no. 3, 1-44
Barnet, R T & R E Müller (1974) *Global Reach: The Powers of the Multinationals*, New York, Simon & Schuster
Baudrillard, J (1975) *The Mirror of Production*, St Louis, Telos Press
Baumgart, W (1982) *Imperialism: The Idea and Reality of British and French Colonial Expansion*, Oxford, Oxford University Press
Berger, J & J Mohr (1975) *A Seventh Man*, Harmondsworth, Penguin
Bergquist, C (ed.) (1984) *Labor in the Capitalist World Economy*, Beverly Hills, Sage
Bernstein, H (1977) 'Notes on Capital and Peasantry,' *Review of African Political Economy*, no. 10, Sept.-Dec., 60-73
Beynon, H (1973) *Working for Ford*, Harmondsworth, Penguin
Birks, J & C A Sinclair (1980) *International Migration and Development in the Arab Region*, Geneva, International Labour Office
Bisharat, M (1975) 'Yemeni Farmworkers in California,' *MERIP Reports*, no. 34, January, 22-6
Blauner, R (1972) *Racial Oppression in America*, New York, Harper Row
Bluestone, B & Harrison, B (1982) *The Deindustrialisation of America*, New York, Basic Books
Böhning, W R (1972) *The Migration of Workers in the United Kingdom and the European Community*, London, Oxford University Press
Borkenau, W (1962) *World Communism: A History of the Communist International*, Ann Arbor, University of Michigan Press
Bowles, S & H Gintis (1970) *Schooling in Capitalist America*, London, Routledge & Kegan Paul
Boyd, R E (1979) 'Introduction,' *LABOUR, Capital and Society*, 12 (2), April
Boyd, R E, R Cohen & P C W Gutkind (eds.) (1987) *International Labour and the Third World: The Making of a New Working Class*, Aldershot, Avebury
Bozzoli, B (ed.) (1979) *The Witwatersrand: Labour, Townships and Patterns of Protest*, Johannesburg, Ravan Press
Brandt Commission (1980) *North-South: A Programme for Survival*, London, Pan Books
Branson, N & M Heinemann (1971) *Britain in the Nineteen Thirties*, London, Weidenfeld & Nicolson
Braverman, H (1974) *Labor and Monopoly Capital*, New York, Monthly Review Press

Brecher, J (1972) *Strike!*, San Francisco, Straight Arrow Books

Brown, G (1977) *Sabotage*, Nottingham, Spokesman Books

Bullock, Lord (1977) *Report of the Committee of Inquiry on Industrial Democracy*, London, Her Majesty's Stationery Office

Bundy, C (1979) *The Rise and Fall of the South African Peasantry*, London, Heinemann Educational Books

Busch, K G (1980) *Political Currents in the International Trade Union Movement*, 2 vols., London, Economist Intelligence Unit

Carr, E H (1951-64) *History of Soviet Russia*, London, Macmillan

——— (1982) *Twilight of the Comintern*, London, Macmillan

Castells, M (1977) *The Urban Question*, London, Edward Arnold

——— (1979) 'Immigrant Workers and Class Struggles in Advanced Capitalism,' in R Cohen et al. (eds.) *q.v.*

——— (1983) *The City and the Grassroots: A Cross-Cuiltural Theory of Urban Social Movements*, London, Edward Arnold

Castles, S & G Kosack (1973) *Immigrant Workers and Class Structure in Western Europe*, London, Oxford University Press

Castles, S et al. (1984) *Here for Good: Western Europe's New Ethnic Minorities*, London, Pluto Press

Chaliand, G (1969) *Armed Struggle in Africa*, New York, Monthly Review Press

Chann, L H et al. (1984) 'Women Workers in Malaysia: TNCs and Social Conditions,' in I Norland et al. (eds.) *q.v.*

Chesneaux, J (1968) *The Chinese Labor Movement, 1919-1927*, Stanford, Stanford University Press

Chilcote, R (1979) 'Review of Casanova's Work,' *Latin American Perspectives*, 6 (1), Winter

Cleaver, E (1971) *Revolution in the Congo*, London, Stage 1

Clegg, I (1971) *Workers' Self-Management in Algeria*, New York, Monthly Review Press

Cobb, R (1970) *The Police and the People: French Popular Protest, 1789-1820*, Oxford, Clarendon Presss

Cohen, R (1974) *Labour and Politics in Nigeria*, London, Heinemann Educational Books

——— (1976) 'From Peasants to Workers in Africa,' in P C W Gutkind & I Wallerstein (eds.) *The Political Economy of Contemporary Africa*, Beverly Hills, Sage Publications, 155-68

——— (1980) 'The "New" International Labour Studies,' Working Paper 27, Montreal, McGill University, Centre for Developing Area Studies

——— (1986) *Endgame in South Africa? The Changing Ideology and Social Structure of South Africa*, London, James Currey

——— (1987) *The New Helots: Migrants and the International Division of Labour*, Aldershot, Gower

Cohen, R & C Harris (1977) 'Migrants, Capital and the Labour Process,' mimeograph

Cohen, R, P C W Gutkind & P Brazier (eds.) (1979) *Peasants and Proletarians: The Struggles of Third World Workers*, New York, Monthly Review Press

Communist International (1919-40) published in several languages by the Comintern

Crawford, M C (1970) 'Rebellion in the Congo,' in R Rotberg & A A Mazrui (eds.) *Protest and Power in Black Africa*, Oxford, Oxford University Press

Cross, M (1988) 'Migrants and New Minorities in Europe,' unpublished paper, Centre for Research in Ethnic Relations, *University of Warwick*

Dangerfield, G (1961) *The Strange Death of Liberal England*, New York, Capricorn Books

Davis, J M (1967) *Modern Industry and the African*, London, Frank Cass

Davis, M (1980) 'Why the US Working Class is Different,' *New Left Review*, no. 123, 3-44

———— (1982) 'The AFL-CIO's Second Century,' *New Left Review*, no. 136, 43-54

Dawley, A (1976) *Class and Community*, Cambridge, Mass., Harvard University Press

Degras, J (ed.) (1956-65) *Communist International 1919-1943*, Selected Documents in 3 vols., London, Oxford University Press

Development and Change (1979) Special Issue on 'Strikes in the Third World'

Dubofsky, M (1975) *Industrialism and the American Worker*, Arlington Heights, AHM Publishing Company

———— (1983) 'Workers' Movements in North America,' in I Wallerstein (ed.) *q.v.*

Duffield, M (1988) *Black Radicalism and the Politics of De-Industrialisation: The Hidden History of Indian Foundry Workers in the West Midlands*, Aldershot, Gower

Dunbar, T & L Kravitz (1976) *Hard Travelling: Migrant Farm Workers in America*, Cambridge, Mass., Ballinger Publishing Company

Ecevit, Z H (1981) 'International Labor Migration in the Middle East and North Africa: Trends, Effects and Policies,' in M M Kritz et al. (eds.) *Global Trends in Migration: Theory and Research on International Population Movements*, New York, Center for Migration Studies, 259-75

Echenberg, M (1975) 'Paying the Blood Tax: Military Conscription in French West Africa,' *Canadian Journal of African Studies*, vol. 9, 171-92

Elson, D & R Pearson (1981) '"Nimble Fingers Make Cheap Workers": An Analysis of Women's Employment in Third World Export Manufacturing,' *Feminist Review*, no. 7

Emmanuel, A (1972) *Unequal Exchange*, London, New Left Books

Epstein, A L (1958) *Politics in an Urban African Community*, Manchester, Manchester University Press

Erickson, C (1957) *American Industry and the European Immigrant*, Cambridge, Mass., Harvard University Press

Ernst, D (1980) *The New International Division of Labour: Technology and Underdevelopment*, Frankfurt, Campus Verlag

Fanon, F (1967) *The Wretched of the Earth*, Harmondsworth, Penguin Books

———— (1970) *A Dying Colonialism*, Harmondsworth, Penguin

First, R (1983) *Black Gold: Migrant Labour from Mozambique*, Brighton, Harvester Press

Flacks, R (1974) 'Making History versus Making Life,' *Working Papers for a New Society*, July

Foner, P (1964) *History of the Labour Movement in the United States*, vol. 4, New York, International Publishers

Forrest, R et al. (1982) *Urban Political Economy and Social Theory*, Aldershot, Gower

Fox, Renée C, W de Craemer & J-M Ribeaucourt (1965/6) '"The Second Independence": A Case Study of the Kwilu Rebellion in the Congo,' *Comparative Studies in Society and History*, vol. 8

Frank, A G (1967) *Capitalism and Underdevelopment in Latin America*, New York, Monthly Review Press

———— (1969) 'Sociology of Development and Underdevelopment of Sociology,' in A G Frank, *Latin America: Underdevelopment or Revolution*, New York, Monthly Review Press

———— (1981) *Crisis in the Third World*, London, Heinemann Educational Books

Freeman, G P (1979) *Immigrant Labor and Racial Conflict in Industrial Societies, 1945-75*, Princeton, Princeton University Press

Friedland, W H & D Nelkin (1971) *Migrant Agricultural Workers in America's Northeast*, New York, Holt, Rinehart & Winston

Friedman, J (1985) 'The World City Hypothesis,' paper for Conference on the International Division of Labour, Centre of Urban Studies, University of Hong Kong (subsequently published in *Development and Change*, 1986)

Fröbel, F, J Heinrichs & O Kreye (1980) *The New International Division of Labour*, London, Cambridge University Press

Galarza, E (1977) *Farm Workers and Agribusiness in California, 1947-1960*, Notre Dame, University of Notre Dame Press

Gambino, F (1970) *Workers' Struggles and the Development of Ford in Britain*, London, Red Notes

Garnsey, E (1981) 'The Rediscovery of the Division of Labour,' *Theory & Society*, 10 (2)

Genovese, E D (1967) *The Political Economy of Slavery*, New York, Pantheon Press

Giddens, A (1979) *Central Problems in Sociological Theory*, London, Macmillan

Gonsalez, R A (1977) 'The Chicana in South-West Labour History, 1900-1975: A Preliminary Bibliographic Analysis,' mimeographed paper, Program in Comparative Culture, University of California, Irvine

Goodman, D & M Redclift (1981) *From Peasant to Proletarian: Capitalist Development and Agrarian Transitions*, Oxford, Basil Blackwell

Gordon, R J (1977) *Mines, Masters and Migrants: Life in a Namibian Compound*, Johannesburg, Ravan Press

Grillo, R (1973) *African Railwaymen: Solidarity and Opposition in an East African Labour Force*, Cambridge, Cambridge University Press

Gutkind, P C W (1967) 'The Energy of Despair: Social Organisation of the Unemployed in Two African Cities: Lagos and Nairobi,' *Civilisations*, 17 (3 & 4)

———— (1968) 'Urbanisation and Unemployment,' *Manpower and Unemployment Research in Africa*, 1 (1), April

———— (1974) *The Emergent African Proletariat*, occasional paper, Centre for Developing Area Studies, McGill University, Montreal

Gutkind, P C W, R Cohen & J Copans (eds.) (1979) *African Labor History*, Beverly Hills, Sage

Gutman, H (1976) *Work, Culture and Society in Industrialising America*, New York, Knopf

Halliday, F (1977) 'Labor Migration in the Middle East,' *Merip Reports*, no. 59, pp. 1-17

Hammar, T (forthcoming) *International Migration, Citizenship and Democracy*, Aldershot, Avebury

Harloe, M (ed.) (1977) *Captive Cities: Studies in the Political Economy of Cities and Regions*, London, John Wiley

Harloe, M & E Lebas (eds.) (1981) *City, Class and Capital*, London, Edward Arnold

Harper, D, B Mills & R Parris (1974) 'Exploitation in Migrant Labour Camps,' *British Journal of Sociology*, vol. 25, 183-211

Harrison, B (1971) *Drink and the Victorians*, London, Faber & Faber

Hart, K. (1973) 'Informal Income Opportunities and Urban Employment in Ghana,' *Journal of Modern African Studies*, 11 (1), 61-89

Hauser, P (1961) *Urbanisation in Latin America*, Paris, UNESCO

Haworth, N & H Ramsay (1984) 'Grasping the Nettle: Problems in the Theory of International Labour Solidarity,' in P Waterman (ed.) *For a New Labour Internationalism*, The Hague, ILERI

Henderson, J (1976) 'Militancy and the Labour Process,' mimeograph

————— (1985) 'The New International Division of Labour and Urban Development in the Contemporary World System,' in D Drakakis-Smith (ed.) *Urbanisation in the Developing World*, London, Croom Helm

Henderson, J & R Cohen (1982) 'The International Restructuring of Capital and Labour: Britain and Hong Kong,' unpublished paper, World Congress of Sociology, International Sociological Association, Mexico City

Hill, P (1963) *Migrant Cocoa Farmers of Southern Ghana*, Cambridge, Cambridge University Press

————— (1970) *Studies in Rural Capitalism in West Africa*, Cambridge, Cambridge University Press

Hilton, R (1975) *The English Peasantry in the Later Middle Ages*, Oxford, Clarendon Press

Hobsbawm, E (1964) *Labouring Men*, New York, Basic Books

Hodgkin, T (1956) *Nationalism in Colonial Africa*, London, Frederick Muller

Hopkins, A G (1966) 'The Lagos Strike of 1897: An Exploration in Nigerian Labour History,' *Past and Present: A Journal of Historical Studies*, no. 35, December

————— (1973) *An Economic History of West Africa*, London, Longman

Hopkins, T (1977) 'Patterns of Development of the Modern World-System,' *Review*, 1 (2), 111-45

————— (1979) 'The Study of the Capitalist World-Economy: Some Introductory Considerations,' in W L Goldfrank (ed.) *The World System of Capitalism: Past and Present*, Beverly Hills, Sage

Horkheimer, M (1972) *Critical Theory*, New York, Herder & Herder

Horton J (1970) 'Time and Cool People,' in L Rainwater (ed.) *Black Experience: Soul, Chicago*, Transaction Books/Aldine

Hughes, A & R Cohen (1971) 'Towards the Emergence of a Nigerian Working Class: The Social Identity of the Lagos Labour Force, 1897-1939,' occasional paper, Series D, no. 7, Faculty of Commerce & Social Science, University of Birmingham

Hymer, S (1979) *The Multinational Corporation: A Radical Approach*, Cambridge, Cambridge University Press

ICIHI (Independent Commission on International Humanitarian Issues) (1986) *Refugees: Dynamics of Displacement*, London, Zed Books

ILO (1962) *African Labour Survey*, Geneva, International Labour Office

————— (1981) *Employment Effects of Multinational Enterprises in Industrialised Countries*, Geneva, International Labour Office

————— (1984) *World Labour Report*, vol. 1, Geneva, ILO

Isichei, E (1976) *A History of the Igbo People*, London, Macmillan

Jenkins, C & B Sherman (1979) *The Collapse of Work*, London, Eyre Methuen

Johnson, H & H Bernstein (eds.) (1982) *Third World Lives of Struggle*, London, Heinemann Educational Books

Jones, G Steadman (1971) *Outcast London: A Study in the Relationship Between Classes in Victorian Society*, Oxford, Oxford University Press

Kapferer, B (1972) *Strategy and Transaction in an African Factory*, Manchester, Manchester University Press

Keely, C B & P J Elwell (1981) 'International Migration: Canada and the US,' in M M Kritz et al.·(eds.) *Global Trends gration: Theory & Research on International Population Movements*, New York, Center for Migration Studies, 181-207

Kendall, W (1969) *The Revolutionary Movement in Britain 1900-21*, London, Weidenfeld & Nicolson

Kerr, C et al. (1960) *Industrialism and Industrial Man*, Cambridge, Mass., Harvard University Press

Kidron, M & R Segal (1981) *The State of the World Atlas*, London, Heinemann Educational Books

Kindleberger, C P (1967) *Europe's Post-war Growth: The Role of Labor Supply*, Cambridge, Mass., Harvard University Press

Kiser, G C & H W Kiser (eds.) (1979) *Mexican Workers in the United States: Historical and Political Perspectives*, Alburquerque, University of New Mexico Press

Kolko, G (1967) *The Triumph of Conservatism*, Chicago, Quadrangle Books

Korman, G (1967) *Industrialisation, Immigrants and Americanizers*, Madison, State Historical Society of Wisconsin

Kushner, S (1975) *Long Road to Delano: A Century of Farmworkers' Struggle*, New York, International Publishers

Lacey, T (1977) *Violence and Politics in Jamaica, 1960-1970: Internal Security in a Developing Country*, Manchester, Manchester University Press

Lefebvre, H (1976) *The Survival of Capitalism*, London, Allison & Busby

Lenin, V I (1918) *The State and Revolution*, Moscow, Foreign Languages Publishing House

Lens, S (1974) *The Labor Wars*, New York, Anchor Books

Levinson, C (1972) *International Trade Unionism*, London, Allen & Unwin

Levy, J E (1975) *Cesar Chavez: Autobiography of La Causa*, New York, W W Norton & Company

Lewis, O (1967) *La Vida: A Puerto Rican Family in the Culture of Poverty*, London, Secker & Warburg

Liebow, E (1967) *Tally's Corner*, Boston, Little, Brown

Lin, V (1985) 'Health, Women's Work and Industrialisation: Women Workers in the Semi-conductor Industry in Singapore and Malaysia,' unpublished paper, Conference on the International Division of Labour, Centre of Urban Studies, University of Hong Kong

Lloyd, P (1982) *A Third World Proletariat?* London, Allen & Unwin

Lux, A (1969) 'Rejoinder to R Cliquet' *Manpower and Unemployment Research in Africa,* 2 (1)

Luxemburg, R (1921) *The Accumulation of Capital,* London, Routledge & Kegan Paul

Lynd, R & H (1929) *Middletown,* New York, Harcourt Brace

———— (1937) *Middletown in Transition,* New York, Harcourt Brace

Magdoff, H (1978) *Imperialism: From the Colonial Age to the Present,* New York, Monthly Review Press

Majka, T (1980) 'Poor People's Movements and Farm Labor Insurgency,' *Contemporary Crisis,* 4 (3), July

Mallet, S (1975) *Essays on the New Working Class,* St Louis, Telos Press

Mandel, E (1978) *Late Capitalism,* London, Verso

Mangin, W (ed.) (1970) *Peasants in Cities,* Boston, Houghton Mifflin

Mann, M (1973) *Consciousness and Action in the Western Working Class,* London, Macmillan

Mao Zedong (1967) 'Analysis of the Classes in Chinese Society,' *Selected Readings,* Peking, Foreign Languages Press (first published in 1926)

Marglin, S (1976) 'What Do Bosses Do?,' in A Gorz (ed.) *The Division of Labour,* Brighton, Harvester Press

Marie, C V (1983) 'L'immigration clandestine en France,' *Travail et Emploi,* no. 17, 27-40

Maroney, H (1983) 'Feminism at Work,' *New Left Review,* no. 141, 51-71

Marshall, R (1974) *Rural Workers in Rural Labor Markets,* Salt Lake City, Olympus Publishing Company

Marshall, T H (1950) *Citizenship and Social Class, and Other Essays,* New York, Cambridge University Press

Marx, K (1967) *Capital,* vol. 1, New York, International Publishers

Marx, K & F Engels (1965) *Selected Correspondence,* Moscow, Progress Publishers

Mather, F (1959) 'The Government and the Chartists,' in A Briggs (ed.) *Chartist Studies,* London, Macmillan

Mauritius (1974) *Conditions for the Setting Up of Industrial Undertakings,* Brussels, Commission of the European Communities, Trade Division

McWilliams, C (1971) *Factories in the Fields: The Story of Migratory Farm Labor in California,* Santa Barbara, Peregrine Smith Inc.

Meillassoux, C (1972) 'From Reproduction to Production: A Marxist Approach to Economic Anthropology,' *Economy and Society*, 1 (1), 93-105

Mihyo, P (1975) 'The Struggle for Workers' Control in Tanzania,' *Review of African Political Economy*, no. 4, 62-85

Mikes, G (1946) *How to be an Alien?* Harmondsworth, Penguin

Mintz, S (1974) *Caribbean Transformations*, Chicago, Aldine

Misham, E (1970) 'Does Immigration Confer Economic Benefits on the Host Country,' in Institute of Economic Affairs, *Economic Issues in Immigration*, London, IEA

Montgomery, D (1974) 'The "New Unionism" and the Transformation of Workers' Consciousness in America,' *Journal of Social History*, Summer

———— (1977) 'Immigrant Workers and Managerial Reform,' in R Ehrlich (ed.) *Immigrants in Industrial America 1850-1920*, Charlottesville, University Press of Virginia

Moore, B (1966) *Social Origins of Dictatorship and Democracy: Landlord and Peasant in the Making of the Modern World*, Boston, Beacon Press

Morse, D A (1970) 'Unemployment in Developing Countries,' *Political Science Quarterly*, 85 (1), March

Munck, R (1988) *The New International Labour Studies: An Introduction* London, Zed Press

Murdock, G & R McCron (1976) 'Youth and Class: The Career of a Confusion,' in G Mungham & G Pearson (eds.) *Working Class Youth Culture*, London, Routledge & Kegan Paul

NACLA (North American Congress of Latin America) (1976) 'Del Monte: Bitter Fruits,' *Latin America and Empire Report*, 10 (7), September

———— (1977) 'Immigration: Facts and Fallacies,' pamphlet

———— (1977a) 'Caribbean Immigration: Contract Labor in US Agriculture,' *NACLA's Report on the Americas*, 18 (8), November/ December

Nash, J (1979) *We Eat the Mines and the Mines Eat Us: Dependency and Exploitation in Bolivian Tin Mines*, New York, Columbia University Press

Nash, J. & P Fernandez-Kelly (1983) *Women, Men and the International Division of Labour*, Albany, State University of New York Press

Nelson, E (1975) *Pablo Cruz and the American Dream*, Santa Barbara, Peregrine Smith Inc.

Norlund, I et al. (eds.) (1984) *Industrialisation and the Labour Process in South-east Asia*, Rosenborg-gade, Institute of Cultural Sociology, University of Copenhagen

OECD (1987) *The Future of Migration*, Paris, Organisation for Economic Cooperation & Development

Offe, C (1972) 'Advanced Capitalism and the Welfare State,' *Politics and Society*, Summer

Olle, W & W Schoeller (1987) 'World Market Competition and Restrictions upon International Trade Union Policies,' in R E Boyd, R Cohen & P C W Gutkind (eds.) (1987) *q.v.*

Ousmane, S (1969) *God's Bits of Wood*, London, Heinemann Educational Books

Ozanne, R (1967) *A Century of Labor-Management Relations at McCormick and International Harvester*, Madison, University of Wisconsin Press

Padmore, G (1971) *The Life and Struggles of Negro Toilers*, Hollywood, Sundance Press (first published in 1931)

Pahl, R (1984) *Divisions of Labour*, Oxford, Basil Blackwell

Paige, J (1975) *Agrarian Revolution: Social Movements in Export Agriculture in the Underdeveloped World*, New York, Free Press

Parson, J (1987) *A Political Economy of Botswana*, Boulder, Westview

Peace, A (1979) *Choice, Class and Conflict: A Study of Southern Nigerian Factory Workers*, Brighton, Harvester Press

Peil, M (1971) 'The Expulsion of West African Aliens,' *Journal of Modern African Studies*, 9 (2), 205-29

Penda-Ofreneo, R (1984) 'Sub-contracting in Export-oriented Industries: Impact on Filipino Working Women,' in I Norlund et al. (eds.) *q.v.*

Perlman, S (1949) *A Theory of the Labour Movement*, New York

Petras, J (1975) 'New Perspectives on Imperialism and Social Class in the Periphery,' *Journal of Contemporary Asia*, 5 (3)

Pfeffermann, G (1968) *Industrial Labour in Senegal*, New York, Praeger

Piore, M J (1979) *Birds of Passage: Migrant Labour and Industrial Societies*, Cambridge, Cambridge University Press

——— (1986) 'The Shifting Grounds for Immigration,' *Annals of the American Academy of Political and Social Science*, vol. 485, May, 23-33

Piore, M J & C F Sabel (1984) *The Second Industrial Divide: Possibilities for Prosperity*, New York, Basic Books

Pollard, S (1965) *The Genesis of Modern Management*, London, Arnold

Portes, A & J Walton (1981) *Labor, Class and the International System*, New York, Academic Press

Powles, W (1965) 'The Southern Appalachian Migrant: Country Boy Turned Blue-Collarite,' in A Shostack & W Gomberg (eds.) *Blue Collar World*, Englewood Cliffs, Prentice-Hall

Rainwater, L (1970) *Behind Ghetto Walls*, Chicago, Aldine

Ranger, T (1975) *Dance and Society in Eastern Africa*, London, Heinemann Educational Books

Ranis, P (1979) 'The Workers and the State in Latin America: Patterns of Dominance and Subordination,' *Civilisations*, 29 (1-2)

Renshaw, P (1975) *The General Strike*, London, Eyre Methuen

Rex, J & S Tomlinson (1979) *Colonial Immigrants in a British City: A Class Analysis*, London, Routledge & Kegan Paul

Rockefeller, N (1963) *The Rockefeller Report on the Americas*, Chicago, Quadrangle Books

Roseberry, W (1978) 'Peasants as Proletarians,' *Critique of Anthropology*, 11 (3), Spring, 3-8

Rothschild, E (1973) *Paradise Lost: The Decline of the Auto-Industrial Age*, New York, Random House

Roxborough, I (1979) *Theories of Underdevelopment*, Basingstoke, Macmillan

Roy, D (1952) 'Quota Restriction and Goldbricking in a Machine Shop,' *American Journal of Sociology*, March

Salaman, G (1974) *Community and Occupation*, Cambridge, Cambridge University Press

Samora, J & P V Simon (1977) *A History of the Mexican American People*, Notre Dame, University of Notre Dame Press

Sandbrook, R (1982) *The Politics of Basic Needs: Urban Aspects of Assaulting Poverty in Africa*, London, Heinemann Educational Books

Sandbrook, R & R Cohen (eds.) (1975) *The Development of an African Working Class: Studies in Class Formation and Action*, London, Longman

Sassen-Koob, S (1979) 'Economic Growth and Immigration in Venezuela,' *International Migration Review*, 13 (2), 314-31

——— (1983) 'Capital Mobility and Labor Migration: Their Expression in Core Cities,' in R Timberlake (ed.) *Urbanisation in the World Economy*, New York, Academic Press

——— (1984) 'The New Labor Demand in Global Cities,' in M P Smith (ed.) *Cities in Transformation*, Beverly Hills, Sage, 139-71

Sau, R (1979) 'Rural Workforce in India: Proletarianisation or Immiserisation of the Peasantry?,' *LABOUR, Capital and Society*, 12 (1), April

Saul, J & R Woods (1971) 'African Peasantries,' in T Shanin (ed.) *q.v.*

Schierup, C-U (forthcoming) *Quest for Return: International Migration and the Yugoslav Crisis*, Aldershot, Avebury

Seeley, J (1883) *The Expansion of England*, London

Seldon, M (1983) 'The Proletariat, Revolutionary Change and the State in China and Japan, 1850-1950,' in I Wallerstein (ed.) *q.v.*

Sennet, R & J Cobb (1977) *The Hidden Injuries of Class*, Cambridge, Cambridge University Press

Serrin, W (1973) *The Company and the Union*, New York, Knopf

Shanin, T (1971) (ed.) *Peasants and Peasant Societies*, Harmondsworth, Penguin Books

——— (1971a) 'The Peasantry as a Political Factor,' in T Shanin (ed.) (1971) *q.v.*

————— (1978) 'The Peasants are Coming: Migrants who Labour, Peasants who Travel and Marxists who Write,' *Race and Class*, 19 (3), Winter

Shanin, T & H Alavi (1982), *Introduction to the Sociology of Developing Societies*, Basingstoke, Macmillan

South African Labour Bulletin, eight times yearly. 4 Melle House, 31 Melle Street, 2001 Braamfontein, South Africa

Spalding, H (1977) *Organized Labor in Latin America: Historical Case Studies of Urban Workers in Dependent Societies*, New York, Harper & Row

Stein, M (1964) *The Eclipse of Community*, New York, Harper & Row

Steinbeck, J (1975) *The Grapes of Wrath*, London, Pan Books

Sturmthal, A & J G Scoville (1973) *The International Labour Movement in Transition: Essays on Africa, Asia, Europe and South America*, Urbana, University of Illinois Press

Sundkler, B G M (1971) *Bantu Prophets in South Africa*, Oxford, Oxford University Press

Tarbuck, K J (1972) *Imperialism and the Accumulation of Capital*, Harmondsworth, Allen Lane

Taylor, R (1976) 'The Volvo Way of Work,' *New Society*, 15, April

Thomas, K (1964) 'Work and Leisure in Pre-Industrial Society,' *Past and Present*, December

Thompson, E P (1963) (1968 edition also cited) *The Making of the English Working Class*, Harmondsworth, Penguin

————— (1967) 'Time, Work-Discipline and Industrial Capitalism,' *Past and Present*, December

————— (1978) *The Poverty of Theory*, London, Merlin

Trapido, S (1971) 'South Africa in a Comparative Study of Industrialisation,' *Journal of Development Studies*, 7 (3), 309-20

United States Department of Labor (1959) *Farm Labor Fact Book*, Washington, Government Printing Office

Valentine, C A (1968) *Culture and Poverty: Critique and Counter Proposals*, Chicago, Chicago University Press

van der Post, L (1958) *The Lost World of the Kalahari*, Harmondsworth, Penguin

van Onselen, C (1976) *Chibaro: African Mine Labour in Southern Rhodesia, 1900-1933*, London, Pluto Press

Vandervelde, E (1929) 'The Second (Socialist) International,' in *Encyclopaedia Britannica*, vol. 12 (14th edn), 511-12

Wallerstein, I (1979) *The Capitalist World-Economy*, Cambridge, Cambridge University Press

————— (ed.) (1983) *Labour in the World Social Structure*, Beverly Hills, Sage

Warren, W (1980) *Imperialism: Pioneer of Capitalism*, London, Verso

Waterman, P (1982) 'Report of a Field Trip to Denmark and Norway,' The Hague, Institute of Social Studies, mimeograph

———— (ed.) (1984) *For a New Labour Internationalism: A Set of Reprints and Working Papers*, The Hague, International Labour Education Research & Information Foundation, 176-209

Weber, M (1958) *The Protestant Ethic and the Spirit of Capitalism*, New York, Scribners

Webster, E (ed.) (1978) *Essays on South African Labour History*, Johannesburg, Ravan Press

Weinstein, J (1967) *The Decline of Socialism in America 1912-25*, New York, Monthly Review Press

———— (1968) *The Corporate Ideal in the Liberal State*, Boston, Beacon Press

Weller, K (1974) *The Lordstown Struggle*, London, Solidarity

Willems, E (1969) 'Religious Pluralism and Class Structure: Brazil and Chile,' in R Robertson (ed.) *Readings in the Sociology of Religion*, Harmondsworth, Penguin

Williams, G (1985) 'Taking the Part of Peasants: Rural Development in Nigeria and Tanzania,' in P C W Gutkind & I Wallerstein (eds.) *The Political Economy of Contemporary Africa*, Beverly Hills, Sage, 144-80

Williams G & C H Allen (eds.) (1982) *The Sociology of Developing Societies: Sub-Saharan Africa*, Basingstoke, Macmillan

Willis, P (1977) *Learning to Labour*, London, Saxon House

Wilson, F (1972) *Labour in the South African Gold Mines*, Cambridge, Cambridge University Press

———— (1972a) *Migrant Labour in South Africa*, Johannesburg, Sprocas

Winn, P (1979) 'The Urban Working Class and Social Protest in Latin America,' *International Labour and Working Class History*, 14/15, Spring

Wolf, E (1966) *Peasant Wars of the Twentieth Century*, New York, Harper & Row

Wolpe, H (1972) 'Capitalism and Cheap Labour Power in South Africa: From Segregation to Apartheid,' *Economy and Society*, 1 (4)

Worsley, P (1972) 'Fanon and the Sub-proletatariat,' *The Socialist Register 1972*, London, Merlin Press

Yinger, M (1960) 'Contraculture and Subculture,' *American Sociological Review*, October

Zeitlin, M (1967) *Revolutionary Politics and the Cuban Working Class*, Princeton, Princeton University Press

Zucker, N L & N F Zucker (1987) *The Guarded Gate: The Reality of American Refugee Policy*, San Diego, Harcourt Brace Jovanovich

Index

Zed Books Ltd

is a publisher whose international and Third World lists span:

- **Women's Studies**
- **Development**
- **Environment**
- **Current Affairs**
- **International Relations**
- **Children's Studies**
- **Labour Studies**
- **Cultural Studies**
- **Human Rights**
- **Indigenous Peoples**
- **Health**

We also specialize in Area Studies where we have extensive lists in African Studies, Asian Studies, Caribbean and Latin American Studies, Middle East Studies, and Pacific Studies.

For further information about books available from Zed Books, please write to: Catalogue Enquiries, Zed Books Ltd, 57 Caledonian Road, London N1 9BU. Our books are available from distributors in many countries (for full details, see our catalogues), including:

In the USA
Humanities Press International, Inc., 165 First Avenue, Atlantic Highlands, New Jersey 07716.
Tel: (201) 872 1441;
Fax: (201) 872 0717.

In Canada
DEC, 229 College Street, Toronto, Ontario M5T 1R4.
Tel: (416) 971 7051.

In Australia
Wild and Woolley Ltd, 16 Darghan Street, Glebe, NSW 2037.

In India
Bibliomania, C-236 Defence Colony, New Delhi 110 024.

In Southern Africa
David Philip Publisher (Pty) Ltd, PO Box 408, Claremont 7735, South Africa.